LOST HISTORIES

LOST HISTORIES

*Exploring the World's
Most Famous Mysteries*

Joel Levy

V
I
S
I
O
N

First published in 2006 by Vision Paperbacks,
a division of Satin Publications Ltd
101 Southwark Street
London SE1 0JF
UK
info@visionpaperbacks.co.uk
www.visionpaperbacks.co.uk
Publisher: Sheena Dewan

A catalogue record for this book is available from the British Library.

ISBN-13: 978-1-904132-93-6
ISBN-10: 1-904132-93-6

2 4 6 8 10 9 7 5 3 1

Cover photo: The Image Bank/Getty Images
Cover and text design by ok?design
Printed and bound in the UK by
Mackays of Chatham Ltd, Chatham, Kent

For the Hooper-Hodson family,
especially Audrey Hooper

Contents

Acknowledgements

Thanks to Louise, Charlotte, Sheena and everyone at Vision.

Introduction

In an average history book most people, places and things can be located. We know where they happened, where they were buried, where they now lie, where you can see them if they have survived. Inevitably, however, many have got lost in history: concealed beneath the dust, vanished below the waves, hidden by fading memory and competing legends. What is left are mysteries.

Everyone loves a good mystery. So much the better if the mystery is real – if it concerns real people or places, or things that really happened. Today it is increasingly hard to know whether the mystery you are being peddled is genuine or simply a house of cards; a pile of baseless speculations heaped upon misreported facts and reified fictions. To some extent history has always been a story, a narrative woven from selected events and selective interpretations, but too much of it is now more like a trashy potboiler. Ideally much of this airport novel-style history would be clearly distinguished and labelled as 'pseudohistory', or at least 'alternative history', but this rarely happens. What is needed, in the words of historian Kevin McClure, is a campaign for real history.

I wouldn't necessarily claim that this book is part of that campaign, but it does attempt to treat historical mysteries without resorting to the pitfalls and clichés of pseudohistory. In fact my initial aim was to cover only topics that fell within the (admittedly arbitrary) remit of 'real history' – ie events that 'really' happened and people, places and things that genuinely existed – but that was never a realistic goal. Firstly, any book on things that are missing in history must at least consider tackling the 300-pound gorillas of the field – popular subjects such as the Holy Grail and the Ark of the Covenant, or topics du jour such as the treasure of the Knights Templar. Secondly, there is of course no clear dividing line between legend and history, as many of the articles in this book clearly demonstrate.

Instead what I have tried to do is look at evidence from the mainstream *and* outside it and consider the plausibility of competing claims and interpretations, to arrive at balanced conclusions about where things might be and whether they still exist or ever did. Each article explains the nature of the historical mystery, and in particular the popular conception of the subject versus the reality, looks at the background, discusses what might remain to be found, examines the efforts that have already been made and assesses the evidence to suggest the most likely solution to the mystery. Each topic is fascinating in its own right, and there is something here for everyone, from the high adventure of the quest for the Holy Grail to the more intellectual pursuit of the true identity of Shakespeare's lost plays.

Most excitingly, some of these mysteries may lend themselves, at least in part, to investigation and solution by dedicated amateurs or even pure dumb luck – it's always possible that you yourself could stumble upon a buried treasure or happen across a long-forgotten grave. If this should happen, though, remember that the true value of any such find is historical and not material, and that this value can only be preserved through expert, professional investigation/excavation, so make sure you call in the authorities before digging for glory.

1

Lost Places

From the Victorian period onwards our era has seen the end of geographical uncertainty; the blank spots on the map have been filled in. Perhaps this accounts for the growth of interest in lost lands, cities and monuments, an enthusiasm that also dates back to Victorian times. As explorers brought back news of cyclopean ruins of cities and temples in the jungles of Central America and South-East Asia, so the romance of the 'lost place' gripped the popular imagination. Legends of such places have been a feature of all cultures throughout history, but when so much of the world was unknown they might have seemed more undiscovered than lost. Such mysteries are most fascinating when there appears to be nowhere left for them to hide, yet they guard their secrets still. This chapter looks at some of the most enduring and fascinating lost places, from the probably mythical – Atlantis – to the historically certain – the Library of Alexandria – and seeks to show that there is more to each mystery than you may suspect.

Atlantis

The archetypal lost land, Atlantis has been located everywhere from Ireland to Antarctica. Its mystery has grown throughout the years, arguably out of all proportion to the actual evidence for its existence, as it has developed into a touchstone of the New Age movement, a key element of the alternative history mythos and an ur-homeland for racist fantasists. So what is Atlantis? The legendary remnant of a genuinely important prehistoric civilisation? A harmless fiction for fantasy novelists? A philosophical conceit for dreamers? Or fuel for dangerous bigotry? And if it really did exist, where was it?

Plato's Atlantis

The original and earliest source for Atlantis is the work of the ancient Greek philosopher Plato (c427–347 BCE). His dialogues *Timaeus* and *Critias* (written c360 BCE) involve discussions between real and (possibly) invented characters. One of the characters in these dialogues, Critias, tells of a story that has come down to him fourth-hand, allegedly from an Egyptian priest from around 600 BCE who in turn was relating knowledge preserved for 9,000 years, which was recorded in inscriptions on columns in the city of Sais. This tale, which is used to illustrate the nobility of the ancient Athenians, describes Atlantis as a great civilisation from the West that conquered the Western Mediterranean from its base 'beyond the Pillars of Hercules'. Normally these pillars are taken to refer to the Straits of Gibraltar, which separate the Mediterranean from the Atlantic, placing the land of Atlantis in what we now call the Atlantic Ocean. Both the name of the lost continent and the name subsequently given to the ocean refer to Atlas, the first high king of Atlantis, equivalent to the Titan of myth who supported the world on his shoulders. (Although Plato gives his Atlas a different parentage to the Titan, it is generally assumed that the two are cognate.)

Plato describes Atlantis in some detail. It was roughly oblong, about 700 kilometres (435 miles) across, with mountains around the coast and a great central plain, the most prominent feature of which was a mount to the south, upon which a great acropolis was built and around which grew the capital city of Atlantis. The central acropolis was guarded by concentric rings of canals, with mighty walls protecting each ring of intervening land. A huge canal connected the circular moats with the ocean to the south, and all the commerce of the world passed up and down the great waterway. At its height, Atlantis was a glorious Bronze Age civilisation, with a mighty army and fleet, rich in natural resources and wealthy from the trade of nations.

Plato also describes how Atlantis was created: Poseidon, god of the sea, took it for his own when the gods of Olympus were carving up the world, and he shaped it according to his needs. His children (the eldest of whom was Atlas) became the kings of the land and ruled according to his precepts. In a familiar tale of decline, however, they became morally corrupt and debased as their wealth and power increased, and so the gods visited disaster upon them, smiting the land with a great earthquake that caused it to sink beneath the waves, becoming an impassable mud shoal that hindered free transport between the Mediterranean and the Atlantic. These arguably shaky foundations have given rise to many libraries' worth of speculation from ancient times until the modern day.

Is Plato credible?

Many classical writers mentioned Atlantis or similar lands, though none appear to predate Plato, suggesting that they may well be based on his account. More importantly, Proclus (c410–485 CE), who wrote a commentary on Plato's *Timaeus*, reports that others claim to have seen the Egyptian column upon which the tale of Atlantis was preserved, appearing to lend credibility to Plato's tale. Proclus, was, however, writing more than 700 years after Plato's time.

Further independent corroboration seems to come from the mythology behind the Panathenaia, the most important festival of ancient Athens. According to some accounts, one of the festival's functions was to celebrate the goddess Athena's role in helping Athens to defeat the nation of Poseidon (ie Atlantis). Since the festival predates Plato, this suggests that he did not invent the story of Atlantis.

So should we take Plato seriously? It seems unlikely that the story could have come down to him exactly as described, as it would have to have survived as a primarily oral tradition for thousands of years. Even if the survival and transmission of the story were credible, the tale itself is not, since much of Plato's account is of a mythical nature (eg the central acropolis of Atlantis being created by the god Poseidon, who moulded the earth with his divine powers). Also, current mainstream history does not recognise any evidence of an advanced Bronze Age civilisation from c9000 BCE that matches Plato's account. One possibility is that Plato invented or adapted a pre-existing fable of an idealised golden land to illustrate moral points (for instance, that Atlantis was doomed when its rulers turned away from the noble precepts of its founders).

Atlantis after Plato

Though Plato's Atlantis may sound like fiction, it has been taken seriously right up until modern times. According to the 4th-century Roman historian Ammianus Marcellus, Atlantis was commonly considered to be a historical fact by educated people of the day. For most of the next 1,500 years or so, however, Atlantis kept a low profile. It was name-checked in the title of Francis Bacon's 1626 work *The New Atlantis*, a novel about a utopian society, but did not really surface again until the 19th century, when a number of theorists and explorers started to put together evidence from cultures widely separated by geography and history, to adduce the possibility of some sort of root or progenitor civilisation, which they identified with Plato's Atlantis.

Donnelly and the antediluvian world

The most influential of these writers was the American politician and amateur historian, Ignatius Donnelly. In his 1882 bestseller, *Atlantis: The Antediluvian World*, Donnelly set out his theory that Atlantis had really existed and had been the 'master' civilisation that founded most of the world's subsequent great civilisations, from Egypt to the Incas. Modern conceptions of Atlantis still owe much to Donnelly's vision of a mighty civilisation with advanced technology and wisdom. He also argued that the myths and legends of many cultures derived from faded race memories of Atlantean history, so that the gods of Norse or classical mythology were based on real kings, queens and heroes of Atlantis, and that when Atlantis was destroyed in a great cataclysm, survivors of the deluge colonised other parts of the world and founded new civilisations.

As evidence for his theory, Donnelly pointed to ancient transatlantic cultural similarities such as pyramid building and sun worship, claiming that Mayan petroglyphs and Egyptian hieroglyphs both stemmed from the Atlanteans, who invented writing (along with astronomy, metallurgy, glass, the compass and various other attributes of civilisation). Donnelly pointed out that many cultures shared myths of great floods and migrant culture heroes who founded civilisations. He also claimed that many plants and animals on either side of the Atlantic were obviously related, pointing to the existence of a now-submerged land bridge across the ocean.

Donnelly's legacy

Most of Donnelly's evidence has since been disproved; he was wrong about the similarities between the Mayan language and Mediterranean ones, and more powerful theories have arisen to explain trans-Atlantic similarities between animals and plants (see page 11). But he had sowed the seeds of Atlantean 'studies' as we know them today.

Several other scholars of varying credibility took up the Atlantean baton, particularly with reference to the Mayan and Aztec cultures. This was due partly to the relative vacuum of knowledge about these mysterious civilisations, and partly to the suggestive presence of pyramids, sun-worshipping and other attributes. But could there also have been a hint of condescension, verging on the racist – the assumption by European/white scholars that the 'inferior' Native American races could not have created their own civilisations from whole cloth, but must owe their achievements to inspiration from an essentially classical/ European progenitor?

Once more was known about the Mayans, Aztecs, Incas and others, however, it was generally accepted that their language, writing, architecture and science were indigenous, and that many of the interpretations and translations of pre-Colombian texts that had appeared to support Atlantean theories were simply wrong.

Madame Blavatsky and theosophy

Racial theories were to take centre stage in the Atlantis mythology, alongside mystical and supernatural elements, thanks to the writings of Madame Blavatsky and her spiritual descendants. Helena Petrovna Blavatsky was one of the most colourful characters of the Victorian era. Often called the 'mother' of the New Age phenomenon, Blavatsky founded the occult/spiritual movement known as theosophy, and helped to create/popularise many of the basic tenets of New Age thought, such as the belief that all religions are the same, and that the spiritual can be reconciled with the scientific.

Blavatsky was descended from Russian royalty and claimed to have spent part of her youth wandering in the East and receiving mystical instruction from Tibetan magi. Later she gained renown as a medium and psychic, and, together with a number of wealthy backers and acolytes, she founded the Theosophical Society to promote her theories and philosophy. Her books, including *Isis Unveiled* (1877) and *The Secret Doctrine* (1888), spelt these out. A flavour of these is indicated by their respective subtitles: 'A Master-Key to the Mysteries of Ancient and Modern Science and Theology' and 'The Synthesis of Science, Religion and Philosophy'.

Blavatsky claimed that various 'ascended masters' and 'hidden teachers' had revealed to her the true history of human development, in which Atlantis and other lost continents played a major part. Supposedly an earlier cycle of human evolution took place on the continent, and Atlanteans constituted the fourth in a series of Root Races. As in Donnelly's conception, Atlantis was the cradle of civilisation and possessed advanced material and spiritual technologies.

Edgar Cayce and the Bimini Road

Atlantis was to get weirder still through the trance-readings of Edgar Cayce (1877–1945), the celebrated 'sleeping seer'. As a young man Cayce had discovered that, when put into a hypnotic trance, he apparently had the ability to diagnose ailments and prescribe cures. Later he developed the ability to read people's past lives and to channel historical and spiritual wisdom, in particular from ancient Atlantis. According to Cayce, Atlantis had enjoyed a 40,000-year history, during which Atlanteans developed from pure energy thought-forms into humans with the sort of high Neolithic culture described by Plato, but with the added twist of advanced technologies such as energy-crystals, lasers, airships and death-rays. Like Donnelly, Cayce said that historical civilisations such as Egypt and the Mayans were founded by Atlantean refugees or colonists.

Cayce also borrowed heavily (though probably unconsciously) from Donnelly in describing the location of Atlantis. Originally it had filled most of the Atlantic between Spain/Africa in the East and the Caribbean in the West, although apparently large tracts of eastern North America had once been part of Atlantis. In particular, Cayce pointed to the Bimini Islands in the Caribbean as being remnants of Atlantis, and claimed that a giant subterranean Hall of Records, a repository of earth-shattering Atlantean wisdom, would be discovered in this area.

There was much excitement among Cayce followers when divers discovered a strange rock formation on the seabed near Bimini, now known as the 'Bimini Road' because of its resemblance to a Roman road. Many claimed that the Bimini Road was proof of the prior existence of an advanced civilisation, which had evidently been submerged beneath the waves just as in the tale of Atlantis. However, most geologists and archaeologists agree that it is simply a curious-looking but natural beach-rock formation.

Atlantis and the Nazis

The story of Atlantis took a darker turn during the 1920s and 30s when fascist ideologues began to use it as one strand of the racist mythology they were weaving. In order to lend some sort of spurious credibility to their half-baked notions of racial superiority, fascist and anti-Semitic writers concocted an alternative version of human history, in which Aryan and Nordic races had been engaged in an aeons-long mythic struggle with debased and corrupt races. Borrowing from theosophy, they declared that Atlantis was one of the homelands where Nordic Aryans had given rise to civilisation and where they had lived in a sort of prelapsarian fascist utopia. Extraordinarily this distasteful fantasy lives on today among neo-Nazi groups in America, Europe and the former Soviet Union.

Could Atlantis have existed?

All of these Platonic concepts of Atlantis – as a great island or continent in the Atlantic Ocean – have at least one thing in common: we now know they cannot be true. The development of plate tectonic theory, the discovery of the Mid-Atlantic Ridge and the mapping of the Atlantic sea floor are the nails in the coffin of the notion of Atlantis as Plato described it. Plate tectonics indicates that while the Americas, Europe and Africa were once joined together (which accounts for some similarities between flora and fauna), active production of new ocean floor has driven them apart and created the Atlantic Ocean. The Mid-Atlantic Ridge is where this new ocean floor is being produced. The physics of plate geology make it impossible for there once to have been a continental land mass that has since sunk into the ocean floor, because the rock that makes up continents is lighter and less dense than the rock that makes up the ocean floor, effectively floating on top of it. The mapping of the Atlantic seabed has confirmed that there are no large land masses lurking beneath the waves.

The new revised version

Atlantis as Plato, Donnelly, Blavatsky and Cayce described it cannot exist, but this does not mean that the tale has no basis in fact. There could yet be a kernel of truth in the Atlantis story that might point historical sleuths towards an exciting discovery: an ancient civilisation unknown to modern archaeology but mighty enough to inspire millennia of myth and legend, perhaps even a civilisation that predates the first known ones in Mesopotamia and Egypt.

It could be that Plato, or one of the many people in the long chain of transmission, got the story slightly wrong. Or perhaps there were errors in translation as the tale was passed from Egyptian priest to Greek traveller. In particular, one well-rehearsed suggestion is that numbers were wrongly translated or transmitted by an order of magnitude, so that Atlantis existed 900 rather than 9,000 years before, and that its dimensions were much smaller, radically increasing the range of potential candidate locations. Some historians, however, point out that such a mis-translation would have been unlikely since, unlike the notation we use today where a decimal point can easily slip, the Egyptian hieroglyphics for different numbers were hard to confuse.

Another suggestion is that, for the parochial Egyptians, 'West' meant anything further than Libya, and could thus include most of the Mediterranean. Alternatively, it is claimed that in ancient times the Pillars of Hercules also referred to the Bosporus Straits that lead from the Mediterranean to the Black Sea.

So by reinterpreting Plato's original account and/or assuming errors, Atlantis hunters are licensed to widen their search to an extraordinary variety of locations, from Ireland to Antarctica and from the shores of the Black Sea to Cuba.

Possible locations of Atlantis

Space precludes more than a brief rundown of some of the most popular, plausible or simply preposterous suggestions as to the true location of Atlantis:

Crete

Working on the theory that, to the ancient Egyptians, Crete would have fit the bill of 'an island far to the west', Irish scholar K T Frost suggested in 1909 that the Bronze Age civilisation of the Minoans (c3000–1450 BCE), based in Crete, could have been Atlantis. The Egyptian name for the Minoans was *Keftiu*, which can be roughly translated as 'people of the pillar', suggesting a link to the Titan Atlas who holds up the sky. Plato describes rituals involving bulls as central to the Atlantean religion, and the Minoans were renowned for their bull cult. More generally, the Minoans were a remarkably rich and sophisticated civilisation for their time, who may well have left quite an impression even after their abrupt collapse, which, it is suggested, was due to a massive eruption on nearby Thera. The associated cataclysm of tsunamis and earth tremors could easily be compared to Plato's description of 'violent earthquakes and floods' that destroyed Atlantis.

The most obvious flaw with this theory is that Crete is very much still there, and doesn't really resemble Plato's description of Atlantis. It is also known that the Minoan civilisation survived for around two centuries after the eruption of Thera, and was well known to the Greeks of Plato's time, who had a whole set of non-Atlantean myths and legends about the Minoans. Finally, while ancient, the Minoans certainly did not date back to 9000 BCE, so it would be necessary to posit that Plato, or someone in his chain of sources, got the date wrong.

Thera

A hundred kilometres to the north of Crete lies modern-day Santorini, known as Thera in ancient times. In 1969 Greek seismologist Angelos Galanopoulos proposed that Thera could have been an inspiration for Atlantis. It too was a centre of Minoan civilisation, but unlike Crete it may have roughly resembled the general shape and layout Plato gives (though not the dimensions), at least until possibly the largest volcanic explosion in the history of civilisation blew a huge hole in the middle of it in about 1640 BCE.

Many of the same objections to Crete as a possible Atlantis apply here, however. The Minoan civilisation as a whole survived the eruption (indeed the evidence is that Therans had plenty of warning and evacuated), and the dates do not coincide with Plato's account. The destruction of much of the island also means that any evidence of the wondrous acropolis or canal system described by Plato may have been lost forever.

Spartel Bank

Given Plato's fairly definite instructions about the location of Atlantis, it seems perhaps strange that it took so long for someone to look carefully at the sea floor just to the west of the Straits of Gibraltar. In 2001 French geologist Jacques Collina-Girard did just that while researching material on the migration routes of palaeolithic people, and found what is known as a palaeoisland – a now submerged island that would have been above sea level around the end of the last Ice Age, when the sea levels were much lower. This island is now a mud shoal (exactly as Plato described) called Spartel Bank, but approximately 11,000 years ago – tying in with Plato's timescale – it was Spartel Island. According to subsequent analysis by Marc-André Gutscher there is even evidence that Spartel Island was hit by a devastating tsunami, which, along with accompanying earthquakes, could have plunged most of the island below sea level within a short period. So far, so good, but here the correspondences end. Spartel Island was nowhere near as large as Plato's Atlantis, and there is certainly no evidence that it was ever inhabited, let alone supported an advanced civilisation.

Tartessos

Tartessos was a city-state in southern Spain that existed c1000 BCE and possibly much earlier. It was a rich trading state, grown fat off the profits of the tin trade (tin was used to manufacture bronze). It was said that the city was fabulously wealthy and rich in metals, as Atlantis was purported to be. It disappeared mysteriously from the historical record in the 6th century BCE, probably as the result of flooding.

In the 1920s Dr Adolfo Schulten made the link between Tartessos and Atlantis, while more recently Dr Rainer Kühne has suggested that satellite photos of a region near Cadiz show the remains of temples and the canal system described by Plato. Kühne argues that the details of Plato's account suggest that it actually refers to the period c1200 BCE and describes a war between Bronze Age Athens and a force from the West who equate to the Sea Peoples – a mysterious group who appear in the historical narrative of a number of Mediterranean cultures around this time. Kühne suggests that the remains shown in the satellite photos may be Tartessos, which was the basis for Plato's Atlantis and the true source of the Sea Peoples, thus solving a clutch of historical mysteries at a stroke. For Tartessos to actually be Atlantis, however, we have to accept that Plato was wrong about the date, location and even the fact that Atlantis was an island.

Tantalis

Tantalis is another lost Bronze Age city. It was probably in Asia Minor (now Turkey), near modern-day Izmir. Historian Peter James fingers it as the source of the Atlantis myth, based on the links between its name/founding myth and the Greek myths about the Titan Atlas. Thanks to Homer, Tantalus is now better known as a mythical figure whose punishment in Hades was to be desperate to eat and drink the grapes and water that were just out of his reach, but other versions of his myth are very similar to those of Atlas, and involve him supporting great burdens and having his city struck down in a cataclysm. James argues that Tantalis was a major Bronze Age kingdom that suffered a calamity and was immortalised in the myth of Atlantis. However, identifying Tantalis as Atlantis means, once again, that Plato was wrong about dates, locations and Atlantis being an island.

Troy and the Black Sea

The Black Sea is thought by many to be a good candidate location for Atlantis, on the basis that the Pillars of Hercules might be a reference to the Bosporus Straits rather than those of Gibraltar. There is also the very real possibility that the Black Sea was a mostly dry basin until around 7,500 years ago when rising sea levels caused a massive breach in the rock dam that separated it from the Mediterranean, resulting in a deluge of biblical proportions that flooded the entire region in a matter of months or years. Several locations around or under the Black Sea have therefore been presented as Atlantis candidates. Nearby, but on the Mediterranean side of the Straits, is the location of ancient Troy, and this was suggested as the basis of the Atlantis story in 1992 by Eberhard Zangger, of the German Archaeological Institute in Athens. Troy was a citadel on a hill surrounded by a plain, and was also an advanced Bronze Age civilisation that fought a great war with the Greeks, just like Atlantis. All of these locations suffer from both a lack of corroborative evidence and the fundamental problem that they require heavy reinterpretation of Plato's account.

Antarctica

From the 1950s on, American academic Charles Hapgood developed a controversial theory of 'crustal displacement', which said that the entire crust of the Earth was subject to periodic sudden and massive reorientations, which could shift continents from the tropics to the poles in a few years. This theory was later linked to the possible provenance of apparently highly accurate maps of far-flung parts of the Earth, such as Antarctica, created by cartographers long before conventional history allows for their accurate navigation and mapping. Alternative historians Graham Hancock and Rand Flem-Ath suggest that Atlantis was an advanced civilisation on the Antarctic continent, which at the time was in a much more hospitable climate zone, but that thanks to crustal displacement 12,000 years ago it found itself at the Pole. Although some refugees escaped, founded other civilisations and somehow preserved their advanced cartographic knowledge long enough to pass it on to 15th- and 16th-century mapmakers, all other evidence for the existence of their once great society is now buried beneath several kilometres of Antarctic ice.

Apart from taking enormous liberties with Plato's account, this extraordinary theory is also handicapped by a lack of evidence, outside of the contentious maps, and by the general scepticism directed at Hapgood's crustal displacement theory.

Ireland

Swedish geographer Ulf Erlingsson's book *Atlantis From a Geographer's Perspective* points out that the only island in the Atlantic that actually comes close to matching Plato's description is Ireland, which is roughly oblong with mountains, a central plain and a great mound in the centre of its ancient capital at Tara. That's about as far as it goes, however, and one of the many obvious flaws in this theory is the fact that Ireland still stands above the waves.

Cuba

Alternative historian and sometime psychic quester Andrew Collins claims that Plato was describing one of the many islands in the Caribbean, among which the best fit is Cuba, which has a great plain bounded by mountains, much of which was possibly inundated in prehistoric times. Following Donnelly, Collins links this putative Atlantis with transatlantic cultural and trading links. The recent discovery on the sea floor near Cuba of what appear to be cyclopean ruins, although they may yet turn out to be natural rock formations, has sparked interest in the Cuba theory, but there is little other hard evidence to back up

Collins' claims. Most commentators would argue that Plato is fairly clearly referring to a location much closer to the Pillars of Hercules than the Caribbean.

Others

There are dozens, if not hundreds, of other candidate locations. The Canaries and the Azores are frequently said to be the last remnants of the Atlantean continent (the Canaries have mysterious megalithic remains which have not been adequately explained), but geography tells us they were never parts of larger land masses.

An expedition to trace Atlantis in Bolivia claimed to have identified a submerged volcanic island in Lake Poopo on the Bolivian altiplano as the fabled lost city, but this means stretching Plato to breaking point. Other candidates include Little Sole Bank in the Atlantic off the coast of Cornwall, and Carthage, ancient enemy of Rome, obliterated in the 2nd century BCE. All make problematic candidates owing to lack of evidence and/or mismatch with Plato's account.

Do we need Atlantis?

One reason for the appeal of Atlantis is that it fills a perceived gap in the conventional historical narrative, namely the question of where civilisation came from. In the conventional account it often seems that the major civilisations, such as Mesopotamia and Egypt, arose very quickly and without historical antecedents, while many other regions only seem to join the narrative when colonised or conquered by these great empires. Prehistory is seen as a blank during which humans had no history, even though we know that, anatomically, modern humans have been around for at least 100,000 years and cognitively modern ones (in the sense of having language, art and religion) for at least 40,000 years. The last Ice Age ended about 12,000 years ago.

What have humans been doing for all this time? Isn't it eminently plausible that civilisations rose and fell and whole histories played out?

From this point of view it makes sense to look for Atlantis, or something like it, but some palaeoanthropologists and archaeologists point out that prehistory is not a blank, and that civilisations did not arise from nowhere. In fact there is considerable evidence for a continuum of intellectual, technological and societal development stretching right back to the early Stone Age. We may not know the details of history during this period, but there is no need to fantasise about Atlantis or any other prehistoric super-civilisation to explain history or fill in the gaps.

Conclusion: Plato's inspiration and the lost city of Helike

Returning to the source, it seems clear from the evidence of Plato's own writings that Atlantis never existed as a real place, and that the theories, speculations, explorations and investigations of Atlantis-hunters can never be successful. By the same token, however, they can never be definitive, so there will always be room for more. We are still left with the question of where Plato may have got his inspiration.

Archaeogeologist Dr Iain Stewart suggests that the lost city of Helike may offer the best clue. Helike was a city in ancient Greece that was entirely levelled by a ferocious earthquake and associated tsunami in 373 BCE. The once-thriving state centred on Helike was divided up between its neighbours, and the site of the city itself was lost, submerged beneath the waters of the Mediterranean according to local belief (though discovered on land by archaeologists in 2000). The 373 BCE earthquake was just one of a series that devastated the region around that time, triggering tsunamis, destroying armies and upsetting the balance of power between warring states. Plato would have been about 50 at the time of the Helike disaster, and must have heard how the wrath of the gods had been visited upon it. It is not hard to imagine that he drew on this event, and the other earthquakes and tsunamis of the era, when creating a fictional civilisation to illustrate his arguments about the history and pedigree of Athens.

Perhaps we can glean a clue from the words Plato puts into the mouth of one of his characters in another work, *The Republic*:

> Now I wonder if we could contrive one of those convenient stories we were talking about ... Some magnificent myth that would in itself carry conviction to our whole community ... Nothing new – a fairy story like those the poets tell and have persuaded people to believe about the sort of thing that happened 'once upon a time'...

The Temple of Solomon

Three thousand years ago Solomon, King of Israel, built a magnificent temple to the Jewish god atop Mount Moriah in Jerusalem. In the heart of the Temple was the holy of holies, the innermost sanctum where the Ark of the Covenant (see page 58) sat on the Even Shetiyah (or Foundation Stone) and where the Shekinah, the manifest presence of God, was said to appear. Solomon's Temple, also known as the First Temple, was destroyed by the Babylonians under Nebuchadnezzar in 586 BCE, but after the Hebrews were freed from captivity and allowed to return to Israel a Second Temple was constructed, standing from 515 BCE until its destruction by the Romans in 70 CE. Today many Jews and Christians believe that building a Third Temple will usher in a messianic age and, according to fundamentalist Christians, even bring the Apocalypse, the Last Judgement and the End of Days. But for this to happen the Third Temple must be built on the precise site of the original Temples and the Ark of the Covenant must be recreated in the exact same spot. The problem with this, however, is that there is intense controversy over the precise location of the lost Temple of Solomon.

The Temple Mount today

Some time after the Romans levelled the Second Temple they built a temple to Jupiter on the site, but by the time of the Muslim conquest there were no buildings standing on the Mount. When the Muslims took possession of Jerusalem from the Byzantine Empire (as the Eastern Roman Empire came to be known), they were shocked to find that the Christian masters of the city were using the area as a rubbish tip, apparently as a deliberate affront to the Jews. Subsequently the Muslims built a number of shrines and mosques there, and the Temple Mount became the Al-Haram al-Sharif (the Noble Sanctuary), the third holiest site in Islam, characterised by the famous Dome of the Rock and the Al-Aqsa Mosque.

Today the Temple Mount is a broad, roughly rectangular platform, with the long axis running north–south. The Dome of the Rock is more or less in the centre, with the Al-Aqsa Mosque at the southern end. To the north of the Mount is the ancient site of the Roman Antonia Fortress. On the western side is the Western or Wailing Wall, widely held to be part of the retaining wall that held up the Temple Mount during the Second Temple, and hence the last remnant of the original Temple complex.

The traditional view

The majority consensus view is that the Dome of the Rock, named for the outcrop of rock it was built to enclose, sits more or less exactly where the First and Second Temples were. This outcrop of rock is variously argued to have been the site of the sacrificial altar in the middle of the Temple, or the Even Shetiyah itself, around which the holy of holies was built. Known as the Sakhra, this rock is steeped in lore and significance.

It was considered to be the exact centre of the world, and the first stone laid in the construction of the Earth. It was also said to have been the rock upon which Abraham was to sacrifice Isaac and the spot where Jacob lay when he had his dream about a ladder ascending to heaven. According to Temple expert Leen Ritmeyer, photos of the Sakhra show the actual depression where the Ark of the Covenant sat.

Identification of the Dome of the Rock site with that of the Temple has important ramifications, both political and eschato-logical (concerning belief in the End Times). If Jewish and Christian Temple rebuilders wish to accomplish their goal they will first have to remove the Dome of the Rock, a move that, it is widely considered, could well trigger World War III or at least a devastating regional conflagration. Even the suggestion that this might be considered inflames opinion in the Muslim world, despite the fact that it is repudiated by official Israeli policy and restricted to fringe groups only. Merely the rumour that an extremist group plans to stage a march on the Temple Mount has been enough to trigger demonstrations as far afield as Indonesia.

The Ophel Mound and the Gihon Spring

In his 1999 book, *The Temples that Jerusalem Forgot*, Dr Ernest Martin propounds the theory that the true location of the Temple was actually to the south of the Temple Mount, on what was known as the Ophel Mound. This is effectively the southern end of the promontory or ridge which becomes the Temple Mount to the north, and sits just above the Gihon Springs, which in ancient times was a major source of water for Jerusalem.

According to Martin, who claims to base his theory on the work of the Mazar family, archaeologists who worked in the Temple Mount area, the Temple could not have been on the Mount because the water supply there was inadequate to supply the 'living' (ie running) water needed for the various purification rituals. Instead it must have been close to the Gihon Springs further down in the valley, while the Temple Mount was only ever the site of the Antonia Fortress. Martin also adduces various Bible quotes and ancient sources to back up his theory.

Martin's theory is generally dismissed by Temple scholars. For instance, Leen Ritmeyer argues that Martin misinterprets or misrepresents his scriptural and ancient sources and simply ignores the mass of archaeological and historical evidence placing the Temple on the Mount. He suggests that Martin's judgement may have been clouded by his religious agenda – namely his desire to find a site for the Third Temple that might be accessible today. In the words of Michael Germano, Martin's book 'may well serve as the awaited stimulus for the building of Jerusalem's Third Temple by shifting our collective focus from the Haram esh-Sharif [ie the Temple Mount] to the area of the Gihon Spring.' Germano, like Martin, is an academic with close links to the Worldwide Church of God, a radically eschatological fringe Christian group linked to many Temple Mount controversies.

The Dome of the Tablets

While Martin's theory is widely dismissed, there are two competing theories concerning the true location of the Temple that are taken much more seriously. One of these places the Temple to the north of the traditional site, with the holy of holies under a small Islamic shrine called the Dome of the Tablets (or the Dome of the Spirits), which covers a small outcrop of bedrock. The name itself is suggestive, for Islamic place names often record connections to previous structures and the holy of holies was the home of the Ark, the dwelling place of both Moses' Tablets of Law and the Shekinah (the divine spirit).

The northern location theory is principally the work of Asher Kaufman, who bases his argument on descriptions of the dimensions of the Temple's outer courts and the space between the Temple and the various gateways that led on to the Mount, as described in a variety of ancient sources. He further argues that the rock covered by the Dome of the Tablets must be the true Even Shetiyah, or Foundation Stone, because it is the highest (and therefore holiest) protuberance on the Temple Mount, and because its pitted appearance matches the description given in the account of a 4th-century pilgrim from Bordeaux, who called it the 'Pierced Stone'.

Flaws in the northern theory

Other Temple scholars have picked holes in Kaufman's theory. In particular, it is argued that the northern location does not leave enough room on the Mount to fit the Temple's foundations without building some sort of massive support structure in the valley to the north. Leading Temple archaeologist Dan Bahat argues that this would have been beyond the means of the ancient Israelites, but Kaufman claims that there is evidence of just such a structure in the valley. Another serious objection to the northern theory is that British archaeologists who explored the area in the early 20th century discovered traces of a filled-in fosse, or moat, dating back to biblical times, which runs across the northern end of the current Temple Mount platform, and which would have cut through Kaufman's proposed location.

As with Martin's theory, Kaufman's hypothesis has been seized on by some Temple rebuilders as a solution to the 'site occupied' problem. In Revelation 11:2 the apostle John is instructed in the dimensions of a new Temple, but told 'the court which is without the temple leave out, for it is given unto the Gentiles.' This is interpreted by some fundamentalists to mean that the Third Temple will not need to include the outer courtyard of the original, which in turn means that it could fit onto a site centred on the Dome of the Tablets without disturbing the Dome of the Rock. Somewhat optimistically, Temple rebuilders of this inclination hope that this will allow reconstruction while avoiding touching off a massive conflict. This is desperately unrealistic, as the Islamic authorities, not to mention international Muslim sentiment, would never compromise the territorial integrity of the Noble Sanctuary in this fashion.

The El Kas Fountain

Perhaps the most plausible alternative to the traditional view is the theory that the Temple was located to the south of the Dome of the Rock, with the holy of holies situated where the El Kas Fountain – an Islamic ablution fountain midway between the Dome and the Al-Aqsa mosque – currently sits. This theory was first proposed in the late 1970s by Father Bellarmino Bagatti, a Franciscan scholar, and more recently championed by Israeli architect Tuvia Sagiv.

Several lines of reasoning support a southern location for the Temple. For instance, Sagiv argues that the traditionally assumed location for the Antonia Fortress makes little sense, and that it was probably sited where the Dome of the Rock now sits. It would make more sense for the ancient fosse, which sits just to the north of the Dome, to have been between the fort and the routes of potential enemy access from the north. Scriptural sources describe distances and elevations between different parts of the Temple complex; while these do not match up with a Dome location, they concur almost exactly with a southern location. The southern location also makes more sense in terms of the water supply the Temple would have needed for its cleansing rituals, as the main Jerusalem aqueduct from the Judean Hills reaches the Temple Mount too low for the Dome site.

The Temple of Jupiter

Sagiv also suggests how the Dome/Temple confusion may have arisen. Thermal infrared scanning of the Dome of the Rock reveals evidence for massive pentagonal foundations beneath it, which match almost exactly the typical layout of Roman temples built in the area. It is possible that when the Muslims gained control of Jerusalem they built on the remnants of the Temple of Jupiter that had sat on the Temple Mount after the Second Temple was destroyed, and that it is these remnants that gave rise to the traditional view that the Dome of the Rock was built on the site of the Temple.

There are objections to the southern location theory, however, including that it ignores the archaeological evidence supporting the traditional location, and that it requires the Temple Mount platform to have previously extended further to the south than it does today.

Temple deniers

An alternative and highly politically-charged strand of thought has come to the fore in the Muslim world since the Six Day War of 1967. Many writers, clerics, politicians and archaeologists are now claiming that the First and Second Temples never existed, and that there has always been an Al-Aqsa mosque on the site dating back to Adamic times. Dismissing the traditional view that the Western or Wailing Wall is the last remnant of the Temple complex, this view effectively denies any special Jewish claim to the Temple Mount, and, by extension, to Jerusalem itself.

There is no evidence for this argument, and it is instructive to point out that prior to the Six Day War and the Israeli occupation of East Jerusalem, Islamic scholars had no issues with the traditional historical account of the Temple Mount.

The dangerous Temple

The Temple Mount continues to be one of the most divisive pieces of geography on the planet, and although most of the debate over its precise location is conducted by evangelicals or extremists of one stripe or another, it should not be dismissed as the trivial twittering of a harmless fringe. An estimated 25–70 million Americans believe that rebuilding the Temple is a sacred duty that will usher in the Messianic Era, and the groups that represent them are hugely influential in Washington, having effectively got George W Bush elected twice. A 1996 Gallup poll found that 58 per cent of Israelis favour rebuilding the Temple. American fundamentalists have donated more than $100 million to Temple rebuilding research projects.

In other words, many serious, well-funded, well-supported, highly placed people are actively pursuing a goal that could trigger a massive confrontation with the Islamic world, against a backdrop of increasing global instability. In this context, the uncertainty over the exact location of the Temple – which is one of the main theological stumbling blocks for rebuilders – looks like a blessed mystery.

The Library of Alexandria

Fabled as the greatest repository of knowledge in the ancient world, the first university and the home of antiquity's wisest scholars, the Library of Alexandria has passed into the realm of legend. Its destruction has been painted as one of the bleakest chapters in mankind's intellectual history, contributing to Europe's plunge into the Dark Ages and setting back the development of science, philosophy, medicine and literature, if not the cause of reason itself, by a millennium. The loss of the Library has even been described as 'the day that history lost its memory'. The Library's legend is enhanced by the layers of mystery that surround it. How big was it? What incredible riches were stored within? How was it destroyed, and by whom? And where are its remains?

The legend of the library

The standard account of the library runs like this. Alexander the Great founded Alexandria in 332 BCE but hung around just long enough to lay out the basic street plan and get construction underway. When he died a few years later, one of his generals, Ptolemy Soter, took control of Egypt and made Alexandria his capital, building great palaces and temples, including a temple to the Muses (or Museum). His son, Ptolemy II Philadelphus (ruled 282–246 BCE), started the library, which was based in or next to the Museum, using Aristotle's personal library as its core. Ptolemy III Euergetes continued the work, determined to gather in the library all the knowledge in the world, and he instituted an aggressive policy of collection that involved acquiring scrolls, copying them and then returning the (inferior) copies while keeping the originals. He supposedly had every ship that passed through Alexandria searched for new scrolls and borrowed the entire scroll collection of Athens, willingly forfeiting his massive deposit in order to keep the originals. Eventually the collection numbered over 500,000 scrolls – 700,000 by some accounts – making it, by a considerable margin, the greatest collection the ancient world had ever known. (The rival library at Pergamon was said to have 200,000 scrolls, which were supposedly transferred to Alexandria as a gift from Mark Anthony to Cleopatra, and the next biggest library in Rome had 20,000 at most.)

Along with the collection of parchment (and later vellum) scrolls, the Ptolemies paid for a permanent faculty of 30–50 scholars to live and work at the library, and over the centuries their number included most of the greatest names of antiquity, including Euclid (father of geometry), Eratosthenes (who calculated the circumference of the Earth), Archimedes (legendary discoverer of the lever, the screw, and pi) and Galen (the most influential medical writer of the next 1,400 years).

Thanks to the library, Alexandria became the centre of learning and knowledge for the entire Mediterranean world for over 600 years, and legends grew up around it. One well-known story comes down to us from the scholar Aristeas (*c*180–145 BCE), the earliest source to mention the library, who tells how 72 rabbis were brought to the library to translate the Old Testament in Greek, and who, despite working in isolation from one another, arrived at 72 identical versions thanks to divine inspiration.

Alongside the Royal (aka Great) Library were 'daughter' libraries, especially one housed at the Serapeum, a magnificent temple to Serapis founded by Ptolemy II. Later Roman emperors, including Claudius and Hadrian, also founded libraries in Alexandria.

Legends of the fall

Although numerous ancient and Byzantine sources mention the fate of the library, they are contradictory, inconsistent and confused, and there is no definitive contemporary account. Traditionally the destruction of the library has been blamed on three people. Julius Caesar is said to have accidentally burnt it down when he set fire to the area around the docks when he was besieged there in 47–48 BCE. A Christian mob under Patriarch Theophilus is said to have destroyed it when razing the pagan Serapeum in 391 CE. Finally, in 640 CE, Muslim forces conquered Egypt and the Caliph Omar is said to have ordered that the contents of the library be burnt in the fires of the city's bathhouses, on the grounds that any scrolls that contradicted the Koran were heretical and any that agreed with it were superfluous.

Myths and mysteries of the Royal Library

Much of the standard/legendary account of the library's development, size and destruction is probably wrong. Sources for the legends often date too long after the events they describe, while many of the claims made have to be viewed with scepticism, given the tendencies of antique scribes to embellish tales or to write with a political/religious agenda.

How big is big?

The Royal Library was probably not as big as legend contends. Historian James Hannam has calculated that storing 500,000 scrolls would require 40 kilometres (25 miles) of shelving, which in turn would mean that the Royal Library must have been a truly monumental building. None of the sources mention such a gargantuan edifice, and since the remains of the library have never been fully excavated its full extent remains a mystery.

Most telling, however, is the evidence from other ancient libraries that have left remains, which show that even those renowned for their wealth and breadth had collections numbering in the thousands rather than the hundreds of thousands. The finest library in the history of ancient Rome was the Library of Trajan, which probably contained around 20,000 scrolls, while the Library of Pergamon, arch-rival of the Alexandrian library, probably had around 30,000. The figure of 200,000 scrolls, which Mark Anthony is said to have taken from the Library of Pergamon and given to Cleopatra as a gift for the Alexandrian library, derives from a writer who recorded the figure as an example of falsehoods levelled at Mark Anthony by his enemies.

We also know that one of the librarians at Alexandria, Callimachus, made an extensive and detailed index of the library's contents, called the *Pinakes*, including summaries and biographical notes about the authors. The *Pinakes* themselves consisted of about 120 scrolls – roughly 1 million words – which is far too small to cover 500,000 or more scrolls. The upshot is that the Royal Library was probably an order of magnitude smaller than popular legend supposes, which may help to explain how it could have disappeared from history without leaving more traces. The inflated figures probably result from a mixture of exaggeration by antique scribes and errors in copying of their works (which for many centuries depended on laborious transcription by hand from versions themselves many times removed from the original). Over time, and in the absence of more concrete evidence to the contrary, these inflated figures became part of the legend of the library.

More than one lost library

As well as debates about the size of the Alexandrian collection, there is an even more fundamental source of confusion in determining its fate, which is that it may be misleading to talk about the library in the singular. We know that there were at least two major libraries in Alexandria – the Royal Library associated with the Museum and the daughter library at the Serapeum. Each of these may have consisted of scattered buildings and/or collections, and so the historical picture becomes very complex.

During the centuries of Roman occupation, Alexandria endured an often turbulent history. It suffered extensive damage when it was conquered by Augustus in 30 BCE and again when Caracalla instituted a massacre of Alexandrians in revenge for a perceived insult in 215 CE. Later it was almost razed to the ground when rebels used it as a base and were savagely put down by the emperor Aurelian in 273 CE, and again, in similar circumstances, by the emperor Diocletian in 298 CE. By the late 4th century it was a much reduced city, and many experts think it likely that if the Royal Library (the one associated with the Museum) did survive beyond the time of Caesar (see page 33) it was probably diminished, broken up and possibly destroyed at some point during these many troubles, but that records of the destruction have not come down to us today.

Other Alexandrian libraries probably survived this period, however, and lasted until the late 4th century, a time of religious fundamentalism and extremism. Descriptions of these libraries, and their destruction, in late antique, Byzantine and medieval sources are probably the cause of confusion over the survival and eventual fate of the Royal Library. It is almost certain that the Royal Library was long gone by this time, but the proud heritage of scholarship in Alexandria lived on in the form of the library in the Temple of Serapis – aka the Serapeum.

The Serapeum was a mighty temple mainly constructed by Ptolemy III Euergetes (ruled 246–222 BCE) on a small hill, or acropolis, in the south-eastern corner of Alexandria. Ancient sources are confused as to when the temple acquired a library. Some experts argue that it was not until the middle of the 2nd century CE, during extensive refurbishment of the Serapeum after a number of fires in preceding centuries, that the Roman rulers of Alexandria founded a major collection there, meaning that it did not come 'into play' until well after the time of Caesar – an important detail when trying to understand what happened to the collections and when.

What really happened to the libraries?

The greatest mystery surrounding Alexandria's great libraries is the issue of their destruction or, perhaps more accurately, their disappearance. For despite their size, fame and importance it is not at all clear what happened to them. Were they destroyed in a single act or disaster? And, if so, who was responsible?

At least one of the traditional suspects can be ruled out immediately, as the Royal Library and any of its daughter libraries had certainly disappeared long before the Muslim conquest of Egypt. The tale of Caliph Omar and the bathhouse ovens is almost certainly a calumny spread by anti-Islamic writers of the Byzantine and medieval era. The guilt or innocence of the other two suspects – Julius Caesar and the zealous mob of Patriarch Theophilus – is much less straightforward.

Caesar the arsonist

The case against Caesar derives from Roman authors writing decades or centuries after the alleged events, who may have skewed their version of events to fit a political agenda, namely painting Caesar as a villain. Caesar's own account of his visit to Alexandria acknowledges that he did start a fire in the harbour area, to defend himself against an attack by Egyptian troops, but does not mention any damage to the library, although this could simply mean that he is covering up a shameful accident. Some historians argue that the Royal Library was far from the docks and too sturdy and fireproof to have been at risk. Others argue that the ancient sources suggest that only a warehouse of scrolls in temporary storage was burnt.

Ferreting out the truth at such a late date is impossible, and there is conflicting evidence that suggests, on the one hand, that the Royal Library had definitely disappeared by around 20 BCE, and on the other that it existed until at least 200 CE. The geographer Strabo, writing about his visit to Alexandria in 20 BCE, does not mention the library as an extant institution but does mention it in another context – *in the past tense.* This suggestive evidence is contradicted by an inscription found in Rome, dedicated to Tiberius Claudius Balbillus, died 56 CE, who is described as having been the director of the Museum and libraries of Alexandria, which seems to indicate that the Museum and its attached libraries must have outlasted Caesar.

Another piece of evidence that is used by both camps in the argument over Caesar's possible guilt is the *Deipnosophistai* of Athenaeus, from around 200 CE, in which he writes: 'And concerning the number of books and the establishment of libraries and the collection in the Museum, why need I even speak when they are all in the memory of men.' For those who argue that the Royal Library lasted well into the Roman era, this passage is interpreted to mean that it was unnecessary for Athenaeus to describe the library as it was still so famous. For those who argue the opposite, the passage is interpreted to mean that the library exists *only* in memory.

Theophilus and the Serapeum

The other commonly named culprit for the destruction of Alexandria's 'library' is Patriarch Theophilus. In practice, the library in question here is the collection at the Serapeum, which was probably endowed, as explained above, by Egypt's Roman overlords and seems to have survived until the late 4th century. According to this version of the destruction of the library, the Serapeum was destroyed in 391 CE when Patriarch Theophilus, the head of the church in Alexandria, led a mob that razed the old pagan temple to the ground. Eventually a Christian church was constructed on the site. It is generally assumed that the books and scrolls kept there were either stolen or burned along with the temple, and the episode is often recounted as a parable on the dangers of fundamentalism, with parallels in the modern era – such as the Taliban's destruction of the giant statues of the Buddha at Bamiyam in Afghanistan. However, while the building itself almost certainly did perish in this fashion, it is less clear that the Serapeum's collection of books was lost at the same time – or even that the collection still existed at this point.

New suspects

The historian James Hannam insists that close reading of the ancient sources does not support either of the traditional suspects fingered for the destruction of the Royal and Serapeum Libraries – Julius Caesar and Patriarch Theophilus respectively. Instead he argues that both collections may have already disappeared before these alleged destructive events took place, and that the real culprits have – in the eyes of history – got away with bibliotechnical murder.

According to Hannam, Pharaoh Ptolemy VIII Physcon (ruled 145–116 BCE) may well have been responsible for the greatest crime in academic history. A bloody tyrant who usurped the throne and visited death and destruction on Alexandria, Physcon may have accidentally destroyed one of his kingdom's greatest treasures during his attacks on the city. There are few convincing references to the Royal Library as an existing entity after his reign, and a list of librarians recovered from an ancient garbage tip suggestively comes to an end at precisely this time.

As for the loss of the Serapeum Library, Hannam accuses one of Patriarch Theophilus' predecessors, George of Cappadocia. George was known to have presided over an earlier ransacking of the Serapeum, and on his death in 361 CE was also said to have in his possession a large collection of books and scrolls. The Emperor Julian (who coveted the collection himself) wrote that it was 'very large and complete and contained philosophers of every school and many historians'.

In summary, there are many suspects for the role of villain in this enduring mystery. Definitively pinning the crime on one of them might be easier if the crime scene itself could be examined, but the exact whereabouts of the Royal Library constitute another great enigma.

Where is the Royal Library?

After the Muslim conquest of 640 CE and the foundation of a new Egyptian capital at Cairo, Alexandria declined in importance and size. Subsequent fires and devastating earthquakes further reduced the once magnificent city, and much of it was swallowed by the waters of the Mediterranean thanks to tsunamis, subsidence and sea level changes (the sea level today is 2 metres, 6.6 feet, higher than it was in Roman times). By the modern era most of Alexandria's architectural treasures, from the wondrous Pharos lighthouse to the royal palaces and temples of the Bruchion quarter, had vanished, including the Museum and the associated Royal Library.

The Bruchion quarter – aka the palace or Royal Quarter – was in the north-east of the ancient city and, according to the Greek geographer Strabo, made up nearly a third of the city. The exact location of the Museum is uncertain, and the location of the Royal Library even more of a mystery because it is not clear from the sources whether it was part of the Museum or actually a separate building, and, if so, how it was situated in relation to the Museum. Until the 1990s there was little archaeological investigation in this part of Alexandria, although bizarrely a group of psychic archaeologists named the Mobius Group did attempt to locate the lost treasures of the city, including the library, back in 1979.

Psychic quest for the lost treasures

The Mobius Group was the brainchild of businessman and explorer Stephan Schwarz, who believed that an alliance between a form of clairvoyance known as remote sensing and conventional archaeological methods such as side-scan sonar and actual physical excavation could produce amazing results. Remote sensing is a form of out-of-body experience, telepathy or astral travel, where the psychic claims to use his or her mind's eye to visualise a target and the surrounding area, and even pinpoint it on a map. According to Schwarz's 1983 book, *The Alexandria Project*, the Mobius Group had considerable success locating sunken relics in the dirty waters of Alexandria's harbour, and divers, following directions from the psychics, even found what Schwarz claimed were the remains of Cleopatra's Summer Palace. Supposedly many of the group's findings were later replicated by a French-Egyptian survey team in 1995, a survey that went on to retrieve many of the relics first spotted by the psychics. How seriously these claims should be taken is a moot point, given that little concrete proof has been produced to back them up. In any case, the team seems to have had less success on land than at sea and did not uncover the Royal Library.

Uncovering auditoria

More conventional archaeological work may have succeeded where psychics failed, with the announcement in May 2004 that a joint Polish-Egyptian team excavating in the Bruchion quarter had uncovered what appeared to be a series of lecture theatres or auditoria. Thirteen lecture halls were discovered, each equipped with a central podium for the lecturer and offering seating for 5,000 students in total, apparently confirming the notion of the Royal Library as an ancient university or academy.

Whether this really is the Royal Library, and if any evidence of the storage of scrolls has been discovered, remain mysteries, because since this initial and much-heralded announcement there has been no more word of the discovery or of any follow-up work. But, as the work of historians like James Hannam reveals, those hunting for evidence of a gigantic book repository of legendary dimensions are likely to be chasing a phantom. The Royal Library of Alexandria probably never existed in the form in which it has been immortalised in popular myth, and the final truth about it remains buried beneath modern Alexandria, awaiting discovery.

Camelot

King Arthur is the central figure in the cycle of myths and legends known as the Matter of Britain. Through latter-day retellings in print and on screen most people are familiar with the basic elements of the cycle, including the tale of Camelot, Arthur's stronghold and the home of the Round Table. In the modern conception, Camelot is usually portrayed as a High Middle Age castle with soaring towers and parapets. But did it even exist, and, if so, would it really have looked like this? Most perplexingly of all, where was Camelot – which of the dozens of claimants to the title is the real one?

Back to basics

The Matter of Britain, as it has come down to us today, is very different from that of previous ages. Arthur himself has accreted so many layers of myth and legend over the centuries that the real Arthur, and by extension the real Camelot, are heavily obscured. To find the real Camelot it is necessary to peel back these layers and examine the historical basis for the Arthur legend.

Tales of Arthur

The Arthurian legends as we know them mostly derive from the medieval versions, beginning with Geoffrey of Monmouth's *History of the Kings of Britain* in 1138, followed by Chrétien de Troyes' *Lancelot* (c1180) and Thomas Malory's *Le Morte d'Arthur* (1470), among many others. In fact it is in Chrétien de Troyes' *Lancelot* that Camelot is first mentioned, and not until later that it assumes its central role in the Arthurian romance.

The earliest references to Arthur come in Welsh poems dating back to the 6th century. In these, Arthur is generally referred to as a *Dux Bellorum*, or 'war leader', and it is in this context that most Arthurian scholars explain the historical basis of the Arthur figure. It is generally accepted that the original Arthur was probably a Romano-Celtic war leader who fought the invading Anglo-Saxons in the period after the withdrawal of Roman forces from Britain and the collapse of the Western Roman Empire. He may have been a tribal chieftain or king, or a general in command of the army of one or more kings, or even the commander of what remained of Britain's Roman military machine. Many pre-existing legendary and folkloric attributes attached themselves to this historical figure (eg magical swords drawn from stones and dragon-slaying), and before long Arthur was a legendary hero rather than a real one. As his legend grew, new elements – some post-dating the original Arthur and relating to other historical figures – became incorporated into the tale.

Did Camelot exist?

What does this mean for the search for Camelot? Camelot seems to be a later addition to the Arthurian romance, which could mean that it was entirely fictional, or simply that it took a while for oral traditions concerning it to be written down. What is certain is that Camelot in the popularly conceived sense of a medieval castle/citadel never existed, as the Britons of the 5th century did not possess the technology to create something like this. The 'real' Camelot, or the historical basis for Camelot, is more likely to have been a hill-fort or an encampment. It would have had earthworks such as ditches and ramparts, wooden structures such as gates, towers and halls, and possibly even stonework in the main walls. It may have been built on a Roman model, perhaps even using pre-existing Roman structures, or it may have been mainly Celtic in form. Probably it was a combination of the two.

Camelot candidates

With this template in mind, where should we look for Camelot? Literally dozens of places around the British Isles claim to have a connection with King Arthur, with many identified (usually by enthusiastic local tourist boards) as the site of Camelot. Which of them to choose partly depends on which of the many candidates one picks as the historical basis for Arthur.

Camulodonum

Perhaps the most obvious candidate is one of the supposed etymological inspirations for Camelot, the Roman city of Camulodonum (present-day Colchester, Essex), at one point the capital of Roman Britain. Several of the models for the Arthur figure were Romano-British generals or leaders. For instance, Magnus Maximianus was the *dux*, or leader, of Roman Britain in the late 4th century, and some of his exploits match those attributed to Arthur by Geoffrey of Monmouth, including fighting a civil war and twice leading military expeditions to Armorica in Gaul to get involved with Continental Roman politics. Maximianus led an army into Gaul after declaring himself emperor, which fits in with early Welsh references to Arthur as *ymerawdwr* (Welsh for 'emperor').

Similar claims and links are made for Riothamus, a late-5th-century British leader who is recorded in 6th-century sources as having twice led an army across the Channel to support the Western Roman Empire, as having been betrayed in battle (as Arthur was) and as having retreated after his last battle to a town called Avallon (Arthur was said to have been carried off to Avalon after his final defeat). The name Riothamus means 'highest king', and so could be a reference to someone whose real name was Arthur.

Finally, there is Ambrosius Aurelianus, a Roman-British general who took control of British forces during the Anglo-Saxon incursions of the late 5th century and who is commonly held to have won a mighty victory against them at the Battle of Badon Hill – the same victory that is attributed to Arthur by early Welsh bards, Geoffrey of Monmouth and others.

All three of these figures make plausible candidates for the historical Arthur, although there are problems with each. Maximianus comes from the wrong period, Riothamus may have been a king in Armorica rather than in Britain, and Aurelianus is clearly identified as different from Arthur by Geoffrey of Monmouth, who wrote that he was Arthur's uncle. He was probably also too old to have fought at Badon Hill, despite what you read in most history books. Nonetheless, if any of them was the basis for the legendary Arthur it is also plausible that he might have made Camulodonum, a major Romano-British city, his Camelot.

The main flaw in this theory is that Camulodonum, located in Essex in South East England, is much too far east to have been

Arthur's base. Most sources agree in basing Arthur in the west of Britain. In addition, the Essex area fell to the Saxon invaders early on in their conquest of England, but Arthur is supposed to have been winning many victories against them at that time.

Winchester

Sir Thomas Malory was very definite in placing Camelot at Winchester, in southern England, and the town proudly displays the Round Table itself in the Great Hall of its castle. In its heyday, Winchester was the capital of the Anglo-Saxon kingdom of Wessex and later of England. It is possible that the Saxons took Arthur's capital as their own.

In practice, Malory's identification is generally dismissed as fanciful. Like Camulodonum, Winchester is too far east to make a convincing Camelot, and the archaeological evidence doesn't back it up either – Winchester Castle was only built in the 12th century, and there is little evidence of Dark Ages activity in the area until the coming of the Saxons. The Winchester Round Table has been dated to c1270, during the reign of Edward I. He was known to have been an Arthur enthusiast, and the table was probably created to amuse him.

Scottish Camelots

Many places in Scotland claim association with Arthur, and Scottish or near Scottish Camelot candidates include Carlisle and Falkirk. One Arthur candidate who might make these northern sites plausible is Artur mac Aidan. Artur was the eldest son of Aidan mac Gabran, who ruled the Celtic kingdom of Dalriada in Western Scotland from around 574–608.

Artur was general of his father's armies, and there are many similarities between his life and that of the legendary Arthur. Artur supposedly had a sister called Morgan; he was a contemporary of a Merlin candidate named Myrddin; he fought a last battle in 582 at the River Allan, also known as Camallan (King Arthur's last battle was the Battle of Camlann), after which his body was taken to an island called Invalone (similar to Avalon).

However, Artur lived too late to be the real Arthur, and is most likely to have acquired his name in honour of the pre-existing tales/legends of Arthur. His kingdom would not have included Carlisle or Falkirk anyway, neither of which have evidence to back up their claims to be Camelot. In fact, since almost all the sources agree that Arthur's base was in the west, in or near Wales, Cornwall or the West Country, it makes sense to look in this area for the best Camelot candidates.

Tintagel

In terms of modern-day tourist lore, Tintagel in Cornwall is the foremost claimant to the crown of Camelot. It is a ruined castle on a rocky windswept headland jutting out into the sea. According to Geoffrey of Monmouth, Arthur was born here. The present castle, however, dates back only as far as the 12th century, and was constructed for Reginald, Earl of Cornwall. Is it merely a coincidence that Reginald was the brother of the patron of Geoffrey of Monmouth, or could this account for Geoffrey's account?

However, there is evidence of an earlier castle or fort on the site, dating back to roughly the correct time, and in 1998 an archaeological discovery seemed to provide strong evidence linking the site with Arthur. Amidst the remains of the 6th-century fort a stone with a Latin inscription was found. Engraved on what has come to be known as the Arthur Stone, was the legend: 'PATER COLI AVI FICIT ARTOGNOU', which roughly translates as, 'Artognou, father of a descendant of Coll, has had (this) constructed' (the 'this' presumably referring to a building on the site).

Artognou (pronounced 'Arthnou') is believed to mean 'descendant of Arthur', while Coll could be Coel Hen, a legendary Romano-British king who is the basis for the nursery rhyme *Old King Cole*, and who is named by Geoffrey of Monmouth as an ancestor of Arthur. The Arthur Stone appears to explain why Tintagel was associated with Arthur, and hence why Geoffrey included it in his account. What's more, other discoveries at Tintagel from the same period as the Stone include fragments of expensive pottery, glasswork and even coins from distant Byzantium, suggesting that it may have been the seat of a rich and powerful kingdom with trade links extending to the Mediterranean.

A worthy Camelot candidate? Perhaps, but Artognou, who-ever he was, was not the same as Arthur (given than his name suggests he was a 'descendant' of Arthur), so we can't make a definite link between Tintagel and Arthur, or conclude with certainty that Tintagel was Camelot. It does, however, seem likely that tales of the Dark Age masters of Tintagel may have fed into the Arthur legend.

Cadbury Castle

Cadbury Castle is actually a hill bearing the earthwork remains of a fort, located next to the village of South Cadbury in Somerset. It was first fingered as the location of Camelot in 1542 by the antiquarian John Leland, who wrote, 'At the very south end of the church of South-Cadbyri standeth Camallate, some-time a famous town or castle ... The people can tell nothing there but that they have heard Arthur much resorted to Camalat.' Arthurian traditions in the locale have been strong ever since. On Cadbury Hill itself there is an Arthur's Lane, an Arthur's Well and an Arthur's Palace (an outcrop at the top of the hill), while folklore speaks of Arthur and his knights sleeping in a cave inside the hill, and of the king leading a wild hunt on Midsummer's Eve.

Some sceptics have suggested that Leland was simply invent-ing this tradition, inspired by the proximity of the villages of Queen Camel and West Camel. Even if he was faithfully record-ing a pre-existing tradition it might seem far-fetched to assume that it was a reliable one spanning a thousand years, except that there is strong evidence to suggest exactly this. Excavations have shown that there was extensive construction on the site during the Arthurian period, with a great hall and many other buildings. The ancient fortifications provided by the earthworks were refurbished and improved at this time. Also discovered were remains of pottery similar to that found at Tintagel, suggesting that, as with the Cornish site, Cadbury Castle was occupied by a lord of wealth and power.

So, although there is no direct evidence of an Arthur, there is strong evidence that during the Arthurian period a powerful king or warlord made Cadbury Castle his base, fortifying and extending it to house a force of more than a thousand soldiers and hundreds more camp followers. Given the local traditions and place-name associations, it seems that Cadbury is a prime Camelot candidate.

Caerleon

Caerleon, a village outside Newport in South East Wales, was an important Roman military town from 75 to 300 CE. Its name is derived from the Welsh for 'Fortress of the Legion'. In early versions of the Arthur myth, such as those of Geoffrey of Monmouth, there is no Camelot, and Arthur's capital is explicitly said to have been situated at Caerleon. It has one of the most impressive amphitheatres in Britain, which by Arthurian times would have been a wide, grassy bowl, where councils and entertainments were held – could this be the origin of the legend of the Round Table?

York

In Roman times York was named Eboracum, but another name for it was *Urbe Legionum*, or 'City of the Legion', because it was the base for the legions guarding Hadrian's Wall and the northern borders of Britannia. Could the early Arthur chroniclers have mixed up 'Fortress of the Legion' with 'City of the Legion', and hence have recorded Caerleon as Arthur's base when they meant York? According to recent theories about the true source of the Arthurian legends this may be the case, as Eboracum was the base of Lucius Artorius Castus.

Castus was a Roman general sent to Britain in 181 CE. He appears to be the first person with an 'Arthur'-type name in recorded British history, and his life story has many parallels with Arthur's. He held the rank of *dux* (Arthur was *Dux Bellorum*). He led expeditions to the Continent, and in particular to Armorica. He led a force of heavy cavalry – horsemen from Sarmatia (modern-day Ukraine) – which was unusual at the time and sure to have made an impression on the people of Britain as they defended the country from barbarian hordes sweeping down from Caledonia (modern-day Scotland).

Castus' Sarmatian cavalry may also have been the source of other elements of the Arthurian legend. They held their swords in special reverence, and had their own folklore about an Arthurian figure with a magic sword that was cast into the water on his death, and who led a band of knights who rode on quests and performed heroic deeds.

There are flaws in the Castus-as-Arthur theory. The Latin form of Arthur is not *Artorius*, but *Arthurus*, so the name is not an exact match. Most significantly, however, Castus lived far too early and fought the wrong enemies. The Arthur legend centres around battles with the Saxons and is firmly attributed to the late 5th century. If Castus did contribute to the Arthur legend it was probably through the folklore passed on by his Sarmatians, and possibly through oral traditions of his exploits kept alive for long enough to feed into the nascent 6th-century Matter of Britain. In this context, York makes an unconvincing Camelot.

Viroconium

In the early 2nd century CE, Viroconium (modern-day Wroxeter, in Shropshire) was the fourth biggest city in Roman Britain. Although it subsequently fell into decline, archaeological evidence suggests that it was reoccupied and heavily restored and fortified during the 480s, exactly the time when Arthur was said to be at large. In their book, *King Arthur – the True Story*, Graham Phillips and Martin Keatman propose that Viroconium was Camelot, and that the Arthur who dwelt there was the Welsh king Owain Ddantgwyn ('Owen White Tooth').

Owain ruled the kingdoms of Rhôs and Gwynedd at the end of the 5th century. He was killed by his nephew Maelgwyn in a battle at Camlan, while Arthur was killed by his nephew Mordred at Camlann. Owain's father was known as the 'Terrible Head Dragon' because he was the pre-eminent British leader, or Dragon, of the period. In Welsh, this translates as *Yrthyr pen-Dragon*, and Arthur's father was said to be Uther Pendragon. In addition, some sources refer to Owain's son as 'Son of the Bear', indicating that Owain may have been known as 'the Bear' – which, in both Welsh and Latin, translates roughly as 'Arthur'. In fact, the first ever mention of Arthur comes in a poem attributed to Owain's tribe, the Gododdin.

In other words there is lots of evidence suggesting that Owain was the historical basis for Arthur. An engraved stone, dated to 480 CE, found at Viroconium records that the city was occupied by a king of the Cunedda family – Owain's family. Was this king in fact Owain 'the Bear' himself, making Viroconium his Camelot?

Arthurian writer Mick Baker points out that of the major cities of post-Roman Britain, only Viroconium shows signs of rebuilding and fortification in the late 5th century, suggesting that it could have become the de facto national capital during this crucial 'Arthurian' period: a Camelot in all but name.

Many Camelots

Tintagel, Cadbury Castle, Caerleon and Viroconium must be considered the leading candidates, but which is the real one? Frustratingly, the nature of Arthur means that *all* of them could be, in part, the real Camelot. If Arthur is, as seems likely, the result of an aggregation of stories about a number of different people, both real and mythical, then the Camelots of each of the Arthur candidates could have contributed to the story of the legendary Camelot. In some senses, then, Camelot has been located in at least four different places, just as Arthur is most likely an aggregate of at least four different men.

Strongholds and regional capitals such as Tintagel, Cadbury, Caerleon and Viroconium could have made a lasting impression on the people of post-Roman Britain, attaining semi-legendary status even during their own time, as did the kings and warlords who dwelt there. As the wealth, power and prestige of both the kings and their fortresses passed into memory they may have been subsumed into a growing national myth, their individual identities lost, replaced by the legend of Arthur and his Camelot.

El Dorado

El Dorado is Spanish for 'the Gilded One'. It is a reference to a man, but has become synonymous with a place: a city or kingdom of fabulous wealth, a hidden land lost to geographers and explorers, deep in the heart of the South American wilderness. More than this, however, El Dorado is a legend, a dream, an obsession, which has driven generations of men to endure terrible hardships and inflict horrible cruelty, and which has led to madness, murder, execution and suicide. In their desperate search for the fabled land of El Dorado, treasure-hunters travelled thousands of kilometres across trackless jungles, hostile mountains and fetid swamps. What were they really looking for, and was it even there to find?

Lust for gold

The Spanish conquistadors who arrived in the New World at the start of the 16th century found wealth beyond their wildest dreams, but success simply fuelled their greed, stoking it into a raging fire that consumed all in its path. This gold lust had first been set off when friendly Native Americans foolishly showed Columbus rich sources of gold on the Caribbean island of Hispaniola (modern-day Haiti and Dominican Republic), but was whipped into a frenzy in 1532 when Atahualpa Inca, lord of the Inca empire, ransomed himself from Francisco Pizarro and his small conquistador army by filling a room with gold. This extraordinary windfall made Pizarro and his men rich beyond imagining, but they were not satisfied. The Incas' ability to gather so much gold implied they must have much more, and when Manco Inca, successor to Atahualpa (who had been murdered by the Spanish, despite his ransom), led the remnants of the Inca army of resistance deep into the western jungle, it was assumed by the conquistadors that he must have carried off a great store of treasure with him.

Tales from the east

In 1538, against this backdrop, the legend of El Dorado was born. An emissary from a Native American tribe to the north-east of the Inca empire arrived with messages for Atahualpa, unaware that the arrival of the Spaniards had turned the South American world order upside down. Interrogated by his captors about possible sources of gold, the Native American told them of a tribe to the east of his who practised a mysterious rite in which their priest-king was covered in balsam gum and coated in gold dust, before diving into a sacred lake to bathe. Golden ornaments and other precious offerings were also tossed into the lake. On hearing the tale, conquistador captain Sebastián de Benalcázar dubbed the man *El Dorado*, 'the Gilded One'.

Legend of the Muisca

This extraordinary tale was true. There had indeed been such a tribe – the Muisca, who lived in the highlands of present-day Colombia – and a sacred lake – Lake Guatavitá, in the hills above Bogotá. Part of the Chibcha peoples, an agrarian culture that traded with the Incas but was not quite as sophisticated as them, the Muisca had been conquered by a neighbouring tribe decades before the conquistadors arrived, and no longer practised the gilded man rite. The captured emissary's tale was a legend – a fading memory of strange ceremonies his father's father might have heard about. It included one vital element – the gold-rich culture in question was not his own, but one beyond it, over the next ridge or around the next bend of the river. This was to become the defining characteristic of the El Dorado legend. No matter how far the European treasure-hunters penetrated into the wilderness, or how many tribes and cultures they interrogated, the fabulous riches they sought were always just out of reach.

Hunt for the sacred lake

Benalcázar soon set off in search of El Dorado, battling through uncharted territory and crossing jungles and mountains, finally reaching the area near modern-day Bogotá in 1539. But other conquistadors were also looking for gold. In 1536 a group led by Gonzalo Jiménez de Quesada had struck inland from the Spanish settlements on the Caribbean coast, and by 1537, after enduring terrible hardships, they had encountered the Muisca. Their well-ordered settlements resembled castles and forts closely enough for de Quesada to consider that he had discovered a civilisation to rival the Incas, and therefore a likely source of gold.

The local chieftain, Tisquesusa, quickly realised the situation and, as was to become standard, directed the Spanish to a land further on, which de Quesada duly invaded. Here he found a temple decorated with enough gold to whet his appetite, and tortured the Native Americans until they revealed the location of a sacred lake not far away: Lake Guatavitá. A few days later de Quesada was the first European to reach the home of El Dorado, but what he found was a disappointment.

Draining the lake – part one

Lake Guatavitá is a deep crater lake (possibly in an extinct volcano or maybe an impact crater – sources differ), the murky depths of which do not give up their secrets easily. Within a few years de Quesada was forced to return to Spanish territory for political reasons but he left behind his brother, Hernán Peréz, who in 1545 made the first of many attempts to drain the lake. Though unsophisticated – a simple-bucket chain was employed – the attempt lowered the lake enough to reveal a little gold. Were these the riches of El Dorado? Had the Native Americans directed them towards the right lake, or was the true kingdom of gold deeper in the uncharted mountains or forests?

Entradas to Hell

By now the legend of El Dorado was common currency amongst the conquistadors, inspiring a number of increasingly daring and dangerous expeditions – or *entradas* – into the interior. A German expedition in 1541 penetrated deep into the Andes and picked up legends of a rich city called Omagua. In the fevered conquistador imagination this became the possible seat of El Dorado, a city paved with gold and dripping with emeralds. Pizarro, conqueror of the Inca empire, had also heard the tales, and in 1541 he dispatched his younger brother Gonzalo on an expedition across the Andes. Gonzalo soon became separated from his co-leader Francisco de Orellana and struggled back to base having lost three-quarters of his party to starvation, Native American attacks, disease and even cannibalism.

Meanwhile de Orellana accidentally made one of the greatest

voyages of discovery in history. Building some riverboats to look downriver for El Dorado, which he believed to be just around the next bend, he ended up following a series of increasingly large rivers all the way to the Atlantic Ocean, becoming the first European to travel the Amazon. The river's name derives from de Orellana's account of meeting a tribe of warrior-women ruled by a fierce queen. Although he did not find the fabled kingdom of gold, he too heard tales of the city of Omagua. Returning to the Amazon in 1546, de Orellana found it less hospitable and perished along with most of his men.

As Spain struggled to assert control over the unruly outposts of its far-flung empire, while also worrying about Portuguese expansion westwards from Brazil, the lure of El Dorado proved a useful distraction for restless conquistadors. By launching *entradas* in search of the legendary land, the authorities could divert potentially dangerous men into opening up new territory. For instance, in 1560 a young soldier named Pedro de Ursua was actually given the title Governor of El Dorado and Omagua, before being dispatched on a suicidal mission into the interior where he was soon murdered by his own men.

Draining the lake – part two

The kingdom of gold seemed to be receding into the east, but Lake Guatavitá still offered the promise of tremendous rewards to those who could plumb its depths. In 1580 a second and more serious attempt was made to drain the lake by cutting a notch in the raised rim surrounding it. The level of the lake was reduced by nearly 20 metres (66 feet) before the workings collapsed with the cost of many lives (the scar can still be seen at the lake today). Golden artefacts and a large emerald were discovered – enough to encourage two more attempts in the 17th century, although these failed to uncover more than a few trinkets.

Guyana and the lost city of Manoa

Enough groups of conquistadors had tramped around Colombia for them to decide that El Dorado was not to be found in this part of South America. The focus now switched instead to another great terra incognito – the area of Guyana in north-east South America. Here the siren call of the golden kingdom would lure two more adventurers to their doom.

The awful inheritance

In 1580 Don Antonio de Berrio arrived in Bogotá to take possession of the estate left to him by his wife's uncle. Unfortunately for him, that uncle was the late Gonzalo de Quesada, one of the original El Dorado seekers, who had stipulated in his will that de Berrio must use part of his inheritance to continue searching for the fabled kingdom.

Despite his advanced years – he was already 60 and the veteran of several European campaigns when he arrived in the New World – de Berrio wasted little time in launching a series of expeditions to reconnoitre the land between Bogotá and the delta of the Orinoco far to the east. This was the area known as Guyana (now modern-day Venezuela and Guiana), an uncharted wilderness within which, it was now assumed, El Dorado must lie. In 1581, 1584, 1585, 1590 and 1593 de Berrio (latterly from his new base on Trinidad, opposite the mouth of the Orinoco) either led or organised tough *entradas* that found little but gathered consistent information about a great city … further inland. Native American sources spoke of a city called Manoa on Lake Paríma, in the mountains at the head of the Caroni River, inhabited by people who had come from the west.

To de Berrio it all made perfect sense. The last Incas, refugees from the Spanish conquest of Peru, had fled far to the east, into Guyana, and built their secret capital, home of the gilded one.

In reward for sending these great tidings back to Spain, de Berrio was made Governor of El Dorado. All he had to do now was find it.

The last survivor

Lending credence to the reports of the Native Americans was the fantastic testimony of a ragged Spaniard who walked out of the wilderness in 1586 and proclaimed that he had spent much of the last few decades living in Manoa. Juan Martinez variantly claimed to be the last survivor of an expedition massacred by Carib Indians, or a different expedition during which he had been punished for a mishap with the gunpowder by being set adrift in a canoe. Captured by Native Americans, Martinez had been led blindfolded to a great city – Manoa – where he met El Dorado himself.

After several months of living in Manoa and enjoying its delights, Martinez had begged to be allowed to return to his own people, and had been sent on his way laden with gold and jewels. Although most of these had inconveniently been stolen by other Native Americans on the way back, he still possessed enough to lend credibility to his tale. Martinez's story had incited gold fever in the region. De Berrio, based on Trinidad, vied with other greedy local governors to build up enough support, funding and men to stage a successful *entrada*.

Sir Walter Raleigh

Unfortunately for de Berrio, alluring New World tales of El Dorado had by now reached the ears of the enemies of Spain, in the person of Sir Walter Raleigh. Raleigh was one of the leading men of Elizabethan England. Privateer, soldier, spy, author, philosopher and courtier, Raleigh was soon to fall victim to the obsession of El Dorado. He had lately fallen out of favour with the queen because of his secret marriage to one of her ladies-in-waiting, and saw an expedition to Guyana as his chance to win back his position at court, as well as securing an incredible fortune and extending English dominion into the territories of the New World. He would find Manoa and entreat with El Dorado to become a vassal of Her Highness.

In 1595 Raleigh arrived in the Caribbean with four ships and a force of men and promptly captured Trinidad and de Berrio. Reconnoitring the estuary of the Orinoco, Raleigh saw enough to convince him that the Spanish had found a rich gold mine in the area, and decided to return to England to muster support for a larger expedition. On his return he wrote *The Discoverie*, or, to give its glorious full title, T*he Discoverie of the Large, Rich, and Bewtiful Empyre of Guiana, with a Relation to the Great and Golden Citie of Manoa (which the Spanyards call El Dorado)*. It was through this book, and subsequent popular adaptations, that the legend of El Dorado entered the European mainstream. In particular, *The Discoverie* included maps showing Lake Paríma and Manoa in such convincing detail that they came to be included in standard atlases for centuries afterwards.

The accession of James I to the throne landed Raleigh in the Tower for 13 years as pro-Spanish and anti-Raleigh factions gained favour. Meanwhile back in Guyana both de Berrio and Raleigh's trusted lieutenant Keymis continued their fruitless search for Manoa, always hearing that it was slightly further on. In 1597 de Berrio, worn out by his constant endeavours, passed away having spent the entire fortune that had brought him to the New World to begin with. 'If you try to do too much you will end by doing nothing at all,' he mused towards the end of his life.

In 1616 Raleigh was released and allowed to venture back to Guyana on a final, ill-fated expedition. He found nothing, while a skirmish with a Spanish settlement (triggered by the soldiers' lust for gold) cost the life of his son, led to a falling out with Keymis, who promptly committed suicide, and provided his enemies back at court with the pretext they needed to doom him. On his return to England he was arrested, tried in secret for fomenting war with the Spanish and, in 1618, executed.

The legend is laid to rest?

Repeated failures to locate Manoa, or even find concrete proof of its existence, did little to dampen the enthusiasm of a stream of adventurers drawn by the old tales and clutching maps descended from Raleigh's. Not until 1800, when the professional explorers and scientists Alexander von Humboldt and Aimé Bonpland arrived to survey the region, was it conclusively proved that there was no Lake Paríma and no Manoa.

Curiously, having dealt a potential death-blow to the legend of El Dorado, von Humboldt then proceeded to trigger a fresh wave of speculation about its original hypothetical location at Lake Guatavitá. After visiting the lake in 1801 he calculated the possible extent of the wealth concealed in its depths, assuming that the legend of the annual offering of El Dorado was true. His musings on the subject sparked wild hyperbole back in Europe. By 1825 one travel guide suggested that the treasure of El Dorado could be worth over a billion pounds sterling (over £60 billion or $113 billion today)!

Gold diggers of 1912

Not surprisingly these extraordinary projections stimulated a number of attempts to harness the power of modern technology to drain the lake and recover the loot. Various concerns were formed to this end, and in 1912 the Company for the Exploitation of the Lagoon of Guatavitá finally succeeded. Once all the water was gone, all that was left was mud and ooze, which hardened into an impenetrable block before more than a handful of gold was recovered. The lake soon refilled. Although treasure hunters continued to sniff around, the lake eventually came under the nominal protection of the Colombian government, and guards its secrets to this day.

The Balsa Muisca

In a kind of post-script to the legend, a pre-Colombian golden artefact was discovered in 1969, near Bogotá, which has gone on to become the visual symbol of El Dorado. It is a model of a raft, upon which are stood the figures of nobles and priests, surrounding a magnificently arrayed king. Probably intended as a ceremonial offering to Muisca gods, the piece is known as the Balsa Muisca.

Proving that popular myths die hard, it has been claimed that the Balsa Muisca was found in Lake Guatavitá, as if cast in by the Gilded One himself. Sadly this is not the case – according to the Bogotá Gold Museum it was found in a cave, hidden in a ceremonial clay jar. Nonetheless, it provides dazzling hard evidence that El Dorado probably did exist, perhaps not in the form of the fable created by the conquistadors' unquenchable greed, but a real man nonetheless.

2

Lost Artefacts, Works and Relics

The works of man are ephemeral, fragile and vulnerable in the face of the passing ages. When an artefact is gone the odds are stacked against it being remembered by posterity. Only in special circumstances – great religious, spiritual, intellectual or artistic significance, or being the creation of someone whose fame is eternal – does an artefact win the renown to live on in memory. In even fewer cases is there a genuine hope that the artefact might still exist and could even be recovered. This chapter looks at four of the most notable of these cases – two religious relics and two cases where the work of great writers is known about but not possessed by the present. These may seem like they belong to disparate classes – objects and writings – but all are artefacts that have been created by humans whose thought, art and craftsmanship have invested them with their inestimable value. This value generates a powerful, almost irresistible lure, driving leagues of searchers over the centuries to hunt for them, as they continue to do today. This chapter explains what people think they are looking for, where they have looked and what their chances are of finding what they seek.

The Ark of the Covenant

Described by archaeologist Leen Ritmeyer as 'the most holy piece of furniture ever made', the Ark of the Covenant was a large chest constructed to hold the stone tablets upon which the Ten Commandments were inscribed ('ark' means chest or container). It was made of fine wood, coated with gold, and had a gold-rimmed lid, atop of which were set statues of cherubim – winged angels that probably looked a lot like sphinxes. Between the wings of these angels, the Old Testament tells us, the spirit of God would manifest.

The Ark had various powers. It could terrify and/or destroy enemies, bring good or bad luck, destroy those who touched it, tell the future and manifest light, sparks and mist. According to some traditions it had a mind of its own. One intriguing theory, first proposed by Nikolas Tesla in 1915, is that the Ark was a giant capacitor, similar to a Leyden jar (invented in 1745), a device that can store electrical charge and discharge it as a single spark or as a continuous glow (effects associated with the Ark). A pint jar can store enough electricity to kill a man, so the Ark, which was 1.3 metres (4 feet 4 inches) long and 76 centimetres (2 feet 7 inches) wide and deep, would be able to store massive amounts of energy.

Known history of the Ark

Whatever the source of its power, the Ark was revered by the ancient Hebrews, who built an elaborate Tabernacle (a sort of tent shrine) for it and carried it before them on their wanderings. When Solomon built the First Temple, the Tabernacle was recreated as the holy of holies and the Ark was stored within. Occasionally, according to some Biblical sources, it was taken out to be used in military campaigns and religious processions, or possibly to keep it out of the clutches of 'wicked kings' who periodically ruled in Israel. It is last mentioned in 2 Chronicles, when King Josiah orders that it should be brought back to the Temple and left there in 623 BCE.

Invasion

Subsequent centuries brought their share of woe for the Israelites as their lands were repeatedly invaded. The first disaster was the Babylonian conquest, which resulted in the fall of Jerusalem and the sacking and destruction of the Temple in 586 BCE. Although it is recorded in the Bible that a great deal of gold, silver, bronze and precious Temple adornments were carried off by the Babylonians, there is no specific mention of the Ark. Later, when the Israelites were permitted to return to Jerusalem and rebuild the Temple, they were allowed to bring much of the Temple treasure back with them, but again, there is no mention of the Ark, nor is there any mention of its fate in Babylon, which seems strange given the importance of the artefact.

The empty chamber

The Second Temple stood until its destruction by the Romans in 70 CE, but the holy of holies was empty when the conquering General Titus marched inside. It is generally assumed that it had been empty all along. In fact by this time the Ark had been absent from recorded history for nearly 700 years. What happened to it? Why is there no mention of its loss? Could it still exist, buried in some forgotten chamber, awaiting discovery by some real-life Indiana Jones?

Missing, presumed lost

The mainstream consensus is that the Ark was destroyed by one of the many invaders to visit the Holy Land, probably the Babylonians. It was common practice for the 'gods' of defeated nations to be carted off by their conquerors, and it seems likely that Nebuchadnezzar would have borne off the Ark in triumph. This is certainly suggested by the 'Apocalypse of Ezra', one of the books of the *Apocrypha*, which explicitly lists the Ark amongst the list of loot, although this book was probably written more than 500 years after the event. Perhaps the Ark was broken up for its precious metals, or otherwise destroyed, and subsequent writers were simply too depressed at its loss to mention it.

If the Babylonians were not responsible for its demise, there are other candidates. The Syrian king Antiochus Epiphanes (174–164 BCE) looted the Temple, as did the Romans under Titus, who carried off some of the prize accoutrements for a triumph in Rome. This has led to the theory that the Ark was removed to Rome, whence it was taken by invading Visigoths, finding its way from them to Constantinople and finally into the hands of the Knights Templar. This theory is not to be taken too seriously, as it seems very likely that the Ark was already missing before the Roman conquest. Friezes depicting the Roman triumph clearly show the Menorah – the candelabrum from the Temple – but there is no sign of an Ark, which would surely have been the most significant piece of loot.

Hidden in the Holy Land

The Bible's lack of comment on the fate of the Ark leaves plenty of room for speculation, and there are several non-canonical (ie writings from the Judaeo-Christian tradition that are not part of the accepted corpus of works that make up the official Bible) and non-Jewish sources that suggest leads.

Solomon's secret

According to the Talmud (a collection of rabbinical commentaries on law and the Bible), Solomon specifically constructed a hiding place for the Ark so that when later calamities came to pass it could be hidden away. One tradition holds that this hiding place was under a wood storehouse on the Temple Mount. The Talmudic tradition goes on to say that King Josiah, anticipating the Babylonian conquest that was to come within decades, removed the Ark to Solomon's secret chamber, where it has been sealed up to this day.

The late controversial 'biblical archaeologist' Ron Wyatt, who claimed to have discovered, among other things, Noah's Ark complete with anchors, said that he had actually seen the Ark in a secret chamber while excavating in a quarry below the alleged site of Jesus' crucifixion. Since he also claimed to have scraped the Messiah's blood off the top of it, and had it analysed to reveal an extra chromosome, his assertion lacks plausibility, but it has inspired subsequent, but so far unsuccessful, attempts to follow up the dig.

Trouble on the Mount

Common among fundamentalist Jews is the belief that Solomon's secret chamber lies within the Temple Mount, beneath the present-day Islamic shrine the Dome of the Rock. The Mount is known to be riddled with chambers and tunnels of various ages. According to archaeologist Leen Ritmeyer, whose analysis of photos of the Rock itself claims to have identified the very spot where the Ark sat (see page 22), the Ark could be in a chamber vertically below the Rock, former site of the holy of holies (or so he believes). This could explain how it was possible for the Second Temple to be fully sacred, despite the absence of its most important artefact. The Ark was spiritually present, projecting its presence through the rock. Bear in mind, however, that Ritmeyer has ideological motivations similar to many who argue for the Ark's presence in the Mount – he wants to hasten the rebuilding of the Temple.

Sharing these motivations was Rabbi Yehuda Getz, who led a 1982 exploration of tunnels in the Mount and claims to have got within 12 metres (40 feet) of the Ark chamber. The authorities called a halt to his explorations, as they have with others, for a mixture of safety and political reasons – the authorities who govern the Temple precinct and the wider Muslim world are massively suspicious of any excavations around the Mount.

Treasure of the Copper Scroll

An alternative view is suggested by verses in the Mishnah, a collection of oral traditions dating back to Old Testament times. According to some rare versions of these, the Ark is hidden in 'a desolate valley under a hill – on its east side, forty stones deep'. Other verses mention a copper scroll which details the location of various treasures. Remarkably, this scroll did indeed exist: it was part of the Dead Sea scrolls discovery (see page 98). The Copper Scroll, found in 1952, proved to be a list of hidden treasures, together with cryptic/unhelpful directions for finding them. According to some (controversial) interpretations the treasures described include the most important contents of the First Temple, the Ark amongst them, and the Scroll repeats the injunction to search in a desolate valley under a hill.

Vendyl Jones and the suspect claims

Another controversial biblical archaeologist, Vendyl Jones, claims to have discovered the exact location, after following an ancient tunnel running from Jerusalem all the way to the shores of the Dead Sea. At the end of the tunnel, he insists, is a chamber he is certain will prove to contain the Ark. 'I just gotta drill a bore-hole into the chamber, drop a pin-camera in and there it is,' he explained to the *Israel National News* in 2005.

Jones is a colourful character who, like so many in this field, has his own religious agenda. He believes that the discovery of the Ark will usher in the overthrow of Israeli democracy and its replacement with a council of religious elders. He also encourages the belief that he was the basis for Indiana Jones (Vendyl Jones supposedly becoming Endy and then Indy Jones), although in practice there is no truth to this. The character's name was originally Indiana Smith, derived from the name of writer George Lucas' childhood dog and the film *Nevada Smith* – the director, Steven Spielberg, then changed 'Smith' to 'Jones'.

Jeremiah and Mount Nebo

Another apocryphal tradition comes from the 2 Maccabees, which tells of how the prophet Jeremiah (who lived from the reign of Josiah to the Babylonian exile) spirited the Ark away to a cave on Mount Nebo, the peak on the eastern side of the Dead Sea where Moses last looked down on the Promised Land and is reputedly buried. When Jeremiah's followers came to mark the spot they could not find it, so its location remains a secret.

Today, Mount Nebo is in Jordan, but there is some dispute over whether this is the Biblical Mount Nebo, and whether either of them are the same place referred to in the Maccabeean verses. A researcher called Tom Croster claims to have seen the Ark in a cave on Mount Nebo, but reportedly his photographic 'proof' shows a relatively modern object.

The Kaba

According to Roderick Grierson and Stuart Munro-Hay, scholars and authors of *The Ark of the Covenant: The True Story of the Greatest Relic of Antiquity,* Arabian sources claim that the Ark did not rest in Jeremiah's cave, but instead fell into the hands of the Jurhum, the tribe that controlled Mecca and the Kaba (now the holiest shrine in Islam, but at that time a polytheistic shrine). Grierson and Munro-Hay make the point that the Kaba closely resembles the design of the Temple's holy of holies, and that the Arab tribes venerated stones that came from heaven (eg the Black Stone that is set into the side of the Kaba), and stored them in wooden chests – aka arks. Might the Jurhum have taken the Ark to Mecca? Could it have inspired their own beliefs, which subsequently evolved into Islam? Could the Ark still be in or around the Kaba?

Into Africa

The Temple had already been sacked nearly 400 years before the Babylonian conquest, by an invading pharaoh described in the Bible as Shishak, thought to be Sheshonq I, who ruled Egypt from 945–924 BCE. Sheshonq made his capital at Tanis in northern Egypt, so if he had looted the Ark he would have carried it there. Interestingly this is the location opted for by Lucas and Spielberg in *Raiders of the Lost Ark*. Since the Ark is mentioned in the Bible subsequent to the depredations of Shishak, however, this option appears unlikely.

Menelik and Ethiopia

A much stronger candidate is the Ethiopian tradition that Menelik, King of Ethiopia and offspring of a union between Solomon and the Queen of Sheba, stole or was given the Ark and brought it to Ethiopia, where it now resides in the Chapel of the Tablet in the city of Axum (aka Aksum). This tale is based mainly on the Ethiopian national epic the *Kebra Negast* (Glory of Kings), which tells the story of how Menelik went to visit his father and encountered the Ark, which decided to accompany him back home of its own free will. There are some objections to this tale. Firstly, the Ark continues to appear in the Bible after Menelik's supposed visit, although the explanation offered is that he substituted a copy and then made off with the real one. A more fundamental objection is that Sheba was traditionally thought to be Arabia, not Ethiopia.

The Ark became an object of intense veneration for the Ethiopians, who based the design of altars for all their churches on it, and made numerous copies, which are still used in religious processions. Some visitors to Ethiopia over the centuries claim to have been allowed access to the contents of the Ark, reporting a variety of stone tablets, some of which were obviously copies shown to placate demanding foreigners. Were any of them genuine, and what of the Ark itself?

The guardian of the chapel, a post handed down through generations, is adamant that he controls access to the real thing, and equally adamant that no one, not even the country's religious and political leaders, should be allowed to see it. Roderick Grierson and Stuart Munro-Hay point out that even if the real Ark had been brought to Axum, the wood would quickly have rotted in the humid climate, but the contents might well have survived. The bottom line is that without access to the contents of the chapel in Axum there is no way to judge the authenticity of the claims. However, Grierson and Munro-Hay argue that 'the traditions that have survived for so long at Aksum should be taken just as seriously as the earliest accounts of the Ark in the Hebrew Bible.'

Multiple Arks

The above is by no means an exhaustive survey of claimed locations for the lost Ark. It is also located, with varying degrees of plausibility, in the ancient temple on Elephantine island in the Nile in Egypt, in Lake Tiberias in Israel, in Tara in Ireland and in Utah in America. What are we to make of this plethora of locations, and of some of the other mysteries surrounding the Ark? For instance, the Bible contradicts itself in describing who constructed the Ark and what was inside it. Sometimes it even seems to be in two places at once.

Grierson and Munro-Hay suggest what may seem obvious in retrospect: perhaps there was more than one Ark. In Ethiopia the copies of the Ark carry their own spiritual significance – in many ways it is the idea of the Ark, the Ark as a symbol, that is important, not its authenticity as an original object. Perhaps the ancient Hebrews felt the same. Multiple Arks would account for the multiple claimed locations. But would the ancients have felt the same about the Tablets of the Law that the Ark contained? Ultimately it is these, and not the container that held them, which are the real historical prize.

Conclusion

Until experts are allowed access to the chapel at Axum and verify the amazing claims of the guardian, or the competing teams of archaeologists in the Holy Land stumble upon something incredible, we must conclude that the most likely solution to the mystery of the Ark and the Tablets of the Law is that they were destroyed by invaders and are lost to history for ever. Perhaps fragments of these ancient relics lie scattered amidst the dust and stones of ancient Babylon.

The lost *Dialogues* of Aristotle

Aristotle was an ancient Greek philosopher who lived from 384 BCE to 322 BCE. He studied under Plato, tutored and advised Alexander the Great and founded the Lyceum (a sort of ancient university). Along with Plato, he is today regarded as one of the two colossi of ancient Greek thought, and is seen by many as the single most important influence on the intellectual history of the West. Yet his surviving writings constitute only a fraction of his original output (as little as one-fifth according to traditional sources), and those that we possess are often fragmentary, cobbled together by later editors from what were effectively Aristotle's lecture notes. Which of his writings are missing, how were they lost, and might they still be recovered?

Lost literary treasures of the ancient world

These questions are not unique to the lost works of Aristotle. The majority of ancient literature is lost to us. Only tantalising clues remain – lists of books given in ancient catalogues; summaries and bibliographies compiled by later writers. Many works of antiquity are known to us today only via passing mentions and odd quotes. Aristotle was one of the most important thinkers of antiquity, so his missing body of work is correspondingly significant, but it also stands as an exemplar of all the other blank spots in the history of classical Western literature, from Homer's lost epics and the missing verses of Sappho to the absent plays of Aeschylus. Investigating the mystery of Aristotle's vanished books may shed light on the field as a whole, helping to answer similar questions for a wider body of lost work.

Public and private Aristotle

Aristotle was a prolific writer who remains famous for the breadth of his intellectual scope (he has been described as one of the first polymaths). He covered subjects from metaphysics, logic, poetry and ethics to zoology, meteorology and economics. His work can be divided into two main groups. His acroatic writings, meaning those taught orally, by word of mouth, and now known as treatises, were mainly composed as study and lecture notes for use in his school (the Lyceum) and as such were not written as 'books' per se and not intended for publication. They were not in a polished literary style and can be difficult to read, self-contradictory and obscure, much as a modern lecturer's course notes for him/herself might be. Some may even be notes taken by Aristotle's students rather than his own work. Ironically, these are the only writings that survive. In classical times they were collected into some 30 works (or 'books'), known as the *Corpus Aristotelicum.*

Aristotle for everyone

The other main category of his work was what Aristotle called exoteric writing – writing designed for public consumption. These were mostly written in the prevailing form of the time, the Platonic dialogue (where the work was framed as a discussion between two or more people). Aristotle's style in these works was admired – the Roman writer Cicero describing it as being like 'a river of gold' – but they are now known only from quotes or excerpts in the work of other writers. Ancient catalogues, such as those written by Diogenes Laertius for the library at Alexandria, list more than 170 works. On top of these are the mass of other writings such as poetry and letters (including many to Alexander the Great and other important figures). In other words, less than one-fifth of Aristotle's writings survive (the exact proportion is disputed by some scholars, but we are still talking about the vast majority).

How were they lost?

The traditional story of what happened to Aristotle's literary estate after his death is derived from the ancient writers Strabo and Plutarch. According to their accounts, Aristotle left his writings to his successor at the Lyceum, and when he died they passed into the hands of Neleus of Scepsis. Neleus' family later consigned the material to a cellar or pit to avoid the attentions of the royal book collectors, where it languished for decades in less than perfect conditions. In the 1st century BCE the writings were sold to a scholar who took them to Athens, where, in 86 BCE, they were snaffled up by the conquering Roman General Sulla, dispatched back to Rome and sold to Tyrannion the grammarian. Not until 70 BCE, some 250 years after the great man's death, did they come into the possession of Andronicus of Rhodes, who compiled the scattered acroatic material into systematically organised books for the first time. It is these versions we know today.

This is almost certainly not the whole story. Some of Aristotle's works would have been available during this time – particularly his *Dialogues*, which had been published as books during his lifetime – and the account does not explain what happened to the majority of them subsequently.

The fragile medium

Presumably the fate that befell the majority of Aristotle's oeuvre was similar to that which afflicted so much other ancient literature. Although we speak of 'books' being 'published', ancient literature was handwritten on expensive papyrus (from reeds) or parchment or vellum (made from animal skin). Few copies would have been produced, and the lending and copying process was fraught with problems, including the still familiar issue of borrowers failing to return material. Since copying was difficult and expensive, only popular/in-demand books would have multiplied. Many parchment and vellum documents were reused as palimpsests, which involved scraping off the top layer so that the new material could be written on the same surface – early medieval Christian scribes were particularly guilty of destroying antique literature in this fashion.

Even copies that *were* produced were highly perishable. Maintaining collections of books depended on well-funded libraries, staffed with professionals; these in turn depended on a rich, stable state. In times of warfare and social instability libraries were vulnerable to looting, fire, flood, wilful destruction and simple neglect.

The chain of transmission

The story of how classical literature was transmitted from antiquity to the medieval era in the West is a complex one. In brief it goes like this. The Roman Empire in the West came under increasing stress from within and without, with mass migrations and barbarian invasions, famines and plagues, religious strife and extremism and increasing economic hardship. In these conditions libraries, books and learning were not highly valued and along the way the great libraries of Rome effectively disappeared.

The Eastern Roman Empire fared better and many scholars and their books ended up in Alexandria and Constantinople, but here too the pressures of economic hardships and religious extremism took their toll (see 'The Library of Alexandria', page 27). By the 8th century the epicentre of scholarship, and the associated movement of literature, shifted to the Islamic world. Here scholarship and particularly book collecting became a passion, and cities and rulers vied to outdo each other with the size of their libraries. The conquest of Samarkand in Central Asia brought with it the secret of paper, a relatively cheap and abundant medium. Libraries such as the one in Cordoba, in Muslim Spain, grew to enormous proportions.

Christian scholars from Europe visited these Islamic centres of learning and translated and copied some of their heritage of literature. Eventually paper came to Europe and some European universities began to rival the Islamic world as centres of copying. The fall of Constantinople in 1453 and the rise of humanism in Italy combined to cause an influx of scholars to a culture primed to value classical knowledge, and the resulting Renaissance together with the invention of printing completed the revival of European scholarship and the dissemination of classical literature. After so many vicissitudes, however, much had gone missing – Gertrude Rawlings, historian of books, comments that what is surprising is, 'not that we have so few ancient writings in our present possession, but that we have any.'

Bestsellers and remainders

Bringing the focus back to Aristotle, there may be specific reasons why some of his works did not survive. As mentioned above, the survival of an ancient work of literature was in some senses a popularity contest. Only those works that were sufficiently in demand would be copied enough to ensure replacement of copies lost to wear and tear, and/or survival of copies in one location in the event of destruction by fire, flood or conquest at another.

From the 3rd century CE the fragile, vulnerable scroll form preferred by the ancient Greeks and Romans was superseded by the sturdier codex form, which more closely resembles today's book. Not all works successfully made this transition, again due to expense. Hungarian scientist Béla Lukács theorises that the teachers at the Lyceum, who were the main guardians of Aristotle's literary inheritance, might have spent their scant budget on transcribing to codex form only those works they used most in their day-to-day teaching – namely the acroatic texts of the *Corpus Aristotelicum*.

The more widely held theory, first proposed by German classicist Werner Jaeger, is that Aristotle's *Dialogues* are part of his early, less mature work – his juvenilia, which were effectively superseded by his later writings. This could explain why they were not copied as much. More recently, A P Bos has argued that it was more a matter of the changing philosophical-literary fashions of antiquity. In his reconstruction of the lost works, the themes and arguments Aristotle uses are mature but the way he illustrates them is through the use of myths and mythical narratives, a mode that went out of style from the 3rd century BCE. Accordingly, later scholars only concerned themselves with Aristotle's later writings.

Whatever the reasons, the consensus appears to be that the rule for ancient literature was 'multiply or die', and Aristotle's early works fell foul of this rule. By the time the Roman Empire collapsed and the Dark Ages swept over Europe, there were simply too few copies of the *Dialogues*, and of his other lost works, to survive the long roll of book-destroying calamities.

Back to life

Just because survival is unlikely does not mean that it is impossible. Might some copies of works thought lost have survived somewhere, against the odds? In the late 19th century, the discovery of ancient papyri in Egypt gave fresh hope to Aristotelian scholars. In 1880 fragments of a copy of a lost work of Aristotle, *The Constitution of Athens*, the most important of a series of 158 treatises on the constitutions of Greek states written by the great man and some of his pupils, were discovered in Egypt and purchased by the Egyptian Museum at Berlin. Then, in 1890, a group of four papyri with a complete copy of the same work was discovered by an American missionary in Egypt and purchased by the British Museum.

Oxyrhynchus

Inspired by this discovery, two young archaeologists from Oxford University, Bernard Grenfell and Arthur Hunt, began to excavate rubbish mounds at Oxyrhynchus, to the south-west of Cairo in Egypt. Oxyrhynchus, which derives its name from the 'sharp-nosed fish' of Egyptian myth that was venerated by the inhabitants, was the capital of a province of Ptolemaic (Greek), and later Roman, Egypt. For over a thousand years it was a centre of administration and bureaucracy, as well as a typical, bustling market town with all the comings and goings of daily life. The inhabitants, and particularly the bureaucrats, made liberal use of papyrus to record everything from tax returns and accounts to school work and love letters. When a papyrus was finished with, it was dumped with the rest of the garbage on mounds outside town. Fortunately for posterity, conditions combined to preserve this material to the present day – the location is far enough from the Nile to have escaped the annual inundations, while the mounds themselves were above the water table, and were eventually covered up by hot, dry sand.

Grenfell and Hunt employed teams of labourers to unearth thousands and thousands of papyri from the rubbish mounds, more or less inventing a new discipline known as papyrology in their efforts to decipher the ancient texts. Keen students of classicism, they nurtured the hope that they would find all the lost works of antiquity. Although they were disappointed to discover mainly tax records, accounts and suchlike, they and their successors (for the project continues to this day) did uncover a wide range of previously unknown ancient literature, including poems of Pindar and Sappho, most of the works of Menander, some Sophocles and some early Christian gospels, including fragments of the 'Sayings of Jesus' (aka the 'Gospel of Thomas').

Hi-tech papyrology

Lost works of Aristotle do not seem to have been among the treasures, but recent advances in imaging techniques are now revolutionising the science of papyrology, so new discoveries may yet be made from the Oxyrhynchus scrolls or from other finds. For instance, imaging the scrolls in light of different wavelengths can reveal previously unreadable writing, while laser scanning can make it possible to read even carbonised material, such as scrolls recovered from the volcanically devastated Roman town of Herculaneum.

Raiders of the lost library

At present there seems to be no specific prospect of uncovering the lost *Dialogues* of Aristotle, but the hope remains that somewhere in the world there may exist an as-yet untapped cache of ancient scrolls or codices that has somehow survived millennia of neglect and strife. The most obvious candidates in Europe and the Near East are ancient monasteries, where books were collected from late antiquity onwards, and where the flame of scholarship continued to burn during the Dark Ages. The hope of discovering a lost Aristotle in some hidden library forms the plot of Umberto Eco's *The Name of the Rose*, in which a Franciscan monk discovers Aristotle's lost work *On Comedy* in the concealed library of a Benedictine Abbey in Italy in 1327. Eco's plot echoes the widespread belief in conspiracy circles that the Catholic Church is concealing a huge cache of material in the Secret Vatican Archives, a real library of material deemed too controversial, sensitive or heretical to be made widely available.

It seems unlikely that there could be a European monastery with hitherto undiscovered chambers, and even if there were the climate is unlikely to have favoured the survival of delicate manuscripts. But perhaps there are monasteries yet to be properly explored/surveyed by modern methods in the Islamic world, which may also have a more conducive climate – for instance, where Egypt, Libya and the Levant were major centres of early Christianity and early monasticism.

The most obvious precedent for such a find is the discovery of the Dead Sea scrolls (see page 98), where a monastic commune in a desert area squirrelled away a cache of documents that were well enough preserved by the arid conditions to be recoverable thousands of years later. Perhaps other such caches are out there, waiting to be stumbled upon by an archaeologist, treasure hunter or simply a shepherd boy looking for a lost lamb.

The Holy Grail

The archetypal lost relic, thanks to its ubiquity as a metaphor in common conversation, alongside the phenomenal success of media such as the third *Indiana Jones* movie and, more recently, the book and film of Dan Brown's *The Da Vinci Code*, the Holy Grail has become the ultimate historical mystery. Fame, however, has failed to bring clarity, for many people are unsure exactly what the Grail is, and most of those who *are* sure are largely wrong. Uncertainty about its identity is multiplied when it comes to its purported whereabouts, for there are a number of artefacts claimed to be the holy treasure itself, together with a catalogue of locations claimed to be its hiding place.

What is the Grail?

In popular conception today the Grail is a cup – the cup that was used to catch drops of Jesus' blood during his Crucifixion, and the same cup that was used by Jesus at the Last Supper when he served the wine (although technically this is called the Holy Chalice). This relic has magical powers: it can produce food and drink, heal wounds, confer immortality and bring prosperity to the land. But this is not the only identity attributed to the Grail, nor even the original one.

Serving up a myth

The first thing to note is that neither the Grail nor the Chalice are specifically mentioned in the New Testament. They are traditions that arose later. The Chalice was the earlier tradition, and can be dated back at least as far as 6th century. The story of the Grail, on the other hand, does not appear until the Middle Ages. The first written source is Chrétien de Troyes' *Perceval, ou le Conte du Graal* (aka Perceval, or the Story of the Grail), written between 1180 and 1191, and in this poem the Grail is not presented as a holy relic, but simply as a dish or bowl.

This points to the original etymology of the word Grail, which is the medieval Latin *gradalis* or *gradale*, meaning a dish or platter used to serve delicacies at a feast. An alternative derivation is from the word *cratalis*, itself a derivation of *crater*, or mixing bowl. So in its earliest conception the Grail was a dish or a bowl, with no particular associations with Jesus, the Last Supper or the Crucifixion.

Royal blood

As the legend of the Grail developed, a new etymology was created. The *Graal* became the Holy (*San*) *Graal*, or *Sangreal*, which could in turn be split into the words *Sang Real*, or Royal Blood. This alluded to the sacred contents of the Grail/Chalice (for the two became conflated), and in more recent times has been taken to be a coded reference to the fact that the 'true' Grail is the bloodline of Christ (ie his descendants).

Other identities

There are plenty of other theories about what the Grail might be. According to Wolfram von Eschenbach's version of the legend, the Grail is actually a stone that fell from heaven and was the refuge of the Neutral Angels in the war between Lucifer and Heaven. Another version claims the Grail was an emerald from the crown Lucifer wore before the Fall. Some writers claim that the Grail is a book, perhaps a lost gospel, perhaps even one written by Jesus himself.

An intriguing theory from the 1953 book *The Ancient Secret: In Search of the Holy Grail*, by Flavia Anderson, is that the Grail is the *Urim ve Tumim* of the Old Testament. Literally translated this means 'lights and perfections' or 'revelation and truth', and it is usually taken to refer to some process of divination or drawing lots. However, Anderson argues that it refers to a specific ancient technology – namely a glass ball full of liquid, held in a tree-like mount, which could be used to produce light effects and to start fires by focusing the sun's rays like a magnifying glass.

Celtic or Christian

The classical conception of the Grail as a cup or bowl with magical powers has close parallels in Celtic mythology, which features several cauldrons that can produce food and drink, give wisdom, heal wounds and bring the dead back to life. Subsequent to the initial Grail romances of Chrétien de Troyes and Robert de Boron (see below) there were Welsh versions that combined Grail and Arthurian motifs with Celtic motifs, which then became a feature of subsequent development of the Grail legend. This has led to a widespread assumption that the Grail legend is basically of Celtic derivation – a recasting of a Celtic myth with a Christian gloss.

In practice, the opposite may be closer to the truth. Several scholars now argue that the Grail legend began with purely Christian motifs, possibly in order to help popularise the sacrament of Holy Communion (which obviously relates to the Holy Chalice, in as far as it concerns the transubstantiated wine for which the Chalice was the first vessel), which later acquired a Celtic gloss.

The history of the Grail

The initial Grail romance by Chrétien de Troyes does not mention the provenance or identity of the Grail. Indeed at this point the object is simply *a* grail, rather than *the* Grail. It was in the subsequent romance *Joseph d'Arimathie*, by the French poet Robert de Boron, that the history of the Grail is first explained. Written between 1192 and 1202, this version tells the story of Joseph of Arimathea and how he brought the Grail to England.

And did those feet, in ancient times … ?

Joseph of Arimathea is a figure from the New Testament whose story was expanded by apocryphal sources (ie gospels that were excluded from the 'official' Bible) and who later developed into a legendary/folkloric figure. He was a wealthy and influential merchant who was a secret follower of Jesus and took charge of his body after the Crucifixion, wrapping it and laying it in his own tomb (thus fulfilling the prophecy by Isaiah that Jesus would be buried in the grave of a rich man). For this service he was imprisoned by the Jewish elders, but Christ appeared to him and fed him (via the Grail, in some versions) before transporting him out of prison.

According to Boron and others, after his escape from prison he joined forces with the Apostle Philip, Mary Magdalene, Lazarus and sundry others, and travelled across the Mediterranean to Marseilles, whence he was sent to Britain, a land he knew from his dealings in the tin trade, to spread the good word. He took with him a cup that was used by Jesus at the Last Supper (ie the Holy Chalice) and which he used to catch drops of blood from Jesus on the Cross. He and his followers landed in the Somerset marshes and ascended the nearest hill, which is now Glastonbury Tor. Here Joseph planted his staff in the ground, whereupon it miraculously sprouted and flowered, and here he founded the first church in Britain.

In later developments of the Grail legend, Joseph and his relatives become the ancestors of the kings of Britain (including Arthur), while the Grail is given into the care of Joseph's son-in-law, first of a long line of Grail Keepers that leads to the Fisher King, Perceval, Galahad and other figures of Arthurian legend. Other tales about Joseph of Arimathea include that he was actually Jesus' uncle, and that he may have brought the young messiah with him on previous trading trips to Britain, a fable that inspired Blake's hymn *Jerusalem*.

The Grail in Britain

The Joseph of Arimathea story states that the Grail ended up in Britain, but there are several different versions and thus several candidate locations.

The Chalice Well

According to local Glastonbury traditions, the Grail was buried deep inside Glastonbury Tor, causing a spring to well up, in what is now called the Chalice Well. Supposedly, it is because the spring flows across the Grail and mingles with the blood of Christ that the waters are reddish. According to geologists, however, the spring water is reddish because it is rich in iron oxides – which precipitate out into the surrounding rock. It is these deposits that are responsible for the Tor's existence, as over millions of years they made the rock harder than the surrounding area, which eroded away leaving the Tor standing proud.

Corbenic, the Grail Castle

According to the Grail romance, Joseph gave the Grail to his son-in-law Brons, the first Grail King, who guarded it at Corbenic Castle. This became the legendary Grail Castle, sought by Arthur's questing knights. Today it is thought that Castell Dinas Bran in North Wales is the location of ancient Corbenic, where a medieval castle now stands on the site of a previous Iron Age fort.

The Nanteos Cup

A much more recent tradition, thought to date from Victorian times, tells the story of how the monks of Glastonbury Abbey, forced out by King Henry VIII's dissolution of the monasteries, dug up the Grail and took it with them to South Wales, where they were eventually forced to entrust it to the care of the local squire, lord of Nanteos Manor. Here it remained until 1952 when the house passed into the hands of a new owner and the Nanteos Cup was removed to a bank vault for safe-keeping.

The Nanteos Cup is actually a small wooden bowl. According to legend it is made of olive wood from 1st-century Palestine. In practice it is almost certainly a witch-hazel mazer bowl (a type of medieval dish) from the 14th century. Several chunks are missing where pilgrims have taken bites from the cup in the belief that it had curative powers.

The Templar connection

The Knights Templar were a military religious order originally set up to protect pilgrims in the Holy Land. They became rich and powerful throughout Europe, and their secret practices and sudden downfall in the early 14th century lent them an air of mystery that, to this day, exerts a powerful influence on the romantic imagination. They first became connected with the Grail legend in Wolfram von Eschenbach's Grail romance *Parzival*, dating from c1210–1215. In this version, the Grail is guarded in the stronghold of Munsalvaesche (sometimes identified with the monastery at Montserrat in Spain) by a group of knights called the *Templiesin*, thought to be a thinly veiled reference to the Templars, who at the time von Eschenbach was writing were at the height of their powers. Since many legends of the Templars talk of their having excavated something from the ruins of Solomon's Temple in Jerusalem, having looted the Grail during the Sack of Constantinople in 1204, or having otherwise acquired secret knowledge that gave them wealth and power, it is not too hard to see how they became associated with the Grail. When the Templars were suppressed in the 14th century, the Grail was supposedly spirited away/hidden.

Rosslyn Chapel

From this starting point the story follows several avenues. According to one version, the Templars took their priceless treasure to Britain, where they largely escaped persecution, and it passed into the hands of the Sinclair family, Scottish nobles with a base in Roslin in Lothian. Supposedly their possession of secret knowledge prompted the construction of the now famous Rosslyn Chapel and prompted them to include all manner of strange Templar and Masonic symbolism in its decoration. Most ornate of all the chapel's fittings is the Apprentice pillar (or Prentice Pillar), a heavily carved column now widely touted as the final resting place of the Holy Grail.

Unfortunately there is no evidence for this, despite unfounded and unsupported claims that 'metal detectors' have 'proved' that there is an 'object' inside the pillar. It is true that there are spaces/vaults beneath the chapel, but these have not been excavated because to do so would threaten the foundations.

Coming to America

Among the many outlandish claims associated with the Templars, the Sinclair family and the Templar survival in Britain, is that Templar ships and navigators were visiting America before Columbus, and that the Sinclairs were behind this. Seeking to hide the Grail in ever more inaccessible locations, the Sinclairs accordingly sent it to the New World, where it was buried in a pit on Oak Island in Nova Scotia, thus connecting the Grail fable with that of the Oak Island Money Pit (see page 145). There is no evidence beyond speculation to support this notion, and in fact it seems unlikely that there was ever anything in the Oak Island Pit.

An even more outlandish claim is that the Grail was smuggled into America by a priest travelling with Captain John Smith to found the colony of Jamestown in 1607. When Smith visited the Piscataway Indian village of Moyaone in Accokeek (now in Maryland), the priest hid the Grail there. Over the following centuries its influence caused the surrounding areas to become the seat of world power (although it apparently didn't do much for the Piscataway Indians, who were wiped out by disease, competition from the colony and other tribes). Who this priest was, how he got hold of the most precious relic in Christendom and why he would want to bury it in Accokeek are questions that remain mysterious.

The Priory of Sion

Thanks to *The Da Vinci Code*, there is currently a vogue for the theory that the Holy Grail was really the bloodline of Jesus. According to this story, first set out in detail in the book *The Holy Blood and the Holy Grail*, Jesus was married to Mary Magdalene. When she and Joseph of Arimathea travelled to Marseilles after the Crucifixion, they were accompanied by Jesus' children and possibly even by Jesus himself, who had not died on the Cross as claimed. The descendants of Christ later became the Merovingian kings of France, before being usurped, after which the bloodline was preserved in secret by groups such as the Knights Templar and the shadowy Priory of Sion. Today, the Holy Grail is said to be, at one and the same time, this secret knowledge about Christ *and* his actual descendants, and the Catholic Church is busily suppressing these 'facts'. Various 'proofs' – which might also be described as Holy Grails – are concealed in Rosslyn Chapel, and possibly somewhere near the town of Rennes-le-Château in Languedoc, France.

This entertaining fiction is largely based on forged papers smuggled into the French national archives by a known fraudster, who invented the Priory of Sion in the 1950s as a vehicle for his own fantasising. It obscures rather than illuminates any genuine search for the Holy Grail.

Real cups and chalices

The Joseph of Arimathea/Arthurian romances, and their associated Templar baggage, form only one skein of tradition regarding the Grail. There are several contenders that claim to be the Grail/Chalice, and which are distinct from most of the Arimathean/Arthurian candidates by virtue of actually existing as real objects.

The Santo Caliz of Valencia

The Cathedral at Valencia, in Spain, hosts a small red agate cup, mounted on a more elaborate structure, said to be the Santo Caliz, or Holy Chalice. It is claimed that 'archaeological studies' of the cup reveal that it dates back to the Near East between the 4th century BCE and the 1st century CE, although this seems to based on an inspection rather than microscopic study or other investigation. The artefact's provenance is fully attested only from 1134 CE, but a so-called certificate of authenticity tells of how it was brought to Rome by Saint Peter himself, and later taken to Spain to keep it safe during the Valerian persecution of Christians in 258 CE.

The Antioch Chalice

A small, plain silver bowl mounted on an elaborate footed shell was supposedly found near Antioch (in modern-day Turkey) in 1908, and identified as a very early (6th-century) Eucharist chalice (ie used during the Eucharist or Holy Communion rite). Perhaps inevitably, there were claims that it was the Holy Chalice from the Last Supper. According to the Metropolitan Museum of Art in New York, where it now resides, the Antioch Chalice is more likely to have been a standing lamp, and its identification as the Holy Chalice is 'ambitious'.

The Sacro Catino of Genoa

The Cathedral of Genoa hosts a hexagonal emerald green dish or bowl known as the Sacro Catino, or Holy Basin, which was identified as the Holy Chalice by medieval writers. Originally thought to be emerald, it was revealed as Egyptian glass when it was broken on its way back to Genoa (after it had been removed to Paris by Napoleon). Its provenance is attested from 1170 CE, and it is said to have been won by Genoese Crusaders

in Palestine or Spain earlier in the 12th century. It was not associated with the Holy Chalice/Grail until the late 13th century.

Conclusion

Arguably the three contenders above have a better claim to the
mantle of the real Holy Grail than the fabled artefacts/secrets of
the Grail romances. The fact remains, however, that there is no
convincing evidence that the Holy Grail ever existed at all. Even if
Jesus is accepted to be a historical figure, and the Last Supper and
the Crucifixion (complete with collection of blood) are accepted
to have really happened, there is no way of knowing what the
cups/bowls involved would have looked like, and what happened
to them immediately afterwards. Only traditions, legends and
stories remain, and most of these can be dated back only as far as
the Middle Ages, whatever antiquity is claimed for them.

The chalice of Arculf

The earliest record of the Holy Chalice comes from Arculf's
descriptions of his trip to the Holy Land in the late 7th century.
Arculf was a Gallic monk who had visited the holy sites and
described them to the monks on Iona. He tells of seeing a relatively large two-handled silver chalice in a chapel in Jerusalem.
What happened to it subsequently is unknown, but it is telling
that none of the candidates above fits the description, and that
Arculf's tale obviously conflicts with the legend that Joseph of
Arimathea took the Chalice/Grail.

Even if an exact match were to be discovered, it is not clear
how its provenance could ever be proved. As with most relics,
from the Shroud of Turin to the various shards of the True
Cross, it is only possible to disprove the claims made for them.
Beyond this, belief in their authenticity is a matter of faith.

Shakespeare's lost plays

The work of William Shakespeare needs little introduction. His plays are the most performed of any playwright ever, and he is regarded as the most important writer in Western literature. The academic edifice devoted to the study of Shakespeare is enormous, while generations of book collectors and antiquarians have sought high and low for material associated with the great man, material rendered more valuable by its very scarcity.

A new Shakespeare play, rediscovered after 400 years, would therefore have enormous literary, academic and antiquarian significance. In some quarters, it would be equivalent to the uncovering of a new Gospel or a new draft of the American Constitution. This makes it all the more intriguing that we actually know of two such lost plays: *Love's Labour's Won*, and *Cardenio*, probably co-written with John Fletcher.

Or do we? Although you will find these officially recorded as 'Shakespeare's lost plays' in almost any biography, there is considerable debate over their identities and whether they existed at all. To understand this debate, and thus to get some idea of whether and where the lost plays might be discovered, it is necessary to delve into the complex world of Shakespeare scholarship.

Quartos and folios

In some ways Shakespeare's oeuvre is like the Bible. There is an accepted canon of works, and there is an Apocrypha (works attributed to Shakespeare by some, but not generally considered by mainstream scholarship to be part of his oeuvre). For the accepted canon, we are mainly indebted to the First Folio, a collection of Shakespeare's plays collated and published seven years after his death, in 1623. This was not definitive however – there were many other plays attributed to Shakespeare both before and after the publication of the First Folio. Most of these are not accepted and belong to the Apocrypha at best. A few, such as *Pericles, Prince of Tyre* have become part of the accepted canon. These are known to us today because they were published separately from the First Folio, often in a cheap form known as quarto (where a sheet of paper is folded into four).

Publication problems

Surely knowing what Shakespeare did and didn't write should be relatively straightforward? It should be a simple matter of looking at quartos and folios and seeing which of them bear his name. Unfortunately the publishing scene of late Elizabethan England makes this impossible. When Shakespeare first came to London and began to write in the 1580s and early 1590s, he was probably something of a jobbing writer; collaborating with other writers was common at a time when playwrights were less precious about authorship than they are today. So his early work was probably largely anonymous.

Later, when he became an established playwright, his very success mitigated against publication of his work. There were no copyright laws during his lifetime, and publishing a play made it all too easy for other publishers and theatre companies to perform without licence, plagiarise and even simply copy. This is why relatively few of his plays were published during Shakespeare's lifetime, and then not always in the most professional editions. Shakespeare's success also gave unscrupulous writers and publishers an incentive to try to ride his coat-tails by falsely attributing works to him. This was a problem well into the 18th century, when the Shakespearean canon became firmly established, and is occasionally still a problem today (see '*The Second Maiden's Tragedy*', page 95).

Promoted from the Apocrypha

Involved scholarship to overcome these textural problems has led to some plays becoming accepted as authentically Shakespearean, effectively gaining 'promotion' from the Apocrypha. In a sense these are 'lost' plays that have been 'rediscovered'. They include *Pericles*, *The Two Noble Kinsmen*, *Edward III* and *Sir Thomas More*. All were probably collaborations, some with a relatively small contribution from Shakespeare.

Ireland's fraud

One of the most remarkable stories connected with lost Shakespeare plays is the tale of William Henry Ireland and *Vortigern*. Ireland was the son of an antiquarian book dealer. Considered a dullard by his father and almost everyone else, he proved to be an expert forger, capable of imitating signatures and ingenious at combining old or aged paper, antique wax seals and antique-appearance ink. To gain his father's approbation he embarked on a series of increasingly ambitious forgeries, leading up to his 'discovery' of a legal document signed by Shakespeare. Other Shakespeariana followed, until in 1795 Ireland produced his most ambitious forgery yet – an entirely new play, supposedly discovered by the spurious benefactor Ireland had invented as the source of his antiquarian treasures.

The play was entitled *Vortigern*, and told of the legendary 5th-century king of Britain. Ireland had based it on the same source that Shakespeare used for many of his history plays: Holinshed's *Chronicles*. Although Ireland was not without talent as a writer, and later went on to write a creditable *Henry II* under his own name (having originally conceived it as another lost Shakespeare play), he was out of his depth and the play was mediocre at best.

The most incredible aspect of the whole affair was the gullibility of the London public and experts alike. The leading impresario and dramatist of the day, Richard Brinsley Sheridan, even bought the rights to perform *Vortigern*, but unfortunately by the time it was actually presented at the Theatre Royal, Drury Lane, in 1796, opinion had swung against the authenticity of Ireland's Shakespeare Papers, and the performance was greeted with such derision that it ran for only one night. Ireland eventually admitted to the fraud and was reduced to hack writing to make a living, although in later years his forgeries were in such demand as collector's items that he forged new copies – forgeries of forgeries. These too are now worth a lot of money.

Proof of existence

Given this mass of confusing evidence about plays that might and might not have been by Shakespeare, how can there be such broad agreement about the two 'official' lost plays? Their identity comes to us via some nifty literary detective work.

Meres' list

The primary exhibit is a list of Shakespeare's plays from a 1598 book, *Palladis Tamia, Wits Treasury,* by Elizabethan cleric and fan of the arts Francis Meres. One chapter of the book compares classical authors with English ones, and gives particular notice to Shakespeare, listing several of his plays, including one called *Love's Labour's Won.* Since this play was apparently not mentioned in any of the usual sources, such as the records of which plays were performed and when, or the *Stationers' Register,* where authors and publishers listed works they wanted to copyright, it was assumed that it was simply an alternative name for an extant play, probably *The Taming of the Shrew,* but at any rate a play written prior to 1598.

The bookseller's list

However, in 1953 a fragment of a bookseller's list – a list of works on offer by a bookseller – was discovered as part of the binding of another book. This list advertised the wares of stationer Christopher Hunt and was dated 1603. Among the Shakespeare plays on offer were: 'Marchant Of Vennis, Taming Of A Shrew, Loves Labor Lost, Loves Labor Won'. Evidently *Love's Labour's Won* (henceforth *LLW*) and *The Taming of the Shrew* were not the same. More importantly, the appearance of *LLW* on a bookseller's list proved that it *had* been published in some form (probably quarto), and could, in theory, yet be discovered.

Paper trail

The existence of a lost play called *Cardenio* is better attested. Contemporary documents record that the King's Men, the theatre company Shakespeare had co-founded and written for, performed a play called *Cardenno* at court in 1613 (bear in mind that in Elizabethan/Jacobean times spelling was often fluid), and again later that year for the ambassador of the Duke of Savoy. In September 1653 a London publisher registered his edition of a play called '*The History of Cardenio*, by Mr Fletcher and Shakespeare' in the *Stationers' Register*.

Suggested contents

So what do we know about the content and character of these apparently lost plays?

Meres listed *LLW* as one of Shakespeare's comedies, and it is often assumed to have been a sequel to *Love's Labour's Lost* (henceforth *LLL*). Tellingly, the ending of that play leaves open the possibility of a sequel, while the final lines actively suggest it. In the extant play, after many misadventures and capers, two sets of couples are finally set to wed, only for the weddings to be postponed for a year, with the brides setting their grooms amusing tasks to occupy them in the meantime. The final dialogue is:

> BEROWNE: Our wooing doth not end like an old play;
> Jack hath not Jill: these ladies' courtesy
> Might well have made our sport a comedy.
> FERDINAND: Come, sir, it wants a twelvemonth and a day,
> And then 'twill end.
> BEROWNE: That's too long for a play.

This is not to say that *LLW* would have been a direct sequel to *LLL*, with the same characters and location. Shakespeare sometimes wrote thematic sequels, that set off the former play with complementary or opposing themes.

Cardenio was probably based on a story from Cervantes' *Don Quixote*. This had recently been translated into English at the suspected time of writing, and John Fletcher was a fan. The plot concerns a jealous husband who resolves to test his wife's virtue by convincing his best friend to seduce her, with predictably tragic results. It was probably quite bloody, as was the fashion at the time.

What happened to *LLW* and *Cardenio*?

The section on Aristotle's lost *Dialogues* (page 66) discusses some of the perils that afflict manuscripts. Many of these would have applied to quartos and folios of Shakespeare's work. They were not always productions of the highest quality – particularly cheap quarto editions – and may not have been treated with much respect at the time. If the plays were unpopular, few copies may have been printed. In the case of *LLW* and *Cardenio*, they evidently did not warrant inclusion in the First Folio, which suggests that there may have been some doubt over Shakespeare's authorship or over who owned the copyright, which in turn might have affected their popularity. Specifically, Shakespeare himself may not have thought too highly of them, which might have affected their chances of reproduction.

Nonetheless, we know from the bookseller's list and the *Stationers' Register* that some copies of each *were* published. According to Stuart Kelly, author of *The Book of Lost Books*, this implies a print run of 1,000 copies or more. So why are there no extant copies? Here the stories of the two plays diverge, for while *Cardenio* almost certainly did exist as an independent play, and may even be around today in altered form, considerable doubt still surrounds the question of whether *LLW* is simply an existing play by another name.

A rose by any other name

The titles of plays, like their spelling, could be fluid, changing in response to unpopularity (ie rebranding allowed re-release) or the whims of patrons (eg if the king preferred one title to another). One suggestion is that the quarto being advertised by the bookseller's list was a 'bad quarto' – the Elizabethan equivalent of a pirate DVD – with confused or misrepresented text, including the title. Perhaps in this 'bad quarto' of *LLL*, the title was given as *Love's Labour's Lost, Love's Labour's Won* – one play with a long name, rather than two plays. Only the second quarto publication of *LLL* has come down to us, so perhaps the lost first quarto was a 'bad' one with a misleading title.

Other candidates

Assuming that *LLW* is not *LLL* but some other play, viable candidates must be comedies written before September 1598, which were not mentioned in Meres' or the bookseller's lists. It would also most likely be of related themes and/or character to *LLL*, although not necessarily a direct sequel. Despite these apparently restrictive criteria, Shakespeare scholars have seriously argued for half a dozen of his plays as the real *LLW*.

The Taming of the Shrew and *A Midsummer Night's Dream* both appear to be ruled out by also being on one or other of the lists. *All's Well That Ends Well* is a serious contender because there are many similarities with *LLL*, but it was probably not written until 1600 at the earliest.

As You Like It is another contender, with the suggestion that its title was originally a sort of subtitle to *LLW*, in the same fashion as the full title of *Twelfth Night* is *Twelfth Night, or What You Will*. Again, however, the problem is that *As You Like It* is dated to 1602.

Shakespearian scholar Professor Leslie Hotson suggested that correct reading of the apostrophes in the title of the *Love's Labour's* plays shows the way. He argued that the apostrophe in 'Labour's' was not possessive but a contraction of 'is' (and there is some evidence that the Elizabethans were not big on possessive apostrophes), so that the title of *LLW* should be interpreted to mean that the characters in the play are 'winning' the labours (hardships) of love – ie they are suffering the travails of love. On this basis, it has been suggested that *LLW* is actually an alternative title for the tragic-historical *Troilus and Cressida*, which would certainly be a strong counterpoint to the frothy comedy of *LLL*.

Yet another suggestion is that *The Merry Wives of Windsor* is the result of a reworking of *LLW*. In this theory, Shakespeare adapted an unsuccessful play – *LLW* – to take account of the fact that Queen Elizabeth was a big fan of the character of Falstaff, and incorporated him into the extant play, also changing its title.

Probably the leading contender is *Much Ado About Nothing* (hereafter *MAAN*). This comedy was probably written in late 1598, which might suggest that Meres could not have seen it in time to include it in his book (which must have been written some time before its publication). However, some scholars believe that Meres was cosy with the cultural elite of London and might well have read the play before its initial performance. As to the plot, *MAAN* could be argued to fit the bill well. It follows a similar pattern to *LLL*'s romantic comedy, with two couples making and breaking up. The characters of Benedict and Beatrice seem to have some considerable back-story, which is not explained – perhaps they are characters from *LLL* with new names. On the other hand, it could be argued that the plots do not mesh, and *MAAN* would certainly not be a direct sequel to *LLL*, if it is a sequel at all.

It should be clear that this debate is both involved and intractable. Unless a version of *LLW*, clearly labelled as such, actually turns up, it will never be possible to settle the argument and say whether it really is an existing play under another name and, if so, which one.

Frankenstein's play

Similarly involved arguments surround the provenance and identity of *Cardenio*. Humphrey Moseley, the publisher who entered *Cardenio* on the *Stationers' Register* in 1653 as a work by Shakespeare and Fletcher, registered two other plays allegedly by Shakespeare at the same time, and another three in 1660. None are thought to be genuine, and it is probable that Moseley was attempting to cash in on Shakespeare's popularity. The original records of *Cardenio* being performed do not specify Shakespeare as the author, so while it definitely existed, perhaps it was by someone else entirely.

The play next appears in history in 1728 when noted Shakespearian editor Lewis Theobald claimed to possess three manuscripts of the play, upon which he based a play of his own devising called *Double Falshood*. Copies of this play still exist, so if Theobald's claims are true, it might actually be possible to at least partly reconstruct *Cardenio*. However, argument rages over the truth of Theobald's claims.

Why adapt?

If he really possessed the originals, why didn't he simply publish those, rather than plagiarise/bastardise them to create his own play? This was hardly in keeping with his life's work of carefully reconstituting the best versions of Shakespeare's plays from the conflicting editions available. It is possible that Theobald adapted the play because he was not certain of its authorship and did not want to 'sully' Shakespeare's oeuvre with an inferior play. In addition, the copies he possessed might already have suffered considerable bastardisation during the Restoration era, when Shakespeare was treated with little reverence and actors and impresarios regularly made sweeping alterations.

Where are the manuscripts?

If Theobald had three copies of *Cardenio*, where are they? Why weren't there more? The answer to both questions may lie in ashes. Many of the original copies may have been lost in a fire at the Globe Theatre, home of the King's Men, which burnt down in 1613. However, the *Stationers' Register* entry suggests new publication well after this. As to Theobald's copies, it is possible that after his death they passed into the hands of John Warburton, a contemporary Shakespeare scholar, whose cook Betsy Baker famously burned a number of his rare manuscripts by accident, using others to line some cake tins. Alternatively, according to Professor Brean Hammond from the University of Nottingham, who quotes newspaper reports from 1770, the copies of *Cardenio* were among a number of manuscripts 'treasured up' in the Covent Garden Theatre Museum. The Museum burnt down in 1808, potentially taking the copies with it.

Was *Double Falshood* the real deal?

Analysis by scholars of Elizabethan drama suggests that the hands of Fletcher and Shakespeare can clearly be seen at work in *Double Falshood*, confirming Theobald's claims. However, other experts argue that the later play is a hoax, and that audiences of the time were intended to be in on the joke. To begin with there is the title, which clearly seems to indicate a hoax. Secondly, there are lines in the play that supposedly allude to the joke and give the game away. This interpretation is backed up by the unusual method employed by the Claremont Shakespeare Clinic, where a battery of stylistic tests are applied to the text and the results are statistically analysed. In the case of *Double Falshood*, the Clinic found that the odds against it being the work of Shakespeare were more than a million to one.

The Second Maiden's Tragedy

Another candidate for the real *Cardenio*, or an adaptation of it, is a Jacobean play called *The Second Maiden's Tragedy* (the name derives from the fact that it was originally untitled and was described as a second version of *The Maiden's Tragedy*), known from a manuscript of 1611. Traditionally this has been attributed to Thomas Middleton, but in 1990 handwriting expert Charles Hamilton published a book claiming that the handwriting on the manuscript is none other than Shakespeare's, and that the play is basically *Cardenio*, but with the names changed. Several companies have since revived *The Second Maiden's Tragedy*, usually under the name *Cardenio*, with Shakespeare given as the author so as to pull in the crowds.

The Shakespearian studies community reacted derisively to Hamilton's claims. The hand in which *The Second Maiden's Tragedy* is written is a fairly generic style called 'secretary', and there is no known Shakespearian secretary with which to compare it. In fact, the only definite examples of the Bard's handwriting are a few signatures on legal documents. Textural analysis points to Middleton as the author, and the general quality of the play is quite poor. Moreover, only the subplot matches the story of *Cardenio*, while the main action concerns a sadistic necrophiliac tyrant.

Attics and old libraries

It should be clear by now that there is little certainty about whether *LLW* and *Cardenio* are genuinely lost Shakespeare plays. But the Shakespeare community is hopeful and many still dream of adding to the greatest theatrical oeuvre in the history of literature. Is this a realistic dream? Might unknown manuscripts turn up even today, after centuries of diligent searching by collectors and librarians?

There are relatively recent precedents. According to the Oxford University Press, the rarest known Shakespeare quarto – the 1594 quarto of *Titus Andronicus* – was only discovered in 1902. Meanwhile in 1909, eight quartos of Shakespeare plays were discovered in the former home of Sir Francis Bacon, an Elizabethan polymath and writer often touted as the 'true' author of Shakespeare's oeuvre. They were wrapped in brown paper and had been hidden behind a bookshelf for at least 155 years. If such a trove can remain undisturbed for so long in a house so prominently associated with Shakespeare, what might yet be found elsewhere, perhaps in a dusty attic, or squirrelled away behind the stacks in the library of a stately home?

3

Lost Treasure

To a historian or archaeologist, all the subjects covered in this book constitute a kind of treasure, an inestimable intellectual and cultural bounty, the discovery/recovery of which would be equivalent to finding untold riches. For the man on the street, however, this simply won't wash. Treasure means money – real riches, not intellectual ones – and few things are more exciting than the prospect of stumbling across a cache of booty worth more than a winning lottery ticket. Hence the popular concept of lost treasure as chests overflowing with gold doubloons and sacks crammed to the brim with gemstones as big as fists.

Incredibly, this is not just a fantasy; there really is treasure out there, lost, buried or otherwise hidden, awaiting recovery; people genuinely have stumbled across amazing caches of loot. In March 2004, for instance, Ken Allen of South Gloucestershire in England found a 'priceless hoard' of 20,000 Roman coins while digging a pond in his back garden, while in June 2000 a farmer in northern India uncovered more than 15 kilograms (33 pounds) of gold and jewellery from the 5,000-year-old Indus Valley civilisation. Even buried pirate loot has genuinely been dug up, as you'll learn from the story of Captain Kidd's treasure.

In this chapter you'll also learn, however, that many legendary treasures are just that. In other words, if hunting treasure, choose your target wisely.

The treasure of the Dead Sea scrolls

The Dead Sea scrolls is the collective name for the mass of ancient writings, mainly early scriptures, discovered in caves on the western shores of the Dead Sea near Qumran, between 1947 and 1956. According to legend, the first of the Dead Sea scrolls were discovered in 1947 by a Bedouin shepherd boy searching for a lost sheep amidst the numerous caves that pepper the hills and canyons of the Dead Sea coast. Venturing into one of the caves, the boy found a collection of broken and intact pottery jars, some stuffed with ancient documents written on papyrus and parchment (animal skin).

By 1948, through a variety of shady intermediaries, some of the scrolls came into the hands of experts who appreciated their significance. It became apparent that there was a whole cache of these documents, and that Bedouin treasure hunters, realising their value, were searching for more. Archaeologists from the young state of Israel and institutions around the world launched their own hunt, hoping to beat the destructive looters to finds of major archaeological significance.

Discovery of the Copper Scroll

In March 1952, one of the most exciting finds was made in a cave in a hill about 2 kilometres (1.2 miles) from Qumran. On a ledge at the back of the cave, partially obscured by a rockfall, beyond a number of jars containing more conventional ancient scrolls, was a jar containing two clay-covered rolls of copper sheet, which later proved to be the two halves of a single, rolled-up sheet of copper inscribed by a stylus with an odd mix of Hebrew and Greek – the Copper Scroll. The writing was not visible when it was discovered, but the indentations caused by the stylus could be seen on the outside of the scrolls, and the archaeologists thought they could make out the words 'gold' and 'silver'.

The excitement this generated had to be put on hold, for the issue of unrolling the scroll proved a thorny one. After four years of head scratching, it was decided to saw through the rolls, leaving strips of copper, which could then be cleaned and analysed. Most of the academics charged with this task were reluctant to publish their translation for fear of sparking off a giant gold rush, but young maverick John Allegro tired of the delay and issued his own version of the scroll's explosive contents.

Directions to incalculable wealth

The Copper Scroll is an inventory of 64 items. The first 63 are caches of hidden treasure, together with directions for finding them, while the last item speaks of a copy of the inventory with further directions and, crucially, 'an explanation'. The treasure listed takes several forms. Most of it is varying amounts of gold and silver, but there are also ornaments and vessels of gold and silver, aromatic substances and scrolls.

What is most astonishing, and problematic, is the quantity of gold and silver listed. The scroll seems to deal in the ancient unit of weight known as the talent. Today no one is sure exactly how much the Copper Scroll talent weighs because it depends on the exact age of the list. The generally accepted academic interpretation puts the total listed weight of treasure at a staggering 26 tonnes of gold and 65 tonnes of silver, together with sundry other items, collectively worth around £1 billion ($1.9 billion) today for mineral value alone. Not everyone agrees with this interpretation, however, because the scroll does not actually spell out the term 'talents', leaving room for speculation. For instance, it has been suggested that the scroll does not deal in talents but in a lesser measure, which would make the quantities more plausible.

Clear as mud

In many respects the Copper Scroll is exactly what a treasure hunter would want to find. There is no preamble, no rubric and apparently no secret code or cipher. It is simply a straightforward list with directions. In practice, however, there are problems with the writing, the language used and the information itself.

The biggest hurdle is that while the directions are fairly clear, they seem to depend on pre-existing knowledge, without which they are largely useless. A sample of the scroll will give the flavour of the text and illustrate the problem:

> In the salt pit which is under the steps: 42 talents. HN
> In the cave of the old Washer's Chamber, on the third ledge: sixty-five ingots of gold. THE
> In the vault which is in the court there is donated firewood, in the midst of which, in the recess: vessels and seventy talents of silver.
> In the cistern which is across from the Eastern Gate, at a distance of nineteen cubits: in it there are vessels, and in the conduit leading into it: ten talents. DI
> In the cistern which is under the wall of the east, in the tooth of the cliff: six jars of silver.

Unless you already know the location to which the scroll is referring, the directions do not make a great deal of sense. In fact, some place names are mentioned, but even these are ambiguous for various reasons. Also, different translators have arrived at different translations. Although the variations are minor, they are crucial when it comes to definitively identifying locations.

Strange writing

Translating the scroll proved to be difficult because the Hebrew in which it is written is strangely archaic (ie for the time at which it was written – probably some time in the 1st century CE) and there are many gaps in the text. Even the writing itself, which was made by pressing a stylus into the copper sheet, is peculiar and hard to read. One suggestion is that it was written by an illiterate scribe who was simply tracing the forms of an original version written on papyrus or parchment. This would make sense in the context of a real treasure list, since the scroll's author(s) would not necessarily want the copyist to know the secrets there inscribed.

Another strange feature is the presence of Greek digrams and trigrams (groups of two or three letters) at the end of some entries, represented in the translation above by the pairs or triplets of capital letters. Even the matter of the scroll itself is mysterious: it is 99 per cent pure copper, which would have been very hard – and very expensive – to obtain in ancient times. Obviously the scroll was meant to last for centuries, but in this case, why did the authors apparently make the directions so personal?

Who hid the Copper Scroll?

The Dead Sea scrolls, including the Copper Scroll, were probably hidden in around 70 CE, to protect them from the marauding Romans who were quashing the Jewish Revolt. It is generally assumed they were collected and hidden by people from the Qumran community, the ruins of which are nearby, who were probably massacred by the Romans shortly afterwards. The identity of the Qumran community is the subject of fierce debate. At first it was assumed that they were Essenes, a Jewish sect mentioned as living in the area by ancient writers such as Pliny and the Jewish historian Josephus. Many historians dispute this interpretation, however, pointing out that there are features of both the Qumran community and the scrolls themselves that suggest that neither the inhabitants nor the compilers of the scrolls (who may or may not have been the same people) were

Essenes. For instance, some of the theological positions espoused by the scrolls seem to clash with those ascribed to the Essenes.

Alternative suggestions for the inhabitants of Qumran include the Sadducees, a Jewish sect associated with the high priests of the Temple in Jerusalem, or some sort of early or proto-Christian community. Maybe Qumran was not a proto-monastery, as is usually assumed, but actually a fort of some kind, possibly for rebels fighting the Romans.

A final possibility is that the Copper Scroll was indeed hidden from the Romans, but at a later date – during the Bar Kokhba rebellion (aka the Second Jewish Revolt) of 132–135 CE, which was triggered by the Roman plan to build a temple to Jupiter on the Temple Mount. At least one cache of Dead Sea scrolls, found in the Cave of Letters, almost certainly dates from this time as the letters found there relate to the Bar Kokhba revolt.

Temple treasure or elaborate hoax?

So is the Copper Scroll for real? The initial academic response was that it was some sort of ancient hoax, or an allegory or per-haps a fable similar to the story of Jeremiah hiding the Ark of the Covenant (see page 63). Partly this was based on the initial assumption that it had been made and hidden by Essenes, an ascetic group who espoused the simple life and were unlikely to have possessed a great amount of treasure. There was also the question of the enormous quantities listed, which would seem to be implausible for any group in the kingdom of Judea.

A possible exception was the Temple in Jerusalem – the cen-tre of Judaism at this time, in both the spiritual and temporal sense. Tithes and tributes were paid to it, and great quantities of ornaments, ritual vessels and other objects of precious metal were also gathered there. This led Allegro, and many subsequent theorists, to argue that the Copper Scroll treasure was real, and consisted of the treasure and ritual objects removed from the Temple ahead of the advancing Romans, squirrelled away to keep it out of their grasp. Why else go to such lengths to create an object as unusual as the Copper Scroll and then hide it away in a cave in the wilderness? The ancient Jews of the area were not known for their sense of humour.

In fact the scroll several times specifically mentions tithes and tributes: eg 'In the ruin-heap of Kohlit: vessels of tribute of the master of nations, and ritual garments. All of this belongs to the tribute and the seventh treasure, a second tithe rendered unclean. Its opening is in the edge of the aqueduct on the north.' Meanwhile, item 32 on the scroll mentions six bars of gold buried in a cave next to the House of Hakkoz. The Hakkoz family, according to some biblical references, were the treasurers of the Temple, responsible for guarding its wealth.

The Temple treasure theory suggests that the Copper Scroll was not hidden by the Essenes/Qumran inhabitants, but by people associated with the authorities in Jerusalem (although it is also possible under the pressure of war the differing groups may have forged an unlikely alliance). It ties in with stories about secret tunnels running from below the Temple Mount as far as the hills by the Dead Sea.

Equipped for the Apocalypse

There are two variations of the Temple treasure theory. One is that the scroll was created during the Bar Kokhba rebellion, and that it refers to the tithes and tributes that were collected for the Temple after 70 CE. This was when the Romans destroyed the Second Temple, meaning that although tithes continued to be collected, there was nowhere for them to go, especially not if they were to be kept out of the hands of the Romans. Perhaps this explains why, according to the Copper Scroll, they were squirrelled away in so many different places, rather than in one or two large caches as might be expected otherwise.

The other version is of potentially far greater eschatological significance, because it suggests that the Copper Scroll booty is the treasure removed from the Temple before 70 CE, and includes the ritual ornaments such as the breastplate of Aaron and the Ark of the Covenant, which otherwise appear to have vanished from the historical record. One objection to this is that the histories of the time clearly record the Romans as having recovered a huge quantity of treasure from the Temple. According to one account, they set fire to the Temple and the precious metals stored within melted and ran through the gutters of the Temple Mount like water. But it could be that the priests left just enough behind to satisfy the greedy conquerors.

This second version is significant because it inspires those who seek to rebuild the Temple and usher in the End Times. In order for this to happen, they believe, many things are necessary, including the recovery of ritual artefacts needed in the Temple or to purify the precincts. So rather than being just an archaeological pursuit, the hunt for the Copper Scroll treasure becomes part of the spiritual quest to bring about the Apocalypse, with all the real-world geopolitical implications that go along with it (see page 20).

Medical expenses

Historian Gloria Moss has a theory that the treasure could have belonged to the Essenes after all, assuming they were not the ascetic monastics of traditional conception. She argues that the Essenes ran a sort of ancient spa/health clinic and were engaged in the highly lucrative trade in medicines such as frankincense, myrrh and balsam, which was worth more than its weight in gold at the time. This would have made them rich, and would also explain the Copper Scroll's references to aromatics, which may have been the raw materials for the Essenes' drug manufacturing. For instance, item 4 on the scroll is: 'On the hill of Kohlit, jar[s] of aromatics, sandalwood and sacred garments; all the aromatics and treasure ...'

However, Temple treasure theory supporters would argue that aromatics and suchlike were important for Temple ritual and as ingredients for incense.

Locating the treasure of the Copper Scroll

Working on the assumption that the treasure is real, is it possible to identify any of the locations mentioned? There are several tantalising references to place names. For instance, the scroll begins with item 1: 'In the fortress which is in the Vale of Achor, forty cubits under the steps entering to the east: a money chest and its contents, of a weight of seventeen talents.' The Vale of Achor is believed to be a valley just to the west of Qumran, and there used to be a fortress there called Hyrcania. The city of Kohlit is mentioned several times – this may be reference to an area east of the Jordan near the Yarmuk River. Item 49 mentions 'the monument of Absalom'. The Tomb of Absalom still stands on the Jerusalem–Jericho road, but it probably post-dates the scroll. Could the 'monument' be a reference to a structure that stood on the same site before the present-day tomb?

Treasure hunters

Clues such as this have been followed by real-life treasure hunters like John Allegro, the maverick scroll scholar who was so frustrated by the official intransigence and foot-dragging that he launched his own expedition. He identified numerous real locations from the scroll, such as those mentioned above, but ultimately came away empty-handed, retreating eventually to bitter academic exile on the Isle of Wight, from where he wrote invectives against religion, based on radical interpretations of the scrolls.

Picking up where Allegro left off, biblical archaeologist Vendyl Jones claimed to have used the Copper Scroll to locate a jug of ancient anointing oil in 1988. In 1992 he uncovered a deposit of what he said was ancient incense. Jones' claims should perhaps be viewed in the light of his eschatological beliefs (see page 62) – for instance, he may have viewed the oil and the incense as substances that could be used to prepare the way for a new Temple.

Academic Richard Freund claims that the Cave of Letters, site of recovery of documents from the Bar Kokhba revolt era, is also the Cave of the Column mentioned in item 25 of the Copper Scroll. When the Cave of Letters was first excavated, bronze ritual objects were recovered alongside stoneware vessels and a scroll. Freund claims that this ties in with what is listed in item 25, and that the archaeologists had unknowingly discovered one of the Copper Scroll treasures – possibly including ritual objects saved from the destruction of the Temple. However, philologist (scholar of ancient texts) Edward Cook points out that Freund has been selective in his interpretation of item 25, which actually lists silver as the buried treasure, and does not mention bronze objects of any sort.

Out of Egypt

Writer Robert Feather has a radical alternative theory about where the treasure is and the true meaning of the Copper Scroll. He argues that the peculiar writing and language used in the scroll are more similar to forms used in ancient Egypt in the 14th century BCE, approximately the time of the Hebrew captivity there. In particular, the strange system used to give quantities ties in with an Egyptian numeral system of the time, referring to a unit called the kite. If this is applied to the quantities in the scroll, it gives a much more plausible total of 26 kilograms (57 pounds) of gold and 13.6 kilograms (30 pounds) of silver.

Feather's theory is that the ancient Jews derived their monotheism from the pharaoh Akhenaton, who attempted to change the Egyptian polytheistic religion to a monotheistic one c1340 BCE, and that the Copper Scroll refers to treasure buried around Amarna in Egypt, site of Akhenaton's capital Akhetaton.

He claims that many of the scroll's descriptions match the area, and that some known finds from Amarna are actually treasures mentioned in the scroll. In particular, Feather explains the cryptic Greek digrams and trigrams. He says that when put together they spell out, in Greek, the name Akhenaton. Feather further develops this theory into a complex account of how the ancient Jews, and later the Essenes in particular, were guardians of this secret tradition of Egyptian lore.

Is the treasure still out there?

Feather's theories notwithstanding, mainstream opinion is that if the treasure does exist it was almost certainly hidden in the area around Jerusalem, Jericho and the Dead Sea. After nearly 2,000 years, however, it may not still be there. There are several plausible reasons why not. The most obvious is that it may have been found/looted by the inhabitants of the region over the course of 20 centuries. For instance, the Bedouin who found the Dead Sea scrolls could have been making similar finds for centuries, not to mention the Jews, Arabs, Christians, Crusaders, Saracens and Byzantines of former ages. Many of the structures in which the treasure may have been hidden have collapsed, been built over or been dismantled in the intervening millennia, any of which could lead to discovery. Any such finds would not have been reported for fear of confiscation/taxation, and would therefore not appear in the historical record.

It may even have been recovered by the very people from whom it was probably hidden: the Romans. If they thought that a large stash of gold had been withheld they might have searched high and low for it. Josephus reports that they tortured captured Essenes – perhaps in order to find out where they had stashed the Temple loot?

Among the items listed in the scroll are caches of documents, and philologist Richard Gwynn-Seary points out that there are some well-attested instances of the discovery of just such caches in the region. During the reign of the Roman Emperor Caracalla (211–217 CE) a jar of scrolls was found near Jericho. It proved to contain early scriptures, much like the Dead Sea scrolls, and was used by Church Father Origen to help create the Bible canon still in use today. In 800 CE, meanwhile, in an almost exact rerun of the Dead Sea scrolls discovery legend, Patriarch Timotheus I of Seleucia records that, 'the dog of a hunting Arab ... entered the cave and did not come out. His master followed him and found a dwelling within the rocks in which were found many books ... The Jews ... came in throngs and found books of the Old Testament and others ...'

Gwynn-Seary even suggests that we *do* have a record of the discovery of the more material treasures of the Copper Scroll, in the form of the tales of Aladdin, Ali Baba and similar stories from *The Thousand and One Nights*, which revolve around secret hoards. He points out that this collection of fables dates back to the 1st century CE (when the Copper Scroll was probably hidden) and might include fictionalised versions of real stories from across the Arab world, including the Near East.

On deadly ground

If the Dead Sea scrolls survived undiscovered until the 1940s, perhaps more carefully concealed treasure could remain hidden until the present day. This is the dream of many archaeologists and treasure hunters who long to unravel the secrets of the Copper Scroll and find some of the fabulous riches listed therein. Some experts speculate that the second scroll spoken of in the last item could be the key, and that only by possessing both scrolls can the treasure be uncovered. Perhaps the original is in a code so subtle that no one has noticed it is encrypted at all.

Would-be treasure hunters are advised, however, that they would be hard pressed to find a more difficult place to search, for the target zone is in the Occupied Territories. Sensibilities are so heightened that excavations of any sort are likely to provoke angry recriminations from one faith or another, while the political and security situation in the area makes it almost impossible to obtain permission to sniff around in secret nooks and crannies. Exploring without permission could be fatal.

The bottom line is that it would probably be a foolish risk to take. Academic opinion is still deeply divided over whether the Copper Scroll is a fake, a fantasy, an allegory of some sort that we still do not understand, or a genuine list of treasure. Even if it is the last, the odds are that anything that could be discovered was already found long ago.

King John's jewels

John, King of England from 1199–1216, is remembered today for many reasons, most of them unfavourable. To children he is best known as the arch-villain in the Robin Hood story, and in history he is remembered as 'bad king John', who lost most of the overseas possessions of the Angevin empire, irritated the barons so much that he was forced to sign the Magna Carta, and lost his Crown Jewels in the Wash.

The royal progress

The basic story, as related by historians from the 13th century onwards, is that King John was travelling in the East of England in late 1216. On 9 October he had journeyed from Lincolnshire to Bishop's Lynn (now King's Lynn) in Norfolk, but when he arrived he began to feel ill. It was decided that he would return back towards Lincolnshire, which was probably thought to be safer at this time, as the French king, Louis, had recently invaded the country to the south.

Calamity in the Wash

On 12 October, John attempted to cross the Wash, the large bay that separates East Anglia from Lincolnshire. At this time it extended much further inland than it does today, and would have been a region of mudflats and marshes, traversable at low tide but dangerous to the unwary, riddled with quicksand and deeper channels and vulnerable to rapid movements of water with the tide. The king is said to have crossed over at Wisbech, where it was possible to ford the Wellstream, one of the rivers running into the Wash.

Meanwhile the king's baggage train, which supposedly included all of the royal treasures including the Crown Jewels (the regalia the monarch bore during the coronation), was also trying to cross the Wash, but was surprised by the tide and got lost amidst the rising waters and quicksand. The traditional account of this disaster is well represented by this passage from Charles Dickens' *A Child's History of England*:

> looking back from the shore when he was safe, he [the king] saw the roaring water sweep down in a torrent, overturn the waggons, horses, and men, that carried his treasure, and engulf them in a raging whirlpool from which nothing could be delivered.

Undone by this tremendous stroke of ill fortune, John was taken to the monastery at Swineshead Abbey in Lincolnshire where he was greeted with 'quantities of pears, and peaches, and new cider'. He was taken ill again, with dysentery, and moved a few more times, eventually dying on the 18 October at Newark.

John's lost loot

Historians disagree about many aspects of this tale. For would-be treasure hunters, one of the most interesting issues is the question of what the king actually lost. Although it is traditionally said that he lost the Crown Jewels, there is no contemporary record that says exactly this. Roger de Wendover's *Flores Historiarum* (Flowers of History), written around 1230, gives the lost loot as 'treasures, precious vessels, and all the other things which he cherished with special care'. Ralph of Coggeshall's *Chronicon Anglicanum* describes it as 'his chapel with its relics ... and diverse household effects'. Another source describes the king's 'pricely carriage and furniture'.

Fast train to nowhere

In his book *Undiscovered*, Ian Wilson surveys the theories about John's lost treasure and points out that the official records of the time show that the king was moving round the countryside at quite a rate – sometimes as much as 60 kilometres (37 miles) a day. This suggests that he was not accompanied by a large baggage train, which in that day and age would have been extremely sluggish. So perhaps the contemporary accounts are exaggerated.

Diamonds are a king's best friends

Set against this is the evidence that genuinely valuable treasure was lost that October day. King John's favourite hobby was collecting jewellery, while as monarch he also owned a hoard of gold and silver plate and other valuables, which he had spent much of 1215 and 1216 gathering together from the various monasteries where it was deposited. Of particular value were the imperial regalia he had inherited from his grandmother, the Empress of Germany, which made up part of his Crown Jewels.

During John's reign all this treasure is listed in the royal inventories called the Rolls (which John himself instituted), but most of it is absent from the inventory of regalia used during the coronation of John's successor, Henry III in 1220. In other words, it seems likely that a priceless collection of royal valuables did indeed disappear.

Crossing point

The central issue is the probable location of the disaster. The coastline in this region is much changed since the Middle Ages. Drainage projects in later centuries reclaimed a lot of land and radically altered the way that sediment was deposited, and the coastline advanced many kilometres. Wisbech in particular, which used to be close to the sea, is now several kilometres inland. For treasure hunters this is potentially encouraging, because it means that where the jewels were lost is now dry land, but it also means that the paths, fords and causeways used to cross the Wash in medieval times now exist as relicts only, occasionally identifiable from the air or as the basis for modern parish boundaries or roads.

On top of this there is serious disagreement about whether John was travelling with or separately from his baggage train, and which route would have been taken in either scenario.

Line of sight

Most modern sources confidently state that John was travelling separately from his baggage train. While he had gone the long way round the Wash, via Wisbech, his train was taking a short cut across the Wash, presumably to make up for the fact that it moved more slowly than he did. As Wilson points out in *Undiscovered*, however, the contemporary sources specifically state that the king barely escaped the disaster, which suggests he was with the baggage train when it was overcome. If the train was indeed carrying his collected loot, he probably would have been loath to let it out of his sight. Safety would have been a particular issue because of the unsettled times and the fact that the fenland of Lincolnshire was hostile territory where the Norman monarchy had never been popular. (This area had been the haunt of the 11th-century rebel Hereward the Wake, a historical figure who was one of the main sources for the legendary figure of Robin Hood.)

These considerations are of prime importance, because it is known that John did cross the Wellstream at Wisbech. If his baggage train was with him, it must have crossed there too. The Wellstream no longer exists, but the River Nene flows more or less in the same course.

Candidate locations

Wilson describes three theories about the exact site of the disaster. For many years the traditional view was that the baggage train crossed separately from John, travelling from Cross Keys on the western side of the Wash to Long Sutton on the eastern side, and being overwhelmed near present-day Sutton Bridge. Many treasure hunters have looked in this area, without success.

Historian Gordon Fowler, assuming that the baggage train was with the king, has pinpointed the likely crossing point of the Wellstream as being just between Wisbech and Walsoken (although today these are now more or less the same town). He even suggested an explanation for the disaster – the sudden appearance of a tidal bore, known as an eagre in that region, which is where a tidal surge funnels water up a river as a series of large, potentially destructive waves.

A third candidate – based on the theory of historian J C Holt that the traditional crossing point of the Wellstream in those days was to the north of Wisbech, between Walpole and Foul Anchor – puts the location near modern-day Tydd Gote. There is evidence in this region of medieval quicksand beds, which ties in with the contemporary accounts of the disaster.

More recently a fourth candidate has emerged, based on a reconstruction of the exact tide tables for that day in 1216, which suggests that the baggage train would have got further than the

Wellstream by the time the rising tide caught up with it, and was probably crossing the mouth of the Welland River at modern-day Fosdyke, to the north-east of Wisbech.

The plot thickens

With so many candidate locations it is hard for a treasure hunter to know where to look, and any search will not be helped by the 10 metres (33 feet) of soil believed to have accumulated over the previous ground level in the last 800 years, which puts the treasure well beyond the range of normal metal detectors. However, this may be only part of the problem. Various sub-plots and intrigues behind the traditional story suggest that the treasure may not be there after all.

Murder most foul

After John's death, rumours proliferated that he had been poisoned, probably via those 'quantities of pears, and peaches, and new cider' laid out for him by the monks of Swineshead. Although most modern historians discount these rumours, not everyone agrees, and medieval conspiracy theories have been advanced, based on the 'coincidence' between the loss of the king's treasure and his untimely death.

Sleight of hand

Another theory suggests that the Crown Jewels were not lost at all, but were either sold/used by John as collateral for loans, with the Wash incident being staged as a kind of misdirection or medieval fraud. Whatever maleficent plan the king was hatching was cut short by his premature death/murder, and the treasure was subsequently stolen. At least one contemporary report speaks of suspiciously heavily laden men seen leaving Newark in the wake of his death.

Mysterious wealth

According to East Anglian folklorist W A Dutt, local legend in the Sutton area talks of King John's Hole, a pool where the jewels were hidden, either by John himself for some nefarious purpose, or by those who recovered them after the disaster in the Wash. The pool is said to be on the southern side of the King's Lynn to Long Sutton Road. But it is possible that this booty hidden in the hole has already been recovered. In the 14th century local baron Robert, third Lord Tiptoft, suddenly became immensely wealthy. There was no apparent source for his sudden affluence, and rumours spread that Tiptoft had discovered King John's lost treasure. So perhaps there is nothing out there left to recover ...

The treasure of the Knights Templar

Thanks to the pseudohistories of *The Da Vinci Code* and the books it draws upon, such as *The Holy Blood and the Holy Grail*, the Knights Templar have found themselves at the nexus of a remarkable tangle of historical mysteries. In the public's perception they have become a byword for hidden history and mysterious knowledge, the core of which is represented by the popular notion of their lost treasure.

The alternative history of the Templar treasure

In very brief form, the narrative that has emerged from the many different 'alternative' histories of the Templars goes like this. The Order of the Knights Templar was founded in the Crusader state of Jerusalem in 1118 by French knight Hugues de Payens and eight companions, and were assigned by Baldwin II, King of Jerusalem, to quarters in part of the Temple Mount compound, hence the name of their order. Despite humble beginnings they rose to power, wealth and prominence with astonishing rapidity.

But in 1307, jealous of their wealth and power – and possibly for darker motives – the French king Philip the Fair and Pope Clement V conspired to destroy them.

On the eve of the simultaneous arrest of all the Templars in France on 13 October, a cadre of knights, alerted to the imminent treachery by an informant, smuggled the Order's treasure out of the Templar stronghold in Paris. This treasure, consisting of both massive wealth and something even more valuable – relics, documents, artefacts or secret knowledge – was taken to La Rochelle on the western coast of France, loaded onto one of the ships in the Order's mighty fleet and spirited away to Scotland. When the Order was finally crushed in 1312 Philip was left empty-handed, while their fleet had apparently vanished off the face of the Earth.

Around the bare bones of this account, a great deal of intriguing and potentially explosive detail has accumulated. In particular, there are fascinating stories behind how the Templars acquired their great treasure, what it consisted of, and what happened to it – and them – in the centuries that followed.

Sources of the Templar treasure

The alternative histories seem rather confused on this issue, with at least three separate sources given for the transmission of the 'ultimate secret(s)' that the Templars supposedly possessed, although it is often suggested that the sources are connected and form a continuous thread.

The Priory of Sion

One suggestion is that the Templars were formed by an even more mysterious and powerful organisation, the Priory of Sion, a secret order set up to safeguard the bloodline of Christ. This in turn had descended from Mary Magdalene and Jesus himself, who were married, had children and came to southern France, and whose descendants founded the Merovingian line of kings (see page 82). Although the heirs of this bloodline were purportedly the rightful kings of the West (if not the whole world), their power had been usurped by the Catholic Church, the whole edifice of which was based on deceptions about the Crucifixion and the true nature of Christ.

The Priory had been set up to guard the actual, physical bloodline of Christ's heirs, but also the various aspects of secret knowledge about Christianity and other mysteries (knowledge which, in some accounts, stretches back much further to the Pyramid- and Temple-builders, Atlantis, etc). The Templars were set up by the Priory partly to increase their power and influence in the Christian world, and partly to build a presence in the Holy Land, and even to carry out specific explorations there – connecting the Priory story to the next explanation.

Raiders of the lost Temple

The second explanation for the secret knowledge/treasure of the Templars is that they uncovered something in the foundations of Solomon's Temple in Jerusalem. According to this theory, the original force of nine knights who founded the Templar order were clearly too few in number to be effective in their avowed mission of guarding pilgrims to the Holy Land. In fact they had very deliberately made Baldwin quarter them on the Temple Mount (possibly using pre-existing knowledge or contacts to influence him), so that they could engage in excavations of the old Temple site.

Quartered in a series of underground halls known as Solomon's Stables, one of the few structures associated with the old Temple still extant, the Templars delved into the tunnels and chambers below the Mount, discovering a secret stash of documents/artefacts/relics. Thus equipped they were able to send emissaries back to Europe to begin their remarkable rise to power and fortune. The lords and princes of Europe apparently fell over themselves to give the Templars grants of land and pledge their help, while the Pope gave them extraordinary privileges, exempting them from any jurisdiction but his own. The Templars were now a law unto themselves in many ways, and recruits flocked to their banner, to be initiated into their strange rituals.

The Cathar connection

A third explanation, also potentially connected to the bloodline of Christ/Priory of Sion story, is that the Templars inherited their treasure from the Cathars. The Cathars (also known as Albigensians) were a heretical Christian sect that became popular and powerful in southern France from the 11th century. Their brand of Christianity, derived from the East, had many Gnostic elements. The basic tenet of Gnosticism (the name derives from the Greek *gnosis*, knowledge) is that the divine is present within every individual, and that the way to achieve union with the divine is through personal *gnosis* or self-exploration. This is in contrast to the Catholic approach, which says that priests are needed as intermediaries between individuals and God.

The Cathars impressed with their piety and purity, gaining many converts and followers and the protection of powerful nobles in the Languedoc region. Numerous attempts by the Church to stifle their spread culminated in the launch of the Albigensian Crusade in 1208, followed in 1229 by the establishment of the Inquisition. The resulting bloody holocaust all but wiped out the Cathars in France, with the last Cathari leader being executed in 1321.

The crucial element in this sad history is the siege of Montségur in 1244. Montségur was a mountain-top fortress of the Cathars, sometimes associated with the Munsalvaesche of Wolfram von Eschenbach's version of the Grail legend (see page 80). The Cathars supposedly kept there a holy cup that was venerated in their rituals, and which has been associated with the Holy Grail. Various other treasures are also attributed to the Cathars – usually similar ones to those associated with the Templars.

According to a popular legend, which bears a strong resemblance to the story of the Templars' midnight flit, just before the stronghold fell to the besieging Catholic forces, four Cathars climbed down the walls and spirited the treasure away to safety. Many Knights Templar came from the region and it is supposed there must have been links between the two groups, and that the treasure was thus passed on to the Templars.

Take it to the bank

In addition to whatever secret/holy treasure the Templars possessed, they also became extremely wealthy in a more conventional, materialistic fashion. They amassed huge estates, extensive properties and valuable ornaments for their churches. In an era before banks, it was customary for the wealthy to store their liquid assets in the safest place possible, which often meant the strong room of a religious order. As a military order with an impeccable reputation and a massive network of commanderies, the Templars were an obvious candidate.

Experience in moving money from Europe (where it was generated) to the Holy Land (where it was spent) gave them expertise in cash transfer, and clever ruses enabled them to get round the prohibition against Christians profiting from usury, so that they were able to lend money all over Europe. They even diversified into shipping, setting up a service to transport pilgrims to the Holy Land, alongside their own men and supplies.

Templar conspiracy theorists look beyond these conventional business methods, and argue that it was the possession of the secret knowledge/relics that made them such a success. The prestige and power derived from the treasure, possibly together with occult sources of information, allowed them to influence, bully or blackmail their way to riches. However it was acquired, some of these vast riches are commonly supposed to have been among the treasure allegedly spirited away on the night of 13 October 1307.

The big secret

What else was carried off to safety that night? Exactly what was the secret Templar treasure? Here the alternative histories are either vague, or of radically different opinions. A remarkable number of suggestions have been made.

The head of Baphomet

When the Templars were brought to trial in France, one of the many accusations levelled at them was that they worshipped some sort of demon called Baphomet. They are also commonly alleged to have been fixated on the worship of severed heads. These allegations have been combined, so that the Templars are imagined to have made the head of Baphomet the centre of strange rituals. Was this strange head the Templar treasure? If so, whose head was it? Candidates include the head of John the Baptist (famously severed to please Salome) and the head of Jesus. There is even a suggestion that the head could speak and prophesy, through either dark arts or some strange technology.

Relics 'R' Us

Perhaps the treasure consisted of/included other relics. Suggestions include shards of the True Cross, the Spear of Destiny (the spear supposed to have pierced Christ's side as he hung on the Cross), the Ark of the Covenant and the Turin Shroud (the face on which is sometimes said to be that of Jacques de Molay, last Grand Master of the Order).

The Holy Grail is an obvious candidate, in both its literal, material form as a sacred/magical vessel, and its metaphorical form as the bloodline of Jesus. Another option is that the Templars possessed Gospels different from, and superseding those, adhered to by the Church, perhaps revealing some other version of history that would shatter the conventional Catholic version. These could have been similar to those recovered in the Dead Sea scrolls (see page 98), and, as suggested by *Da Vinci Code* style historians, could have told the story of Christ being married and having children.

Secret knowledge

On top of all this, it is suggested that the Templars were inheritors of an ancient tradition of esoteric wisdom passed down from the Atlanteans, via the Pyramid- and Temple-builders. Not only did this give them the secrets of monumental masonry, but it also accounted for their strange mystical, Gnostic and otherwise non-Christian practices, among the most famous of which were their initiation rituals, which involved spitting to the side of the Cross, parodies of the Mass and, allegedly, denying Jesus.

What happened next?

How and what the Templars acquired is just the start of the tale. The real story is what happened afterwards, although again, there are several different versions, each with different implications for the site of the Templar treasure today.

The Scottish connection

Scotland is often touted as a potential destination for the fleeing Templar treasure fleet. At the time, Scotland was in the midst of a row with the papacy and was therefore excommunicated, meaning that once there the Templars would be beyond the Pope's authority and over the next few years of torture and trials on the Continent the Order could escape persecution in Scotland. Moreover, the rulers of Scotland were believed to be friendly to the Templars, to the extent that the Knights are said to have fought alongside Robert the Bruce against the English at Bannockburn in 1314.

The mysteries of Rosslyn Chapel

Rosslyn has already featured in the discussion of the Holy Grail in Chapter Two, but according to alternative historians its true significance is as some sort of Templar cryptogram. It was built between 1440 and 1480 by William Sinclair of the Sinclair family, Earls of Orkney and also Lords of Roslin in lowland Scotland between Edinburgh and Glasgow. The Sinclair family were supposedly important Templars in the 13th century, and Freemasonry in Scotland was purportedly founded by William Sinclair, thus connecting the Templars with their supposed successors the Masons. Many Masonic and quasi-Masonic groups today claim this Templar ancestry.

Rosslyn Chapel represents the Sinclair's use of the architectural secrets of the Templars and is riddled with Masonic symbolism. It is said to be a copy of the Temple of Solomon, deliberately left unfinished to look like the ruined original. The ornately carved Apprentice Pillar (or Prentice pillar) within the Chapel is suggested as a hiding place for the Templar loot, as are several large chests said to be buried about the property, possibly in secret crypts beneath.

The American connection

Rosslyn Chapel also apparently displays carvings of American flora, made before the voyages of Columbus. This ties in with legends about Henry Sinclair, ancestor of the chapel's builder and an alleged Templar, who is said to have made secret voyages across the Atlantic, possibly using secret knowledge obtained from the Templar treasure (eg Biblical/pre-Biblical accounts of transatlantic voyages or Atlantean navigational lore, contained in the ancient scrolls they excavated from beneath the Temple), possibly in order to inter there the Order's treasure, safe from grasping European hands.

Rennes-le-Château

Before Rosslyn became the focus of Templar/Grail hunters, the village of choice was picturesque Rennes-le-Château in Languedoc, the old Cathar region. Here the mystery of Bérenger Saunière has excited treasure hunters for decades. Saunière was the village priest of the poor parish of Rennes from 1889–1905. He should have spent most of his life in obscurity and near poverty, given his official income, but during the 1890s Saunière began to spend lavishly, first renovating the church, which included making some bizarre alterations, such as putting a statue of a demon over the door, and later building himself a luxury villa. In cosmopolitan Paris he hobnobbed with the rich and famous, occultists and the demi-monde, and at home he threw lavish parties. When he died he was said to be worth millions of francs.

The source of this wealth was alleged to be a mysterious scroll that Saunière found hidden inside a pillar in the village church. The scroll in turn led the priest to discover some hidden treasure nearby – possibly the lost Cathar-Templar treasure. Armed with the knowledge/power this brought, he was able to make influential friends and become enormously rich. With his death in 1917, however, the secret of the treasure was lost, perhaps buried under Rennes or somewhere in the surrounding countryside.

Take your pick

In conclusion, the Templar treasure is now hidden/buried in or around Rosslyn Chapel in Scotland, somewhere in North America (see 'The Oak Island Money Pit', page 145) or somewhere underneath Rennes-le-Château. Alternative sites include any of the numerous Templar commanderies in Europe – many of which are said to sit atop warrens of tunnels and caverns – particularly those in countries like Scotland and England where the Order largely escaped persecution.

House of cards

These alternative versions of history make exciting reading, but the truth is that this convoluted web is constructed almost entirely of unfounded speculation, simple errors or outright fictions. Nearly every aspect can be debunked, although it is hard to know where to begin.

Did the Templars really discover or inherit something amazing?

Despite the various theories there is no evidence that they did. The three main suggested sources for the treasure are the Priory of Sion, the Temple Mount and the Cathars. All rest on shaky or non-existent ground.

The Priory of Sion story is the invention of a convicted French conman and fantasist named Pierre Plantard. After World War II Plantard concocted an elaborate fantasy version of history in which he was the descendant of the Merovingian kings and, by extension, of Christ himself. He then invented a secret society with supposedly mystical and portentous antecedents, called the Priory of Sion, and recruited a few members for quasi-religious activities of vaguely distasteful nationalist-royalist political character. He even had forged documents smuggled into the French national archives at the Bibliothèque Nationale.

When later researchers unearthed these it lent credence to the tale Plantard himself was spinning for them. Although he eventually fell foul of the law and was ordered to stop perpetrating his scam, by then the Priory of Sion and its long guardianship of the bloodline of Christ was firmly established in the popular imagination. The Priory–Templar connection was another element of the tale concocted by Plantard. It should be pointed out that while there was, briefly, a real Order of Sion, it had nothing to do with Plantard's Priory. It was a monastic order based around an abbey on Mount Zion in the Holy Land, which collapsed after the Saracen victories of the late 13th century.

One of the most common elements of the Templar story is that the founding knights excavated beneath the Temple Mount. In practice, however, there is not a shred of primary evidence (eg records from the time) to suggest that any excavations were ever carried out by the Templars, beyond whatever building works they undertook later in their history to enlarge or outfit their quarters on the Temple Mount. While there are tunnels in the Mount, there is no evidence that the Templars ever explored or were even interested in them.

Some literary detective work by historian Kevin McClure has uncovered the real source of many of these excavation myths, and it is an unsettling one. McClure traces the claims made by many alternative historians to a passage in a book on the Templars by Guy Delaforge, who later went on to set up the quasi-Masonic Order of the Solar Temple, which claimed to be inheritor of the Templar tradition (and secret knowledge), and which was eventually responsible for the terrible murder of more than 70 people. Delaforge's book, in which he describes the excavations, is pure fantasy and he does not attempt to give a source. However, he in turn was apparently used as a source by several subsequent writers.

Assertions about the excavation are often backed up by the assumption that the nine founding knights were too few in number to be there for their avowed purpose of protecting pilgrims, and therefore must have had ulterior motives. This is suspect logic, especially given that each knight might have had a retinue of men-at-arms, making them a more formidable force than suggested; and more importantly their initial task was simply to escort pilgrims from Jerusalem to the Jordan River, for which an army was not necessary.

The Cathar connection is equally suspect. There is no evidence that the Cathars possessed any secret treasure, nor for the tale of the escape from Montségur, which seems to be pure romantic fiction. Nor is there evidence of special links between the Templars and the Cathars – only the circumstantial support that they co-existed and that there were Templar strongholds in the Cathar area, as there were all across France. Much is made of religious similarities between the two groups, but these are probably overplayed. The Templars were devout Christians and many of the heresies laid at their door can be put down to the hyperbole of their French prosecutors.

The 'in' thing

The Templars' rise to wealth and power was indeed remarkable, but was it really inexplicable? Perhaps they were simply the right group at the right time. The *Catholic Encyclopaedia* explains: 'The order owed its rapid growth in popularity to the fact that it combined the two great passions of the Middle Ages, religious fervour and martial prowess.' Also, it was the practice at the time for charitable donations to be given on an institutional and not personal basis, which favoured institutions such as the Templars.

Was there any Templar treasure?

Another common conceit about the Templars is that they were immensely wealthy when they were suppressed, and that this wealth mysteriously vanished. This is a myth. In fact, by the time of their dissolution the Templars were in the red for a variety of reasons, from inflation to changing economic policy around Europe. Most of their assets were in non-liquid form, and they needed whatever rents or income their properties earned for their enormously expensive adventures in the East. By the end of the 13th century they, along with the other Crusaders, had been kicked out of the Holy Land with a concomitant loss of prestige and therefore donations. There is considerable evidence that by 1307 the Templars were struggling to pay for basic upkeep of their commanderies and many of their members were living in penury.

The Templar fleet

The famous Templar fleet proves to be equally mythical. Although they were heavily engaged in shipping and trade thanks to their constant travelling to and from the Holy Land, it is unlikely that they ever had more than a handful of ships. In 1312 their great rival order, the Knights Hospitaller, who were specifically engaged in naval operations, possessed only four warships, and it is thought unlikely that the Templars would have had many more. There are few records that explicitly state how many ships they had, but the most that are mentioned at any one time are *two*. When they needed extra ships they would hire them. Also, their ships were galleys, entirely unsuited for the kind of oceanic exploration attributed to them by some alternative historians.

Going out with a whimper

More misconceptions gather around the fate of the Templars. Their demise arose partly because of their very weakness, rather than through fear of their strength. It was when they became vulnerable due to money problems and loss of prestige that their enemies could take action, and – although in France the Templars did indeed have a rough ride, with many executed for heresy – in much of Europe they were not found guilty and did not suffer persecution. Pope Clement initially tried to stop the persecution, but Philip the Fair had done too good a job of blackening the name of the Templars in France through slander and acquisition of confessions by torture (a legal means of obtaining evidence at the time), and he was eventually forced to wind up the Order, which is not the same as utterly destroying it. What few assets it had were shared between other Orders, including a couple of successor Orders in Portugal and Spain, about which there was nothing secret or clandestine. This, and the fact that there was little to go round to begin with, accounts for the fact that Philip ended up empty-handed.

Did the Templars really have secret knowledge or relics?

There is no evidence that the Templars possessed any great secret. The strange practices that gave rise to many of the suppositions and legends about the Templars were exaggerated by Philip's prosecutors as part of the plot to blacken their names. Baphomet, the so-called demon, was probably a word used to describe Mohammedans (ie Muslims), with whom the Templars necessarily had many dealings in the Holy Land. The alleged worship of heads may be an over-interpretation of their possession of a couple of relics – the heads of two female martyrs, in particular the head of St Euphemia, which were well known and in no way secret.

The secret knowledge they were said to have possessed and passed on to the Masons is pure speculation. Links between the Masons and the Templars are themselves purely fictional – invented by some Masonic groups/writers from the 18th century onwards in an attempt to give themselves a more impressive provenance.

Does Rosslyn Chapel have any links to the Templars?

In fact there is no evidence for this, according to Evelyn Lord, author of *The Knights Templar in Britain*. It was built more than a hundred years after the Order was suppressed. The alleged Scottish connection is generally tenuous. Contrary to legend, there is no record of Templars fighting with Robert the Bruce, which there would have been had they done so, and, in fact, the Templars were generally on good terms with the English kings Robert the Bruce opposed. In particular, the Sinclairs of the time were no friends of the Templars and are on record as having testified against them in the trials of 1309. Having said which, one of the early Sinclairs may well have been a Templar, but this applied to many noblemen of the period.

Rosslyn Chapel itself is almost certainly a copy of nearby Glasgow Cathedral's choir, which would have been a handy reference for the masons building the chapel, rather than a version of the Temple. It was probably left unfinished because of shortage of money, which was common for private chapels. It would be difficult for the chapel to have any connection with Freemasonry, since this was not founded until hundreds of years later. Alleged connections between the chapel's builder, William Sinclair, and Freemasonry in Scotland are thought to be spurious and based on later fictions, like so much of Masonic 'history'. There is no evidence that any treasure or other secrets are buried in or around Rosslyn Chapel. There is also no evidence beyond some letters of extremely doubtful authenticity that an early Sinclair travelled across the Atlantic.

Is there a real Rennes-le-Château mystery?

Much like the Plantard–Priory of Sion fraud, it seems that most of the Rennes mystery can be traced to a 1950s French hoax. In this instance Noël Corbu, the owner of a newly opened restaurant in Saunière's old villa, thought that a good treasure mystery might boost custom. In practice none of the 'mysteries' are that mysterious. Saunière's inexplicable wealth came from his practice of selling indulgences, where, in return for a fee, a priest would say a mass to shorten the payer's stay in purgatory. This was outlawed by the Catholic Church and indeed Saunière was suspended and eventually fired for persistent violations. Also, he did not die a wealthy man. Quite the opposite, for he lived many of his later years in near poverty, desperate for money.

The strange alterations he made to his church owe more to symbolism linked with his radical pro-royalist, antidisestablishmentarianist views. The hollow pillar in which he supposedly discovered the parchment, and which is exhibited to visitors to this day, is almost certainly a complete fake that was never part of the church. There is no evidence of any treasure ever having been buried or found in the area.

The Templar deception

The lies and deceptions of Plantard and Corbu, together with their repetition and elaboration by subsequent authors, which is now reaching its ultimate synergy in the work of Dan Brown, means that much of genuine interest about the Templars and the various related mysteries is obscured. For instance, it is possible that the Templars adopted some unconventional approaches to Christianity due to their experiences in the East. Little is known about the Cathars beyond the tragedy of their brutal suppression. Rosslyn Chapel is indeed an extraordinary and beautiful piece of architecture, genuinely rich in strange symbolism. But the way that pseudohistorians uncritically recycle fiction, speculation and misinformation means that the so-called Templar mystery is like a snowball rolling downhill, gaining mass and momentum, but with nothing more than slush at its core.

Montezuma's hoard

The 16th-century Spanish conquest of the New World was driven by greed for treasure. The conquistadors won incredibly vast wealth from the subjugated and destroyed peoples of South and Central America, yet it was not wealth beyond their wildest imagination. Their lust for gold was unquenchable, clouding their minds with a siren call that could not be silenced. In South America the greedy conquistadors convinced themselves of the reality of El Dorado (see page 47). In Mexico they were fixated on the idea that the Aztecs had somehow hidden a great store of treasure. The legend of Montezuma's hoard was born.

Whose hoard is it anyway?

The most common form of this legend is that in 1520 the Aztec emperor Montezuma II gathered the bulk of his treasure and sent it northwards to keep it out of the hands of the invading Spaniards. It was secreted or buried in a cave or some other spot, where it still rests to this day, waiting for a lucky or intrepid treasure hunter to stumble across what would probably be the greatest trove of all time.

Most of this tale is probably wrong. To begin with, Montezuma's actual name was Moctezuma (or even more properly, but prohibitively unpronounceable, Motecuhzoma), meaning 'he who makes himself ruler by his rage' in Nahuatl, the language of the Aztecs. 'Montezuma' was a Spanish adaptation. Secondly, there is considerable confusion about what was hidden/lost, and where. There seem to be several different versions of the story, and in most of them the hoard is not Moctezuma's at all.

The return of the king

Moctezuma II had been the ruler, or *tlatoani*, of the Aztecs for 17 years when he received the first reports of strange foreigners penetrating his territory in 1519. For a variety of reasons, from a slew of omens to coincidences with Aztec myth, he identified Hernán Cortés, leader of the Spanish force, with the god Quetzlcoatl. This god, a hero of the Aztecs, said to have journeyed into the east in prehistoric times, was prophesied to return one day and claim his rightful possessions, including the vast wealth in tribute, holy artefacts, temple ornaments and the like, which the Aztecs had accumulated through conquest and labour.

According to Spanish accounts of the conquest, Moctezuma welcomed Cortés to the capital at Tenochtitlán (now Mexico City), made obeisance to him, showered him with tribute and offered to turn over all the Aztec wealth to him. In the *Florentine Codex*, one of the most important sources of information for the history of the conquest, compiled by Spanish monk Bernardino de Sahagún using Aztec sources, it is recorded that the Aztec ruler told Cortés, 'My lord ... to the land you have arrived. You have come to your city ... here you have come to sit on your place, on your throne. Oh, it has been reserved to you by a small time, it was conserved by those who had gone, your substitutes … Come to the land, come and rest: take possession of your royal houses …'

If this account is accurate it seems unlikely that at the same time Moctezuma would be sending the bulk of his treasury to safety in the mountains to the north. Except that we also know that, while the Aztec ruler did indeed equate Cortés with Quetzlcoatl, he was nevertheless none too keen on receiving a visit and tried to deflect the Spaniards from approaching the capital. He sent gifts, ambassadors and more gifts, but only succeeded in inflaming the conquistadors' greed. Perhaps his honeyed words to Cortés were a ruse to buy time and protect the treasure – later on the Spaniards certainly suspected the Aztecs of just this sort of dissemblance.

The traditional account of the hoard legend sometimes includes unverifiable and probably entirely fictional details, such as Moctezuma dispatching the treasure with a force of 1,000 elite warriors, who carried it far to the north to lands of the present-day United States. This is the rationale behind the extensive treasure hunting that goes on from California to Texas (see page 136), but pinning down a hard source for these legends is impossible.

The Night of Sorrow

Soon after the Spanish force arrived in Tenochtitlán, Cortés began to throw his weight around, making Moctezuma a prisoner, installing Christian accoutrements in the temples and issuing constant demands for treasure. The mood amongst the Aztecs soured and things turned increasingly ugly. Cortés was forced to leave the capital to head off a Spanish force at the coast who had been sent to arrest him by a rival would-be conquistador. While he was away his lieutenant Pedro de Alvarado had hundreds – possibly even a thousand – Aztec nobles massacred, triggering a revolt. Cortés arrived back just in time to get caught up in it.

As the days wore on, the situation for the Spanish – holed up in Moctezuma's palace and surrounded by hundreds of thousands of angry Aztecs – grew increasingly desperate. Tenochtitlán was a city built on the swampy Lake Texcoco. A number of islands were connected by causeways and bridges, most of which had been destroyed by the besieging mob. The Spanish were running low on food and their water supply had also been cut.

On 1 July 1520, Moctezuma was sent out to calm the people but was pelted with rocks and suffered an injury. The Spanish claim he died of this injury, but most historians suspect that Cortés simply realised he was no longer useful and had him murdered. News of his death inflamed the Aztecs further and the Spanish decided to make a break for it that night. Loading themselves up with as much of their loot as they could carry, the conquistadors tried to slip out along one of the causeways, but were spotted. Canoes full of hostile Native Americans closed in on all sides. The fighting was fierce and the desperate Spanish tried to press forward. Many threw their loot into the water to lighten their loads, or were pushed, dragged or fell in and sank like stones thanks to the gold they were carrying. As many as a thousand Spanish died (alongside many more Native Americans) in what is now known as the *Noche Triste* (the Night of Sorrow).

According to some sources, Montezuma's hoard is actually the treasure that the Spanish lost in Lake Texcoco. Through their constant demands for tribute and treasure, the greedy conquistadors had amassed great quantities of gems and gold. Although much of the gold was probably in the form of Aztec artefacts, the Spaniards had it melted down and made into wedge-shaped bars of gold bullion. How much of these gems and bullion ended up on the lake bed alongside the bodies of thousands of Spaniards and Native Americans is unknown, but there seems little chance of recovering it. After the conquest Cortés had the lake drained, and present-day Mexico City, possibly the largest city in the world, now sits atop it. Supposedly attempts have been made in the past to search the former lakebed for treasure, and people living in the area still dream of finding it. According to an article in *México desconocido*, in March 1981, workers digging the foundations of the Bank of Mexico found a golden disk of Aztec craftsmanship, which was explicitly described as 'the first discovery of Moctezuma's treasure'. But beyond the discovery of single artefacts such as this there is no sign of the greater mass of treasure.

Cuauhtémoc's hoard

After the Spanish fled in disarray the Aztec capital was ravaged by a smallpox epidemic brought by the foreigners. Moctezuma's successor quickly succumbed and his young nephew Cuauhtémoc was left in charge. According to some versions of the hoard legend, it was he who dispatched the Aztec treasures – which had been withheld from the Spanish – to keep them out of the invaders' hands should they return.

Return they did, Cortés having built up a massive force of native allies and a small fleet of ships with which to invade the Aztec capital. The siege of Tenochtitlán began in around May 1521 and lasted for 80 days. Eventually, exhausted by smallpox, drought and the bloody fighting, the city fell on 13 August. Many of the inhabitants fled and Cuauhtémoc was taken prisoner.

The Spaniards certainly believed that the Aztecs had hidden a hoard of treasure from them, although it is not clear whether they believed it was loot that had been held back from them on their previous visit, or simply that which they had lost on the *Noche Triste*. Spurred on by his dissatisfied men, Cortés had Cuauhtémoc and his deputy put to torture. Their feet were covered in oil and roasted over a fire. According to one account, Cuauhtémoc took his punishment remarkably well, rebuking his companion for groaning with the words, 'And do you think I, then, am taking my pleasure in my bath?'

All that the Spanish could get out of Cuauhtémoc was that the Aztecs had thrown what treasure they possessed into the lake rather than have it fall into Spanish hands, giving the hoard the same provenance as the *Noche Triste* explanation. Like Mexicans long after him, Cortés had the lakebed searched by the best divers he could find, all under his watchful eye, but all that was brought up was what the Spanish described as a 'golden sun', probably an Aztec calendar wheel, strangely coincident with the Bank of Mexico find some four-and-a-half centuries later.

The treasure of Río Medio

A final theory about the fate of the supposed Aztec hoard is that it is actually loot that the Spanish *did* amass, but which they subsequently lost in transit, while attempting to ship it back to Spain. Transatlantic shipping was a hazardous business and the Caribbean is hurricane territory, so wrecks were common. However, it seems clear from the various accounts that Cortés did not believe that he had recovered the full Aztec hoard, so this interpretation of Montezuma's hoard would not be the traditional one.

Even more contentiously, the hoard may already have been recovered 30 years ago only to be lost – or stolen – again. In August 1976, gold objects were recovered from the sea floor off the Mexican coast at Río Medio, near the city of Veracruz. Eventually a remarkable haul was brought up, consisting of several gold Aztec artefacts, many ingots of gold, probably created by Spanish conquistadors melting down their loot, and many pieces of jewellery. The find was explicitly linked with the lost treasure of Moctezuma. Theories advanced to explain the find include the possibility that it was loot collected by a Castilian adventurer and ship's captain named Figueroa, who was known to have perished in a storm in 1528 in the Río Medio area. How the treasure got from the bed of Lake Texcoco, or wherever else it may have been hidden, into Figueroa's ships, however, is unclear.

The treasure was sent to the Bank of Mexico in Mexico City (or possibly the branch in Veracruz) for safekeeping in 1976, but was never seen again. In 1982, six years on, enquiries by journalists came up against a brick wall. The museums and universities involved in the recovery pointed to the bank, which denied ever having received any such treasure. It has not been mentioned since. Was it somehow lost in a bank, museum or university vault, or, more likely, stolen from the state and sold off illegally to private collectors?

Gold in them thar hills

Many American treasure hunters choose to believe the version of the legend that has the hoard transported out of danger and secreted in the far northern extremes of the Aztec dominion. Local legends, based on little or no concrete evidence, link Montezuma's hoard to literally dozens of locations in Arizona, California, Colorado, New Mexico, Texas and, above all, in Utah. Many landmarks in the region are named after Montezuma (eg Montezuma's Castle in Arizona, a Sinaguan pueblo ruin). One of the most persistent rumours puts the hiding place near Kanab, in South West Utah near the Arizona border, either in a cave in the surrounding hills, or in one of the Three Lakes nearby. These two sites have given rise to some far-fetched tales of treasure hunting.

Tall tales

In this part of the world there are many promising spots – caves, old Native American sites and petroglyph (rock marking/painting) sites. It was a photo of some petroglyphs in the Kanab area that apparently led a prospector named Freddie Crystal to explore nearby Johnson's Canyon in 1914. When he came into town with tales of having found a cave full of sacks of treasure, he triggered a mini-gold rush. By 1924 most of the town had moved to temporary residences at the head of the canyon, frantically digging for treasure. Needless to say, none was ever found.

More recently another set of petroglyphs led a treasure hunter called Grandt Child to explore a lake to the north of Kanab. According to an article by Max Bertola, a writer on the lore of Southern Utah, one of the Three Lakes Chain was marked with an Aztec sign for treasure, leading him to suspect they had constructed some sort of ingenious water trap to protect their hoard. In 1989 diver friends of Child's made repeated attempts to explore a tunnel they claim to have found, which ended in a chamber according to scanning equipment. However, they reported being rebuffed by supernatural interventions including invisible hands choking and pulling at them.

Conclusion

Make of these tales what you will. Local tourist boards love this sort of thing as it draws in the tourists, and treasure hunters discuss, recycle and embellish such rumours on internet forums. As we've already seen, however, claims about Moctezuma's treasure in the southern States or anywhere else are built on shaky foundations. There is no evidence that the Aztecs ever had a secret hoard that was dispatched anywhere.

The most likely scenario is that the Spanish recovered most of the Aztecs' wealth both during their initial stay in Tenochtitlán and in the years after the conquest. Some treasure may have been thrown into Lake Texcoco and never officially recovered, but much of this may have been surreptitiously dug up and pocketed by Native Americans and Spaniards alike after the lake was drained. More treasure may lie on the seabed amidst the wreckage of Spanish treasure galleons – and a significant chunk may have already been salvaged and then stolen. In conclusion, the scenario that there is a cave in Utah, Arizona or New Mexico stuffed with sacks of Aztec gold and gems is the least likely of the bunch.

Captain Kidd's buried treasure

The notion of buried treasure is irrevocably bound up with the romantic concept of the pirate, but for the most part it's a fictional notion, largely deriving from the enormous success of Robert Louis Stevenson's *Treasure Island*. This adventure novel introduced several now ubiquitous elements of pirate lore, such as treasure maps and 'X's that mark the spot. One of the few recorded instances of a pirate who actually did bury some treasure is William 'Captain' Kidd, a privateer turned pirate of the late 17th century. Kidd's story has inspired over 300 years of treasure hunting and given birth to a rash of local legends that would see caches of gold squirrelled away in almost every nook and cranny of the coastline of New York State and surrounding areas, not to mention much further afield. Have these treasure hunters simply fallen for a romantic fiction, or is there really a stash of pirate gold waiting to be discovered?

The true history of Captain William Kidd

Although born and raised in Scotland, by the late 1600s William Kidd, a respected and experienced sailor, privateer and merchant, had made his home in the colony of New York City. Maritime trade was burgeoning, with vast wealth traded back and forth across the high seas from the New World and the Far East to Europe and back. Privateering, a sort of legal piracy where the captain of a privately owned ship was issued with a letter of marque authorising him to capture and loot the ships of enemy nations, was a profitable profession. Its near cousin, piracy – where ships and crews respected no boundaries of nationality or allegiance, and simply preyed on whatever ships they could catch – was a growing problem.

Against this background Kidd was induced to sign up to a scheme to outfit and dispatch a well-armed privateer ship, which would sail the Indian Ocean capturing pirates, confiscating their loot and supplementing it with any other 'legal' prizes (for an English ship of the time this primarily meant French ships, or ships sailing under a French flag). Kidd received backing from a number of wealthy English patrons, including, it was rumoured, King William himself, and also invested most of his own fortune in the project.

An ill-starred voyage

In 1695 he left London in the *Adventure Galley*, a formidable war-ship armed with 34 cannons, but almost immediately his luck ran out. He was stopped by a Royal Navy vessel and much of his hand-picked crew of honest able seamen was press-ganged into naval service. New York, Kidd's next port of call, was at that time a favourite haunt of pirates, so replacing the lost men meant recruiting criminals, former pirates and other ne'er-do-wells. In September 1696, Kidd finally set out for the East Indies with his mixed crew of honest seamen and miscreants, but soon after arriving in the Indian Ocean misfortune struck again and he lost a third of his crew to cholera. The *Adventure Galley* itself proved to be poorly built and leaky.

Overstepping the marque

Kidd's cruise in the Indian Ocean, intended to target pirates ply-ing the seas around Madagascar and infesting the routes to and from the Red Sea, did not go well. He encountered few legitimate prizes, and his crew grew quarrelsome after watching one fat merchant ship after another sail past. At one point Kidd argued with the ship's gunner over prizes they had passed up, striking him with a bucket – a blow from which the man later died.

On 30 January 1698, Kidd finally seemed to have struck gold when he boarded and captured the merchant ship the *Quedagh Merchant*, laden with a valuable cargo of rich fabrics, silver and gold. There was enough loot here to make Kidd and his men rich, but the legitimacy of the prize was open to question – although it sailed under a French commission, it had an Indian cargo and an English captain.

By this time the captain's reputation was already in tatters. On his passage across the Atlantic, Kidd had quarrelled with the commander of a Royal Navy squadron, who reported back to England warning of his piratical air. In addition, he had long overrun the term of his official commission, and his subsequent exploits earned him further poor reports. Back in London, meanwhile, the political landscape had shifted and the party to which his backers belonged was out of favour. Accounts of Kidd's piratical ways were embarrassing powerful men when they could least afford it. He was officially declared a pirate.

The voyage home

After an encounter with a pirate, during which most of his crew mutinied and defected, Kidd abandoned his now decrepit galley and sailed back across the Atlantic in the *Quedagh Merchant*. Arriving in the Caribbean in the spring of 1699 he was apprised of his legal status and resolved to return to New England, explain himself and use his network of influence, along with the considerable wealth he now possessed, to get himself off the hook. Most of the valuable cargo was sold off and the collected booty was loaded onto a new ship, in which Kidd sailed back to America. Before approaching the authorities, he spent some time arranging affairs to best suit him. He seems to have visited several spots along the coast of New England, most notably Gardiners Island at the tip of Long Island, where he buried a large cache of treasure, marking the spot with a cairn. He also communicated with the Governor of Massachusetts via an attorney, claiming to have in his possession 'goods to the value of 30,000 pounds'. As well as the treasure he had buried, Kidd is believed to have given away a lot of loot around this time.

The end of Kidd

Convinced that he would be protected by his money and his possession of documents showing that the prizes he had taken in the Indian Ocean were legitimate, Kidd surrendered to Governor Bellomont in Boston. But powerful forces were marshalled against him. Bellomont confiscated the documents and had him clapped in irons and shipped back to London. The documents, which were central to Kidd's defence, were mysteriously lost and only showed up hundreds of years later, conveniently misfiled amidst government paperwork.

Unable to defend himself properly, and testified against by former shipmates, Kidd was sentenced to death. From his cell in Newgate Prison he wrote a desperate letter to the Speaker of the House of Commons, promising to lead a committee to a place in the Indies where he had 'lodged goods and Tresure to the value of one hundred thousand pounds'. It was to no avail, for on 23 May 1701 he was executed by hanging. In a grisly postscript, the rope broke at the first attempt and he had to be hanged again, before his body was tarred and hung up in an iron cage as a warning to all.

Counting the loot

So what of the treasure? How much was there to begin with, and what happened to it? The primary cache would seem to have been the loot buried on Gardiners Island, but this was dug up by a party under Governor Bellomont shortly after Kidd's capture. Some £20,000 was recovered, estimated to be more than £2 million (more than $3.8 million) today. Via his lawyer, Kidd had claimed to have £30,000 of loot, so this would suggest that £10,000 was not recovered. However, he gave away or spent a lot of money and, more to the point, Bellomont obtained a manifest of the cargo Kidd had brought back with him to America, and it was almost all accounted for.

Does this mean that there is, in fact, no outstanding treasure left to seek? In Kidd's letter to the House of Commons he claims to have cached £100,000, while rumours back in New England spoke of him possessing a fortune three or four times this size. Should these last sums be discounted as the last gambit of a desperate man and the baseless speculation of idle gossip-mongers? Did Bellomont truly possess the full measure of Kidd's loot?

Villainy on the high seas

Much of the account of Kidd's doings in the Indian Ocean derives from his own testimony, which naturally attempted to portray him in a favourable light. If he is to be believed, he never willingly or deliberately entered into piracy, and in fact took only legitimate prizes, even if their legitimacy was later disputed. What's more he refused numerous opportunities to take heavily laden East Indiamen, even though this caused tension with his crew and eventually led them to mutiny.

This may not, however, be the whole story. Perhaps Kidd wasn't the innocent he proclaimed himself to be, nor the reluctant pirate posterity deems him. We know, for instance, that on 15 August 1697, Kidd menaced a convoy of British-protected merchant ships and only withdrew after receiving the attentions of their armed escort. Perhaps Kidd, whether egged on by his villainous crew or as result of his own felonious character, attacked other illicit prizes that were not recorded at the time.

Even if he captured only the ship we know about – the immensely valuable *Quedagh Merchant* – and at least one other, lesser prize, he may not have returned to America with all the loot. He could have secreted caches of treasure somewhere in the Indian Ocean or the Caribbean, prior to sailing back to New England. He might well have also held back from Governor Bellomont the true extent of his wealth, and might have squirrelled some of it away in caches other than the one on Gardiners Island. Even a 'small' trove of money/gems/trinkets would be worth a considerable amount today.

The hunt for Kidd's gold

This is the rationale that has driven thousands of people over the years to hunt for Captain Kidd's legendary buried treasure in every nook and cranny of the New Jersey–Connecticut shoreline. An amazing plethora of places claim to be linked to Kidd and/or to house a portion of his booty. Partly this is because Kidd is known or believed to have stopped at several places in the area before he gave himself up to the governor – spots where it was common for ships to lie to and/or for landing parties to come ashore for fresh water and victuals. These included: Gardiners Island, Block Island, Charles Island and the Thimble Islands, all in Long Island Sound; places in Raritan Bay in New Jersey; places up the Connecticut River such as Clark's Island (sometimes called Kidd's Island); and places up the Hudson River valley.

In some of these places (eg Money Island, a now vanished islet in Raritan Bay), some old coins have actually been found, but given the history of ships, seafarers, merchants and settlers in the region, there is no way of knowing if these have any link to Captain Kidd.

The mysterious maps

Adding real spice to the story is the discovery in the 1920s and 30s of four apparent treasure maps hidden by Captain Kidd or his family/associates in pieces of furniture that supposedly belonged to him. Guy and Hubert Palmer were English brothers who ran a pirate museum and were devoted collectors of pirate-related memorabilia. Through one of their regular suppliers, antiques dealer Arthur Hill-Cutler, they came into possession of items such as Kidd's sea chest and bureau, which had supposedly accompanied him back to Britain on his final voyage (although their provenance was unclear). Even more remarkably, they discovered a series of scraps of parchment bearing maps secreted in hidden bottoms and hollow runners, all of apparently the same island.

The Palmer brothers had the maps checked by a British Museum expert who proclaimed them genuine, but they were in such poor condition that they could not be handled, so slides were taken and copies made by tracing over the photos. These copies have been pored over relentlessly by generations of treasure seekers, but so far without leading anywhere.

One obvious interpretation of all this is that the whole affair was a crude hoax. Apparently Hill-Cutler was not always above suspicion in his dealings, and it requires little imagination to envisage that, knowing of the Palmers' obsession with all things piratical and their desire to believe, he screwed fake brass plates onto the items of furniture, hid fake maps about them and sold them to the gullible brothers. The alleged treasure-maps are simply too good to be true, bearing intricate codes and such tantalising legends as 'Smuggler's Cove', 'Wrecks' and 'Turtles'. All that is missing is a large 'X' and a skull and crossbones.

This is certainly the opinion of the British Library today, where Peter Barber, the Curator of the Map Department, has declared the maps to be fakes. Treasure hunter Paul Hawkins disagrees, and points out that since the original documents appear to have vanished, leaving only copies, any judgement on their authenticity must be suspended. The appropriately named Hawkins further claims to have deciphered the codes and located the treasure island, which he says is in the Indian Ocean.

Conclusion

So far no one has successfully unearthed any of Kidd's dozens of alleged buried hoards. The truth is that they are unlikely to, because in all likelihood Governor Bellomont has already dug up all the buried loot there was. The only treasure we know to have definitely existed has been accounted for. The rest is rumour, supposition, speculation and the wild claims of a condemned man clutching at straws. Kidd's legacy lives on, however, for his story is supposed to have helped inspire *Treasure Island*, fixing for ever in the minds of the public the romantic notion of buried pirate treasure.

The Oak Island Money Pit

One strange mystery ties together many of the stories already encountered in this book, from the Holy Grail and the Knights Templar to Captain Kidd's pirate gold and the works of Shakespeare. All these treasures have featured in theories about what lies at the bottom of the Oak Island Money Pit.

The Oak Island story

Oak Island is a small, tree-covered island in Mahone Bay off the coast of Nova Scotia, in Canada. Since the mid-19th century stories have circulated about a shaft or pit on the island that might contain buried treasure of some sort, and over the last two centuries an extraordinary amount of money and effort has been spent on attempts to recover that treasure – attempts that have cost no less than six lives.

An intriguing discovery

The original story of the Oak Island pit comes from accounts in mid-19th-century newspapers, which vary slightly in their details but agree on the main elements of the tale. In 1795 a young man named Daniel McGinnis, who was exploring the island, came across a slight depression in the ground next to a tree, above which, according to some versions, a pulley hung from a projecting branch. Putting two and two together, McGinnis recruited two friends and began to excavate the depression, which proved to be a pit loosely filled with soil. A few metres below the surface they found flagstones, and 3 metres (10 feet) below them a layer of oak beams or logs.

A many-layered mystery

Convinced that the pit was man-made, and imagining connections to lore of buried pirate treasure, which was prevalent along the New England/Newfoundland coast, the three sought more help. It took a while, but by 1803 (or 1810, depending on the source) they had formed a business venture with a partner and returned to excavate in earnest, uncovering layers of clay, charcoal, fibrous material identified as coconut fibre and more platforms of oak beams. Strange markings were allegedly found in or near the shaft. About 24 metres (80 feet) down they thought they had struck a chest, but when they returned to dig it out the next day they found the shaft flooded and could not drain it.

Subsequent, increasingly elaborate and hi-tech, ventures experienced essentially the same sequence of events. More evidence of a man-made shaft or pit would be followed by discovery of something intriguing, whereupon disaster would strike and the pit would collapse or get flooded again. Drilling to obtain cores allegedly recovered some links from a golden chain, but flooding disrupted operations. Numerous parallel shafts were sunk to try to access the original shaft – now named the Money Pit – but these also flooded. A man was killed when a boiler blew up.

At one point the miners thought they had reached the bottom of the pit, but it apparently collapsed into some sort of subterranean void and flooded again. It was assumed that the pit's builders had rigged up an elaborate water trap system, so that sea water from the nearby Smith's Cove would flood any 'unauthorised' attempt to recover the mysterious treasure, and would help to plunge the putative chests of loot still further beyond reach.

The 20th century saw multiple expeditions and ventures to Oak Island, involving such unlikely figures as Franklin D Roosevelt (who actually spent some time on the island helping with the excavations) and John Wayne. A man had died in 1897 when a hoist device broke and four more died in 1965 when overcome by gas. During the 1960s a causeway was built to allow a mechanical digger to be brought onto the island and dig out the entire area of the original pit, although its exact location was by now lost amidst the hundreds of parallel and diagonal shafts and bore holes that had been sunk.

Finds and clues

Apart from the small bits of gold, other finds have been made in the pit, including fragments of parchment, old tools and, most significantly, a stone tablet inscribed with a coded message, dug up in the early 19th century. Although the tablet was lost, then found, and then lost again in 1919, a record of the markings was subsequently produced in 1970. It proved to be a simple code, which when cracked spelled out the encouraging message: 'Forty Feet Below Two Million Pounds Are Buried'.

In 1971 a video camera was lowered down a borehole into a subterranean cavern to obtain murky footage of what was claimed to be a severed hand and a chest, at which point the cavern collapsed. For the time being, explorations have ceased and the island has recently been put up for sale.

From pirate's loot to alien technology

The original theories about the contents of the Money Pit were of limited scope. The early reports seem to assume that there must be pirate treasure buried there, and Captain Kidd – famously supposed to have secreted loot all along the east coast of North

America (see page 138) – is specifically mentioned. Other pirates, such as Henry Morgan and Blackbeard, are also referred to. Related candidates for the constructors of the pit include Spanish sailors from a treasure galleon caught in a gale or British sailors who had captured/recovered Spanish treasure but didn't want to declare the full extent of their finds. Both pirates and the British Navy are known to have frequented Mahone Bay, while one analysis claims that the reported structure of the Money Pit, with its regularly spaced levels of oak beams, resembles British military engineering of the 17th century.

The Templar connection

As the excavations wore on and the workings appeared to be on an ever grander scale, complete with water traps and collapsing caverns, the theory that pirates or sailors had dug the pit began to lose favour. This was too complex to be the work of a few men, and must therefore involve large, well-funded and organised groups with extensive engineering and construction knowledge.

Among the most popular candidates to fit these criteria are the Knights Templar. In historical mystery circles the Templars are said to have inherited the monumental masonry and architecture secrets of King Solomon and the Pyramid-builders. They are also linked to the site through the rumours and legends about their lost fleet, ocean-going prowess and transatlantic connections. It is often pointed out that when Columbus arrived in the New World his ships bore the Templar cross upon their sails.

In particular, Oak Island is linked to the legend of Henry Sinclair, Earl of Orkney and ancestor of the Sinclairs of Rosslyn Chapel, whose Icelandic heritage gave him access to Viking knowledge of Newfoundland. Supposedly he was given navigational secrets by the Templars to enable him to secretly explore the New World in the 1390s, and deposit there the treasure they had entrusted to him. Evidence for this claim includes a set of medieval letters, an allegedly pre-Columbian rock carving in

Westford, Massachusetts, which apparently depicts a knight, and the prevalence of Templar crosses on tombs in a graveyard for early settlers in Nova Scotia. According to this theory, the Money Pit hides nothing less than the lost treasure of the Templars, which could be anything from the Holy Grail or the Ark of the Covenant to the True Gospels or the Talking Head of Jesus (see page 120).

Such theories of pre-Columbian contact with the Americas are not simply harmless fun. They have sometimes been co-opted by far-right white supremacists and other racists to bolster absurd theories that the Americas were originally settled by Nordic types, thus somehow legitimising the destruction of Native American cultures and underpinning offensive racist agendas.

More outlandish theories

Other groups who may have had the wherewithal and inclination to construct the Money Pit include, according to some theories, the Incas, seeking a place to hide their gold from the greedy conquistadors, and the ancient Atlanteans, caching their secret knowledge/technology – possibly of extraterrestrial origin – after the destruction of their continent.

One of the most intriguing claims, however, is that the pit contains a collection of documents proving that the true author of Shakespeare's plays was Sir Francis Bacon. This theory is mainly the work of Dr Orville Ward Owen who claims to have decoded Baconian ciphers revealing that the Elizabethan philosopher and writer had secreted a stash of documents in some subterranean place. Bacon is sometimes said to have been the illegitimate son of Sir Francis Drake (a frequent visitor to the Americas), suggesting one route by which he may have acquired knowledge of Oak Island, while he is also linked to Newfoundland by virtue of a grant of land there made to him by King James I. Perhaps he devised the pit as a way to hide the proof of his Shakespearian authorship. Perhaps he was a member of some Invisible College that had inherited esoteric knowledge from the Templars and hence knew about the pit already.

Pitfalls

Some of these theories fail to impress for reasons explained elsewhere in this book (eg it is highly unlikely that any of Captain Kidd, the Templars, the Incas or the Atlanteans ever had any secret treasure to hide). More to the point, however, they are probably largely redundant, because the Money Pit is almost certainly not a man-made treasure depository, but a natural formation. What's more, almost every element of the Money Pit legend that suggests otherwise is dubious, from the initial accounts to the alleged evidence.

Natural caves and collapses

The most obvious explanation for the Oak Island mystery is that the pit is an entirely natural formation that has been misunderstood and built up through imaginative retelling. The geology of the area favours the formation of underground caverns and eroded faults and cracks in the rock. If one of these caverns collapses through natural processes it can cause a sinkhole or pit to open up on or just below the surface as the soil and rock fall into the newly opened void. This pit will then fill up over time with new soil, while tree trunks and other debris can easily fall in/get washed in as well. It is easy to imagine a scenario where all that is left of the natural pit is a shallow depression on the surface, such as the one McGinnis is said to have found, and that when this was excavated the newer soil within the pit, together with the occasional layer of wood deposited during a storm or flood, would give the whole formation the appearance of having been artificially constructed. Several different sinkholes and voids could easily join up with each other and the sea via narrow cracks, explaining how water could get in and flood the Money Pit and other boreholes, especially given the level of disturbance and digging in the area.

Such processes and formations are well known in the Mahone Bay area and have been observed on Oak Island itself. One of the few attempts to do any scientific survey of the site, by the Woods Hole Oceanographic Institute in 1995, concluded that natural forces were the most likely explanation.

Discounting the evidence

If the Money Pit was a natural formation to begin with, what of the suggestive evidence and finds? Most of it is highly problematic. Prior to the late 19th century, all the details depend on a few newspaper articles of uncertain provenance, written long after the events they refer to. Some simply recycle the same information, while several disagree on basic 'facts'. For instance, the suggestive finding of a pulley hanging from a tree branch above the pit, which supposedly first alerted the young McGinnis to its presence, is disputed, and if the pit really were constructed to hide something why would its builders have left such obvious clues lying around? The same applies to markings allegedly seen in or near the pit, and to the cipher stone.

The stone itself is deeply suspect. There is no proof that it ever existed, and the supposed record of the code carved on its surface is probably a 1970s invention. Other findings pulled out of the pit could either be fictional embellishments designed to encourage investors and/or perpetuate the yarn, or the detritus left by 200 years of cack-handed excavations. The video evidence obtained in 1971 is also considered spurious, since there is no sense of scale and nothing can be made out in detail – identification of a hand and chest are said to owe much to wishful thinking.

Telling tales

In fact there is something altogether fishy about the origin of the Oak Island myths. It was not unknown for 19th-century newspapers and journals to embellish or even invent stories, especially if it was a bit of harmless fun in the interest of spinning a good yarn. In North America, particularly, there was a tradition of tall-tale-telling competitions where people would endeavour to invent the best yarn. This tradition also ties in with the literary antecedents of the Oak Island tale, which closely resembles Edgar Allan Poe's popular short story *The Gold Bug* (1843), first published in a newspaper.

Poe's tale tells of a scrap of parchment that bears a cipher in invisible ink, which leads an ingenious and determined young man to track down the location of Captain Kidd's buried treasure. To find the hidden cache, he has to locate a spot directly beneath the branch of a mighty tree, and subsequently dig a deep hole.

Did the Oak Island story begin as a journalistic riff on *The Gold Bug*, perhaps augmented with local knowledge of a filled-in sinkhole, only to spiral out of control into an obsessive treasure hunt that would claim lives?

The Masonic connection

A fascinating theory by Joe Nickell of *Skeptical Inquirer* magazine is that the whole tale bears a strong Masonic imprint. Many of those involved in the Oak Island excavations over the years have been Masons, while the original story has many parallels with Masonic allegories and fables about initiates seeking to recover hidden knowledge/artefacts. In particular there are similarities with the allegory of the Secret Vault and the initiation rite for the Royal Arch degree, which is based upon it. For instance, in the original Oak Island tale the miners uncover soft stone, charcoal and clay as they excavate the pit, before hitting what they think might be a chest, striking it with a crowbar to test its composition. Nickell points out that in Masonic allegory chalk, charcoal and clay signify freedom, fervency and zeal, while in the Royal Arch initiation ceremony the Secret Vault is located with a blow from a crowbar. There are many other similarities and links between the Money Pit mystery and Masonry.

If the original story was indeed a 'tall tale', perhaps it was written as an attempt to disseminate a Masonic allegory in the guise of a popular story, which then got out of hand. Nickell goes further and suggests that the whole saga of Oak Island up to the 1930s has been some sort of elaborate Masonic performance. But for what purpose? Perhaps there is a great mystery here after all: perhaps the Masons got so heavily involved because their secret tradition of esoteric lore, stretching back via the Templars to ancient Israel, Egypt and beyond, led them to believe that something truly extraordinary genuinely *is* buried there! Or perhaps there was never anything at the bottom of the Money Pit except seawater, limestone and broken dreams.

4

Lost People

Few people achieve sufficient glory, renown or infamy to be remembered after their death. Fewer still achieve all this but come to rest in an unmarked or unknown grave. For graves are what this chapter concerns. Since all of the people discussed in this section are historical personages, quests to find them inevitably become quests to find their resting places. The chapter might arguably have been entitled Lost Graves, except that not all of the subjects sought for herein were afforded the dignity of a proper burial, and hence do not lie in a proper grave or tomb.

There is something particularly touching about a lost person. Perhaps it is because most cultures have some version of the belief that a person's soul or spirit cannot rest easy unless the body is properly interred. Or perhaps it's that personal stories seem unfinished if they lack the concrete ending a defined resting place provides. When they finish in mystery, there is a natural urge to want to solve it, partly to 'tie up' historical loose ends, and partly to help to lay that person's spirit to rest.

For some of the lost people in this chapter the hunt for their grave is not just about tying up loose ends. Rulers such as

Boudicca or Genghis Khan might well have been buried with considerable grave goods, so tomb raiders can savour the prospect of treasure. Groups of people, such as the lost army of Cambyses or the Lost Colony of Roanoke, bring the prospect of major archaeological finds – a kind of treasure in themselves. But the true reward for the discoverer of any of these final resting places would be a place in the history books of his or her own.

The lost army of Cambyses

Cambyses II was the emperor of Persia (ruled 530–522 BCE) and successor to Cyrus the Great. Eager to emulate his father's deeds of conquest, and to extend Persian rule across all the known nations (ie civilisations) of the world, Cambyses invaded Egypt in 525 BCE, defeating the last true Egyptian pharaoh Psammetichus III. Yet today he is remembered not for his feats of conquest, but for his lost army – a force of 50,000 warriors, dispatched to conquer a tiny oasis kingdom, that vanished into the desert and was lost without a single survivor or the slightest trace being discovered for more than 2,000 years.

Desert explorers and adventurers including Count László Almásy – the model for the English patient in the book and film of the same name – have sought to uncover their final resting place and solve their mysterious disappearance.

Herodotus and Cambyses

The primary source for the tale of Cambyses and his lost army is the ancient Greek traveller and historian Herodotus, an intrepid man who travelled all over Egypt just 75 years after the Persian invasion. Herodotus followed in Cambyses' footsteps and recorded the local tales and histories of the invader. Unfortunately his impartiality is questionable; he had the typical ancient Greek antipathy towards the Persians and his *Histories* slander Cambyses remorselessly, painting him as a despot, madman and general ne'er-do-well.

Herodotus first recounts how Cambyses managed to cross the difficult Sinai desert region and meet the Egyptians with his army intact, which is relevant because it shows that the Persians were capable of coping with desert transits. They recruited Arabian tribes to create water depots at regular spots along the route – in effect, artificial oases – and in this manner were able to arrive at the battle site in good order and defeat Psammetichus.

Later, Cambyses travelled to the major Egyptian cult centres to be crowned pharaoh but, according to Herodotus, made only a perfunctory effort to learn about or pay respect to their customs. He then decided to launch military expeditions against the Ethiopians (to the south), the Carthaginians (along the coast to the west) and the 'Ammoniums' – ie the inhabitants of the Siwa Oasis, a small fertile enclave deep within the Western Desert, which was famous for the Oracle of the Temple of Ammon (the Siwan name for the Egyptian god Amun-Ra, whom the Greeks equated with Zeus). The priests of the temple were used to commanding respect from Egypt's rulers, who were supposed to obtain 'divine' favour to legitimise their overlordship. Alexander the Great made sure to do this when he conquered Egypt 200 years later, but Cambyses, it seems, failed to follow the proper forms and disdained the Siwans.

The Siwan expedition

Cambyses took his army south along the Nile to launch his Ethiopian expedition, stopping at Thebes to detach a force to send to Siwa in 524 BCE. According to Herodotus, in Book III of his *Histories*, an army of 50,000 men was ordered to 'enslave the Ammonians and burn the oracle of Zeus'. Led by guides, the army set off into the desert, reaching 'the city of Oasis', known to the Greeks as 'The Isles of the Blest' (modern-day Kharga), seven days' march to the west. After this, they were never seen again, although the Siwans themselves were somehow able to give Herodotus a rough account of what happened next:

> this is what the Ammonians themselves say: when the Persians were crossing the sand from the Oasis to attack them, and were about midway between ... [Siwa] and the Oasis, while they were breakfasting a great and violent south wind arose, which buried them in the masses of sand which it bore; and so they disappeared from sight. Such is the Ammonian tale about this army.

This is the full extent of what we know about the lost army, which has led many scholars to doubt the episode ever happened. Perhaps Herodotus was simply inventing the tale to make Cambyses look more foolish. Why would the Persian emperor waste his time launching a strike on Siwa? Why would he send such a huge army to conquer such a small place (probably only a few thousand residents at most)? Above all, why would he send them via such a perilous route with so little preparation or precaution?

Herodotus himself suggests, albeit indirectly, some of the answers. A possible motive for the expedition is that Cambyses was angered by the attitude of the priests of the Temple of Ammon, who – themselves angry at a perceived lack of due deference – may have been spreading the word that his kingship was illegitimate. They may even have predicted his death. Herodotus also drives home the point that Cambyses was an irascible drunk, given to fits of spite and cruel rage, and quite capable of nursing a lethal grudge. He was also unhinged enough to doom his men with inadequate planning and preparation.

An alternative explanation is that Siwa was only intended as a way point on a longer journey. Perhaps the real targets were lands further to the west. Cambyses' intended assault on

Carthage had been called off because the Phoenicians who provided his navy refused to move against their kin who had set up the colony at Carthage. Perhaps he intended to approach them by land instead – this would account for the apparently disproportionate size of the expeditionary force.

If Herodotus is right, the Persian army met a bleak end. The region they were travelling across includes barren depressions of bare rock and boulders; wind-sculpted buttes; plains of salt and dust; vast sand seas of impassable dunes; searing desert winds hotter than 40°C that blow for days on end; massive sand storms that will bury anything that stands still; and an utter absence of water. How the Ammonians knew the fate of the lost army is unclear, given that they specifically told Herodotus that not one soldier had reached Siwa, but perhaps they simply assumed the most likely scenario.

The army in the desert

Apart from being a great unsolved mystery, the miserable desert fate of the lost army of Cambyses also presents the intriguing likelihood that there could be a huge find of skeletons, armour, clothing, weapons and equipment from the ancient Persian era awaiting discovery. The army would have included in its number soldiers from many different parts of the antique world. In the uniquely arid conditions, with the possibility that sand may have covered and protected, the remains could be amazingly well preserved. There could be an archaeological treasure trove somewhere in the Sahara.

Hard target

Herodotus provides a few clues about the possible location of the lost army, describing the army's route from the oasis known as 'Island of the Blest', which is today a major agricultural town known as Kharga. From here they would presumably have tried to follow the traditional caravan route to Siwa, which goes via the oases at Dakhla (a few hundred kilometres to the west) and then Farafra (a few hundred more to the north-west). From Herodotus' account it sounds as though the Persians may have got to Dakhla or even Farafra, but were then lost as they attempted to complete the final leg of the journey. Even narrowing it down this far, however, leaves a dauntingly vast area to examine. If the Persians got lost out of Dakhla and started going in the wrong direction they could have ended up pretty much anywhere in the Western Desert.

The Western Desert is one of the hardest places in the world to be looking for lost relics. It is vast, covering about two-thirds of modern-day Egypt: an area of 680,000 square kilometres (263,000 square miles), equal to the combined size of Austria, Belgium, Denmark, Greece, the Netherlands, Norway and Switzerland. The conditions, as described above, are incredibly harsh and desolate. Even modern vehicles with four-wheel drives and special equipment cannot cope with some of the dunes found in the sand seas. Much of the area is restricted owing to the security issues of the region: millions of landmines from World War II, the proximity of the border with Libya and sensitivities about oil operations and terrorism. And there is always the likelihood that any finds that are stumbled across will soon be covered up by the shifting desert sands, never to be seen again.

The enigmatic Count Almásy

Undaunted, many desert adventurers have dreamed of solving the mystery of the lost army. Probably the most famous was the Austro-Hungarian playboy, pilot and desert explorer Count László Almásy, whose life and times provided the model for the Ralph Fiennes character in *The English Patient*. Almásy started off as a self-taught dabbler in the exotic world of desert discovery, but his expertise with motor vehicles and his reckless disregard for personal safety led him to pull off some amazing escapades.

During the 1930s he was part of a crowd mainly composed of genteel British officers interested in desert travel and exploration, who were primarily fixated on locating the semi-legendary Zerzura, the Oasis of Little Birds, alluded to in medieval writings. Almásy amazed the other members of the Zerzura Club, as they had named themselves, by successfully discovering this hidden oasis, but his search for Cambyses' army was less successful and even more dangerous.

Almásy was an avid fan of Herodotus, and in 1936 determined to follow the tracks of the army as described by the ancient Greek. His journey is described by Saul Kelly in the book *The Lost Oasis: The Desert War and the Hunt for Zerzura.* Kelly tells how on a previous expedition Almásy had discovered pottery fragments that suggested how the Persians had hoped to cross the waterless desert. By burying huge caches of amphorae (jars) along the intended route, and employing local tribesmen to ferry water to them, they could effect a similar operation to their successful crossing of the Sinai.

This at least was Almásy's theory, but when he ventured into the desert from Farafra on his 1936 expedition, he discovered not caches of jars but a series of cairns that he described as 'ancient hollow, circular pyramids of stone about the height of a man', which seemed to mark the route across the forbidding sand seas. Perhaps the Persians had employed scouts to build them, hoping to follow them all the way to Siwa.

Kelly relates that the Almásy party then ran into problems that gave him an insight into the probable fate of Cambyses' force. Their progress was halted by impassable giant dunes, and the hot desert wind called the khamsin (or khamaseen) blew up, whipping their vehicles with scalding, 44°C+ storm-force winds. All but one of the vehicles broke down and they were lucky to make it out of the desert alive in the third, following a corridor between two towering dunes until they reached Siwa four days later. Almásy planned a further expedition, but war broke out and he never got another chance.

Disputed discoveries

In the last decade there have been some slightly confused reports about discoveries in the Western Desert that sound almost too good to be true. According to Professor Mosalam Shaltout, chairman of the Space Research Center at the Desert Environment Research Institute of Egypt's Minufiya University, an Italian-led expedition in December 1996 which was surveying for meteorites stumbled across archaeological remains in the El Bahrein Oasis area of the Western Desert. Aly Barakat, a geologist with the team, found a dagger blade and hilt, pottery shards, apparently human bone fragments, burial mounds, arrowheads and a silver bracelet, which, on the basis of a photograph, was identified as 'most likely belonging to the Achaemenid period' (ie ancient Persian).

Meanwhile, in 2000 there were widespread reports that a team of oil-prospecting geologists, said to be from Helwan University, in Cairo, had stumbled across similar finds in the same area, spotting scattered arrow heads and human bones.

In 2003 geologist Tom Bown led an expedition to the area, accompanied by archaeologist Gail MacKinnon and a film crew, to follow up Aly Barakat's discoveries, which they, controversially, said had been suppressed by the Egyptian authorities. Bown claimed to have found remains at the same site, near the El Bahrein Oasis, at a place later named Wadi Mastour, the Hidden Valley. In fact he reportedly went as far as describing seeing thousands of bones littering the desert.

Yet another follow-up expedition in 2005, however, cast serious doubt on the claims of both Barakat and Bown. A team from the University of Toledo, in Ohio, together with British and Egyptian associates, travelled to the site near El Bahrein. They located a broken pot found by both Barakat and Bown, although they identified it as Roman, but they failed to find any other suggestive remains beyond a few burial sites, which they claim are common in the desert. Instead of fields of scattered human bones they found large numbers of fragments of fossilised sand dollars (sea urchin-like creatures that leave distinctive round calcite cases), which are apparently easy to mistake for human bones and could explain the previous claims.

Can Herodotus be trusted?

So despite tantalising claims and hints, the lost army of Cambyses has apparently not been found yet, nor any definitive proof that it really existed. The cairns and pottery found by Almásy and the weapons and bones allegedly seen by Barakat and Bown may not be what they seem, or perhaps they simply belong to some of the many other groups who have made the perilous desert crossing – for instance, the notorious Forty Days Road slave caravan used to follow the route through the Western Desert via Kharga.

Ultimately the credibility of the tale comes down to Herodotus. In this sense he was not highly regarded even by other ancient writers, some of whom felt the sobriquet 'the Father of History' bestowed upon him by Cicero should be changed to 'the Father of Lies'. As already noted, he was biased against the Persians and his portrait of Cambyses has a touch of the pantomime villain. In fact it seems from other contemporary sources that many groups in Egypt welcomed the invader, and an inscription specifically records Cambyses as honouring the Egyptian religion and customs in a praiseworthy manner. This does not mean that Herodotus made up the story about the lost army, or even that his sources deceived him, but it does add another layer of uncertainty to an already difficult search.

Should you choose to believe him, however, you may be able to join the hunt yourself. In 2004 a tour operator called Aqua Sun Desert set up a desert safari to explore the Western Desert area around Dakhla, Farafra, Siwa and El Bahrein and to look for evidence of the lost army. It was reported at the time that the tours would continue for five years. As Aqua Sun manager Hisham Nessim says, 'If we discover anything about the lost army, it will be the discovery of the century.'

Boudicca's grave

Boudicca – the academically preferred version of the better-known Boadicea – is a legendary figure of British history, famous as an archetypal warrior woman who supposedly embodies the spirit of Britannia with her motto, 'Britons never, never shall be slaves!' In 60–61 CE she led her tribe the Iceni and other Celtic allies in a bloody revolt against the occupying Roman forces, but was defeated in a final battle and met her end. Her final resting place has never been discovered, but its location has triggered speculation from the informed to the ridiculous.

The revolt of the Iceni

Boudicca was Queen of the Iceni, a tribe of British Celts who lived in what is now Norfolk in East Anglia. Her name derives from the Celtic word *bouda*, meaning 'victory', and was hence was an Iron Age equivalent of Victoria – a fact made much of by the Victorians, who popularised her legend. The better-known version of her name, Boadicea, is probably the result of a mis-transcription of Tacitus, the Roman historian who is the primary source for her story. (The other source is Dio Cassius, a slightly later Greco-Roman writer who probably based his version mainly on Tacitus, although he added some extra details.)

After the Romans' conquest of Britain in 43 CE they had occupied most of South East England, but left client kings in charge of some peripheral areas. This was common practice. What usually followed was that the king in question would will his kingdom to the Romans on his death, ensuring an orderly transition of power. In the Iceni area, King Prasutagus had been left in charge as a client king; Boudicca was his wife. In return for subjecting to Roman overlordship and making the Roman emperor co-heir to his kingdom, he was allowed to rule and was even lent considerable sums of money with which to enjoy himself.

When he died, however, he left his people in a parlous state. Roman law did not recognise inheritance by females, and Prasutagus had only daughters (although the Romans probably would have annexed his kingdom anyway). On top of this, the Iceni were faced with the debts he had run up. Accordingly the Romans took over, and the Iceni suddenly found that their jealously guarded freedoms had disappeared. Their lands were now considered Roman property and they were treated like slaves. They were ruthlessly taxed and, according to Tacitus, Boudicca and her daughters were flogged and raped.

In 60 CE, while the Roman governor Suetonius Paulinus was away in Northern Wales campaigning against the Druids on Anglesey, the Iceni and their neighbours the Trinovantes rose up in revolt. Leading them was the charismatic and forceful Boudicca, whom Dio Cassius describes as cutting a striking figure:

> Boudicca was tall, terrible to look on and gifted with a powerful voice. A flood of bright red hair ran down to her knees; she wore a golden necklet made up of ornate pieces, a multi-coloured robe and over it a thick cloak held together by a brooch. She took up a long spear to cause dread in all who set eyes on her.

First the British horde fell on the Roman settlement of Camulodunum (modern-day Colchester), razing it to the ground and massacring most of the inhabitants. They defeated a Roman legion sent to deal with them, and in 61 CE moved towards the recently founded Roman trading post and administrative centre of Londinium (modern-day London).

Hearing the news of the revolt, Suetonius had called off his campaign and marched from Wales to Londinium at speed, travelling the entire length of the Roman road known as Watling Street, arriving there just before the British host. Realising that he did not have enough men to defend the city, he retreated, evacuating as many as possible. The Britons burned Londinium to the ground and again massacred everyone they found, before moving along Watling Street to Verulamium (modern-day St Albans) where they did the same. In all, Boudicca's forces are said to have killed around 70–80,000 people.

The Battle of Watling Street

Suetonius retreated back up Watling Street, gathering what forces he could, eventually mustering 10,000 men. Boudicca's horde was said to be 230,000 strong. The Roman governor knew that if he took on the Britons in open country they would surround him and cut his force to pieces, but he also knew that if deployed on the right ground, superior Roman military tactics would nullify the imbalance of forces.

Tacitus records that Suetonius 'prepared to break off delay and fight a battle. He chose a position approached by a narrow defile, closed in at the rear by a forest, having first ascertained that there was not a soldier of the enemy except in front of him, where an open plain extended ...' This is the only description we have of the site of what is commonly called the Battle of Watling Street, on the basis that since Suetonius was retreating up this Roman road he would probably have picked a site not far from it. The pursuing British horde, confident of victory, drew up the wagons carrying their women, children and old folk in a huge ring around the battlefield so that they could view the fight.

Unable to cope with Roman tactics, discipline and armour, the British horde was defeated and tried to flee, but were impeded by their own wagons. The Romans slaughtered 80,000 of them in one of the worst single days of carnage ever recorded on British soil. Tacitus records that Boudicca survived the carnage but committed suicide with poison (according to tradition, her daughters committed suicide alongside her). Dio Cassius reports that she fell sick and died, presumably of despair at the great defeat. Tantalisingly, he also records that she was buried with great ceremony and riches, raising the questions: where does Boudicca's body lie, and might the rich hoard of grave goods still be recovered?

The great unknowns

Assuming that Boudicca was interred somewhere (as opposed to being cremated), there seem to be two main possibilities. One is that she fell at, or near, the battlefield and thus might be buried there, perhaps among the tens of thousands of other corpses that might have been either left for carrion or dumped in mass graves. Alternatively she may have escaped to relative safety amongst other Britons, and been buried by them.

Where would she have fled? Common sense would suggest back to her homeland amongst the Iceni, but it is not certain if she came from there originally. It is quite possible that she was from another tribe and had been married to Prasutagus to cement an alliance, for instance. So this option does little to help pinpoint her grave.

The original sources, Tacitus and Dio Cassius, offer little help. Tacitus' account is probably fairly accurate. He was writing c100 CE, well within living memory of the events, and he had a first-hand source in the person of his father-in-law Gnaeus Julius Agricola, who had been at the Battle of Watling Street as a young tribune, and was later Governor of Britain. But Tacitus provides frustratingly few details to help locate the battle site beyond the topographical information quoted above. Instead it is necessary to turn to less direct sources – archaeology and folklore.

Local legends

Folklore as a source of 'hard' historical evidence must be treated with caution, but it can preserve local traditions that date back centuries – maybe even millennia.

King's Cross station

Perhaps the most prevalent bit of folklore regarding Boudicca's grave is the tradition that she is buried beneath one of the platforms in King's Cross station, one of the main railway stations in London, from where trains head north along the busiest rail route in the country. (It is also now famous internationally for being where Harry Potter catches the train to Hogwarts in the popular books and films.) Absurd though it sounds, this legend is remarkably widespread, although the actual platform number that is given varies considerably. Usually it is Platform 10.

A former place name for King's Cross is Battle Bridge, which is given as a possible location for the Battle of Watling Street – perhaps this is the basis of the legend. Alternatively, the original source of the legend may be Lewis Spence's 1937 book *Boadicea – Warrior queen of the Britons*. Spence was a folklorist and writer on occult and pseudohistorical topics such as Atlantis and fairy traditions, and is not now noted for his academic rigour.

The story received an added impetus in 1988 when an article in British newspaper *The Daily Telegraph* claimed that contractors working on Platform 10 at King's Cross station had unearthed the skeleton of the warrior queen. This has since been quoted widely, usually with the date of the discovery given as 22 February. Things become clearer, however, when we learn that the actual date given was 28 February, meaning that the article itself ran on 1 April.

Gop Hill

Britain is littered with burial mounds and tumuli that date from the Stone Age right up to the late Iron Age (when the Romans arrived). Some of these have become linked in local legend and folklore to Boudicca. One intriguing set of traditions links Boudicca and the Battle of Watling Street to Flintshire in North Wales. A major prehistoric earthwork called Gop Hill used to be known as Gop Paulini (from the Welsh *Coperleni*), suggesting it was named after Suetonius Paulinus. Other old place names in the area are suggestive, such as the 'Hollow of No Quarter' and the 'Hill of Carnage', and the topography is said to fit Tacitus' description. Some carved stones from the region also seem to be lexically linked to Boudicca or the battle – one is called Buddig's Stone, and another the 'Stone of the Place of Lamentation'. A golden torc (a type of Celtic neck ring) found in the area was added to local legend and attributed to the dead queen's grave goods. There are also local legends about the ghosts of Boudicca, Suetonius and assorted Roman and Celtic warriors seen wondering the area.

Antiquarians writing in the journal *Mercian Mysteries* have exposed these North Welsh traditions as spurious at best. They seem to result from a combination of mistranslations and wishful thinking by earlier antiquarian authors, whose work then becomes the basis for local traditions picked up by others. So, for instance, Gop Hill's older name, Coperleni, is more likely to derive from *copa'r* ('summit' or 'top of') *Leni* (perhaps a personal name of local significance) than from Paulinus. In addition, Buddig's Stone is actually a corrupted version of Vuddig's Stone and there is nothing to support an association with Boudicca. The torc is from Ireland and dates to well before Boudicca's time.

Barrow girl

Barrows are prehistoric burial mounds that often garner folk-loric or legendary associations, and several of them have become associated with Boudicca in folklore. For instance, a little-known barrow on Hampstead Heath is known in local folklore as Boadicea's Grave, but the dating appears to be wrong as it resembles a Bronze Age barrow, making it 2–3,000 years too old to belong to Boudicca. On the other hand, it may also be too young – it does not appear on maps until 1725 and the only excavation of the mound in 1894, by Sir Hercules Read, the Keeper of the British Museum, found that the top layer was modern debris. In other words, it may be a 17th- or early-18th-century fake or rubbish tip.

Boudicca's home region of East Anglia also boasts barrows linked to her. A barrow in Quidenham, Norfolk, is variously known as Viking's Mound, the Bubberies or Quidenham Mount and is reputed to be the resting place of Queen Boudicca 'and all her jewels'. Meanwhile in Garboldisham a barrow sometimes known as Soldier's Hill is also said to be her grave.

The Lady of Birdlip

Archaeological discoveries can be more convincing than local folklore because of the presence of material evidence. However, unless archaeologists are fortunate enough to find inscriptions or other definite information at the same time, attributing identities to tombs or bodies is a matter of pure speculation. A good example is the Lady of Birdlip, a skeleton dug up near Birdlip in Gloucestershire in the late 19th century. Along with the bones were found a variety of grave goods, and the grave itself was flanked by two other graves. The grave seems to date to the 1st century CE, which is the correct time, and the grave goods – which included a mirror, brooches, a necklace and bowls – led to the identification of the skeleton as a woman.

Perhaps inevitably it was suggested that the Lady of Birdlip was none other than Boudicca, buried with her two daughters alongside her. The region had been the home of the Dobunni in late Iron Age times – perhaps these were Boudicca's original people, to whom she had fled after the disastrous defeat somewhere nearby? Intriguingly, anomalous amounts of Dobunnic currency have been found in East Anglia, suggesting some sort of link between the Dobunni and the Iceni.

The problem with this identification, apart from the total lack of any actual evidence, is that on viewing the Birdlip skull most experts assume it is male. Only when the context is known – ie the apparently 'feminine' grave goods – do attributions change. Antiquarian Malcolm Watkins argues that the Lady of Birdlip might have been a shaman/priest, rather than a warrior queen.

Up and down the Roman road

Mainstream academic opinion locates the Battle of Watling Street – and therefore the probable region of Boudicca's grave – as being along the route of the old Roman road of Watling Street, probably somewhere in the Midlands and most likely somewhere near a Roman fort or camp. Suetonius and his outnumbered force might have been making for the relative safety of the Roman fortress at Viroconium (modern-day Wroxeter), placing the site somewhere between there and Verulamium (St Albans) along the route of Watling Street.

Several candidates have been suggested. Venonis, now High Cross, in Leicestershire, is where Watling Street intersects with Britain's other major Roman road, the Fosse Way. This would have been a good place for Suetonius to meet reinforcements he might have hoped would arrive via the Fosse Way from the legion based in Exeter. There is evidence that there was a Roman camp/fort at Venonis as well. Another candidate is Lactodorum (modern-day Towcester), in Northamptonshire, which was a Roman fort along Watling Street to the south of Venonis.

The most favoured candidate, however, is the Roman fort of Manduessedum, which is now the site of Mancetter, near to Atherstone in Warwickshire. Finds date the fort to the correct period, while the topography here is said to match the description given by Tacitus, and it is suggested that a special corral for horses at the nearby camp called the Lunt (near modern-day Coventry) was built to house animals captured from the defeated British host. This theory is mainly the work of historian Graham Webster, but beyond the circumstantial evidence set out here there is no proof to back it up.

The cameo queen

As Webster himself has commented, only the discovery of a mass burial with associated weapons and other datable artefacts is likely to settle the issue of the location of the Battle of Watling Street. Similarly, the final resting place of Queen Boudicca is likely to remain a mystery unless it is found that the ancient Britons helpfully buried her with some written identification.

In practice, Boudicca herself is a historical problem. She is known only from the two Roman sources given and is not recorded or attested from any other sources. Indeed, until the work of Tacitus was rediscovered in medieval Europe during the Renaissance, British historians and chroniclers such as Bede or Geoffrey of Monmouth seemed to be unaware that she had ever existed. Given such a slim historical profile, it is hardly surprising that Boudicca should be so difficult to locate. Her final fate remains surrounded by unknowns. Where was the final battle? Did she die at the site? Was she buried, and, if so, by whom and with what ceremony? Perhaps she was cremated, dumped in a mass grave or simply fell somewhere in the wilderness. It is doubtful we will ever know.

The tomb of Genghis Khan

Genghis Khan was a Mongol warrior from the vast steppes of Central Asia, who amalgamated the disparate tribes and nations of his native lands into a potent army, and used it to conquer an empire that stretched from the Pacific to the Caspian. The peoples of Europe quailed at the mention of his name, while the inhabitants of the Middle East, Central Asia and China knew the full force of his wrath and might.

When he died on 18 August 1227, on campaign in Western China, he was taken back to his native land to be buried. According to one legend, his tomb was built into the bed of a diverted river, which was then allowed to resume its course; another tells of how hundreds of horses were stampeded across the grave to utterly flatten the mound and render the site invisible, and an impenetrable forest was planted atop it. In both versions, the slaves who built the tomb were then massacred, as were the soldiers who killed them, so that no one should know where the great Khan was buried and to keep safe the secret of the vast hoard of spoil and tribute believed to have been interred with him. A curse was placed on those who should try to disturb his eternal slumber, so that in Mongolia the tomb of Genghis Khan became known as *Ikh Khoring*, the Great Taboo.

Genghis woz 'ere

This is the legend of the lost tomb of Genghis Khan, the precise whereabouts of which remain one of history's great mysteries. For many years the area of Genghis' homeland was largely inaccessible to Western scientists since Outer Mongolia was a client state of the Soviets, while Inner Mongolia remains a jealously guarded part of China. The impoverished local governments did not have the resources to undertake archaeological explorations of their own. With the fall of the Soviet Union, however, Outer

Mongolia became much more accessible, triggering a new wave of interest in the tomb of the great conqueror.

This interest is twofold. Firstly, remarkably little is known about the era of early imperial Mongolia, owing in part to the lack of direct sources of information. The Mongols of Genghis Khan were largely illiterate and did not go in much for keeping records or writing histories. Almost everything we know about this period comes from foreign sources or from histories written after the time of Genghis. There is also little archaeological evidence, partly because of a lack of exploration, and possibly also because Genghis and his hordes were nomadic, used perishable materials and were relatively light on massive construction projects.

The second reason is the romance of the potential discovery, or, as Indiana Jones might put it, 'fortune and glory'. Apart from being the final resting place of one of the great figures of world history, Genghis' tomb could also hold a hoard of loot that might, as would-be tomb-raider Maury Kravitz puts it, 'eat the Tut [Tutankhamun] exhibit for breakfast.' In the course of his conquests, Genghis and his generals looted and despoiled empires and kingdoms in China, Central Asia, Persia and well into Eastern Europe, bringing back huge quantities of tribute and loot to Mongolia. Academics are divided over whether Genghis would have been buried with grave goods but legend says that he was – and, if so, it could be the greatest collection of grave goods in history. Kravitz, the sponsor and leader of a long-running project to investigate early imperial Mongolian sites and search for the tomb, points out that none of the Mongols' accumulated loot from around Eurasia has ever been recovered or even rumoured, suggesting that a large quantity of it may still be out there somewhere in the steppes or mountains.

Locating Genghis' tomb might also solve a related but subordinate mystery – the whereabouts of the tombs of the emperors of the Yuan Dynasty (1279–1368), founded by his descendants (who included the great Kublai Khan). According to legend, the

Yuan emperors wanted to follow Genghis' example and be buried in the same secret location. In other words Genghis and his burial trove might be only the tip of the iceberg.

Clues from history

There are few hard facts about Genghis' life or death. He probably came from Hentiy aymag in northern Mongolia, near the sources of the Onon and Kerulen rivers, and as a youth was forced to take refuge from his enemies in the Hentiyn Nuruu range, at a mountain called Burkhan Khaldun, or Buddha's Cliffs, which remained one of his favourite places. According to legend he asked to be interred in a place that held special meaning for him when he died – this has been interpreted by some to mean Burkhan Khaldun. Unfortunately there are dozens of places that go by this name and are linked by local tradition to the Great Khan.

The main source of information on his life and death is a work called *The Secret History of the Mongols*, written 13 years after his death and not known in the West until the 19th century. According to this work, which is believed to weave fact with liberal doses of fiction and mythology, Genghis (or Temujin as he was then known) was born and later crowned Great Khan near the present-day town of Batirsheet, near the border with Russia. This is regarded as another possible location for his tomb.

According to other near-contemporary texts, a mausoleum to the memory of Genghis was built on the site of his former palace, and court officials would commute from here to his actual resting place to carry out rites and ritual observances. This obviously contradicts the traditional legend that no one knew where he was buried, but this does not mean it is not accurate, and it suggests that anyone who can find Genghis' palace will be on the right track for his tomb. In fact the Chinese have built their own mausoleum to Genghis Khan in the Autonomous Region of Inner Mongolia, at a site they claim is near where he died. They say it houses relics associated with him.

Nature's way

Many scholars do not believe the tomb of Genghis Khan exists at all. According to Morris Rossabi, professor of Mongol and Chinese history at Columbia University, New York, 'There was no tomb culture among them [the Mongols] at the time of his death.' Instead it was traditional to leave the body to the wild animals and to nature, by tying it to a horse and sending it into the wilderness or leaving it in the desert. Whether they would have applied such brusque treatment to the corpse of their greatest leader, a godlike figure, is unclear, but two factors suggest they might have. Firstly, Genghis Khan made a virtue of his simplicity, his espousal of the traditional Mongol lifestyle and his closeness to the common warriors who served him. In a letter probably written for him, addressed to a Taoist monk, Genghis says, 'I, living in the northern wilderness, have not inordinate passions. I hate luxury and practise moderation. I have only one coat and one food. I eat the same food and am dressed in the same tatters as my humble herdsmen.' Secondly, Mongolian tradition holds that after death the body is not important, only the soul, so that it might not have seemed disrespectful to Genghis' men to dispose of his mortal remains in such an unceremonious fashion.

If there was no burial, how do we explain the legends about his tomb? One approach is to look at the parallels between these stories and other folklore. Great figures like Genghis Khan can quickly become more than historical personages and achieve mythic status. Alexander the Great's exploits, for instance, gave rise to a rich heritage of legend and folklore about him in all the lands he touched. The same is true of Genghis. The story of his burial bears a strong resemblance to that of the Sumerian hero Gilgamesh, who was interred in the bed of a temporarily diverted river. Folklore speaks of early Iron Age Celtic kings being similarly entombed. In this context it is more difficult to take Genghis' burial legend seriously.

Tomb raiders

Plenty of people, however, disagree, and since the 1990s there have been a number of serious attempts to find the lost tomb. Between 1993 and 1996 an extensive Japanese operation employed everything from satellite imagery and magnetometers to helicopter spotting, but came away empty-handed. Then in 2000 the ongoing Chinggis Khan Geo-Historical Expedition began (Chinggis is the spelling of Genghis preferred in Mongolia). This was a joint American–Mongolian venture, instigated and driven by a remarkable American character, Chicago gold-trader Maury Kravitz.

Kravitz has been obsessed with Genghis Khan since reading about him during his national service days. During the late 1990s he put together a board of academics and experts and struck an agreement with the Mongolian government to allow them to start excavations at sites linked to the early imperial era. The expedition's first discovery was the site of the Kurultai, or Great Convention, where Genghis was acclaimed Khan in 1206. Later they explored one of the mountains called Burkhan Khaldun, where some academics believe the tomb might be hidden (although it is uncertain which mountain). In 2001 they made their most exciting discovery: the Ölögchiin Kherem, or Almsgivers' Wall – also known as the Ulaan Khad (Red Rock), and, most suggestively, Chinggis' Wall.

The Kherem site

The Kherem or 'Wall' site – about 320 kilometres (200 miles) north-east of the Mongolian capital Ulan Bator, near the sites of Genghis' birth and coronation – is a 180-metre (600-foot) high hill encircled on three sides by a wall. The wall is 3 kilometres (2 miles) long and varies between 2.5 and 3.5 metres (9 and 12 feet) in height, although it is in a state of advanced disrepair, and the expedition experts insist that nothing like it has been seen in Mongolia before. Within the walled compound preliminary surveys revealed more than 40 graves, together with a roadway leading from the lower part of the apparent graveyard to the higher elevations, where the highest status burials are likely to be. Pottery found on the site dates it to the early imperial era, as does carbon dating on some of the skeletons. Kravitz and his team are convinced that one of them could be Genghis himself, and point to a nearby burial site containing a tomb said to belong to the 100 soldiers executed to preserve the secret of the Khan's final resting place. If they are right the other graves could be high-ranking Mongol officials/generals of Genghis' time, or even his descendants.

The Avraga Palace

In 2004 a rival Japanese–Mongolian expedition discovered the remains of what it claims was Genghis Khan's palace at Avraga. According to some reports, the team also found a mausoleum there and – on the basis of the ancient accounts of how officials would commute from the mausoleum to the nearby tomb – suggested that Genghis' tomb might be nearby. Pottery found at the palace site confirms the date, and the local topography reportedly matches contemporary accounts.

Genghis in China

To further confuse the issue, a Chinese report from 2000 claimed that Chinese archaeologists in the Xinjiang Uygur Autonomous Region had found the 'real' tomb of Genghis Khan between two lakes, not far from an above-ground mausoleum belonging to one of his grandsons.

Playing politics with Genghis Khan

So there are at least three groups claiming to be on the track of Genghis Khan's tomb, and at least four possible locations:

Burkhan Khaldun, where the Chinggis Khan Geo-Historical Expedition supposedly found the ruins of an old temple before being driven away by a plague of biting blackflies, Ölögchiin Kherem, Avraga Palace and the Chinese site.

The last of these can probably been dismissed. It has not been heard of since the isolated 2000 report, and such claims should probably be seen in their political context. The Chinese authorities are nervous of the prospect that Genghis' tomb will be found in Outer Mongolia and become a focus of Mongol nationalism, threatening their territorial claims in Inner Mongolia. By the same token they are keen to emphasise anything that validates their claim to be the true caretakers of Mongolian heritage – hence their recent plans to radically enlarge their ersatz mausoleum to Genghis Khan.

Politics are equally important in Outer Mongolia. In 2006 the country celebrated 800 years of Mongolian unity, dating from the coronation of the Khan. Genghis himself is a massively popular cult figure. Apart from holding artefacts that could be of great significance for the study and reputation of the early imperial era, the tomb might become a sort of national shrine and place of pilgrimage. On the other hand, there is considerable disquiet over the perception of the archaeologists as desecrators of sacred ground, going against the tradition of leaving material remains undisturbed, together with suspicion that they want to loot treasures that belong to the country. The Chinggis Khan Geo-Historical Expedition has already run into trouble, finding itself unceremoniously booted out of the country in 2002 following accusations by a former prime minister of Mongolia. Kravitz had to employ all his PR skills to get the Mongolians back on side, despite the fact that one of the expedition's founding principles is that any finds will belong to the indigenous government.

Looking for Genghis

At present the main focus of the hunt for Genghis' tomb remains the Kherem site. Kravitz's expedition returned again in the summer of 2006 for another season of exploration – at the time of going to press what they've found is unknown. But is this really the best place to look? While the Kherem burial ground may well be an important site, it does not tally with the legends of Genghis' entombment. The presence of at least 39 other graves would suggest that the site was far from secret, while the fact that none of the graves stands out as being of particular magnificence does not fit with expectations.

Kravitz himself has spoken of his personal belief that Genghis was buried on Burkhan Khaldun, his youthful mountain redoubt. Those who would beat the driven American to his life's goal might do well to identify which Burkhan Khaldun is the real one, and explore there. But be warned – this is difficult territory: dangerous mountains set in an isolated wilderness, plagued with maddening swarms of flies and, perhaps, protected by the curse of the Khan.

The Lost Colony of Roanoke

Sometime between 1587 and 1590 the population of the first English colony in the Americas vanished, almost without trace, leaving behind little but the cryptic message 'CROATOAN' carved onto a timber post. Four hundred years on, what has been called 'America's oldest mystery' remains an enigma, but the latest technology finally promises answers.

The first settlement in America

In the late 1500s Elizabethan England was greedy for a piece of the New World. The vast flow of treasure from her New World empire was making Spain, England's arch enemy, rich and power-ful, and the English were desperate to establish a strategic toehold in the new lands, together with the possibility of discovering lucrative new sources of mineral, agricultural and human wealth. In 1584 the queen's favourite, Sir Walter Raleigh, was awarded a licence to establish a colony. He promptly dispatched an expedi-tion to the newly claimed territory of Virginia. The good relations with the natives that were established and the favourable reports brought back induced him to dispatch a colonising party, and in 1585 the first English colony in America was established on Roanoke Island (now in North Carolina).

Raleigh's first colony, under the captaincy of Ralph Lane, did not fare well. They struggled to find enough food and soon fell out with neighbouring tribes. They waited impatiently for the return of their supply/relief fleet, and when Sir Francis Drake called in at the colony on his return from raiding the Spanish Caribbean in April 1586, they decided not to wait any longer and gratefully accepted his offer of a lift home. In fact they missed by only a short while the actual resupply fleet, under Sir Richard Grenville. Finding the colony abandoned, Grenville decided to return to England but left a force of 15 men to maintain England's – and Raleigh's – claim to the area.

The White colony

In 1587 a second group of colonists assembled by Raleigh stopped off at Roanoke Island to check on Grenville's men. A landing party came ashore and made a grisly discovery: the only traces of the 15 were the bones of a single man. The one local tribe of Native Americans who were still friendly – the Croatans from nearby Hatteras Island – later explained that the small group had been attacked and the nine survivors had sailed off up the coast in their pinnace (small boat), never to be seen again.

In fact the new colonists did not intend to re-establish the Roanoke colony and had their sights set on the mainland

Chesapeake Bay area (where the plan was to establish the 'Cittie of Raleigh'). But the commander of the ships that had brought them, Simon Fernandez, refused to take them any further, claiming that he would miss his window of favourable weather to make the return trip across the Atlantic (although it is more likely that he wanted more time to spend privateering, which was his true occupation).

The main body of colonists went ashore on 22 July. In all there were 91 men, 17 women and 9 children, under the leadership of John White, a friend of Raleigh's who had been the official artist on the original colonising expedition and would have been familiar with the area. They set to work rebuilding the colony. On 18 August, White's daughter gave birth to a girl, Virginia Dare, the first English child born in the Americas. But the tense relations with the natives, epitomised by the murder of a settler who was out gathering shellfish, prompted the colonists to elect to send Governor White back to England with Fernandez to petition for more support and supplies. He set sail on 28 August. White was never to see his family again.

The disappearance

White made every effort to get back to America as quickly as possible but was dogged by bad luck. War broke out with Spain and almost all available ships were requisitioned to protect England against the onslaught of the Armada. By the time White made it back to Roanoke, travelling with a small squadron of three ships under Captain Abraham Cooke, it was August 1590.

A landing party, including White (who recorded the episode in his journal), went ashore, '& sounded with a trumpet a Call, & afterwards many familiar English tunes of Songs, and called to them friendly,' but no response was forthcoming. At the north end of the island they found the site of the colony. The first sight that greeted White was an odd one. On a tree on a sandy bank were carved the letters 'CRO'. Further on they came to the remains of the actual settlement. A palisade of wooden timbers had been erected since his departure, but within it, all the houses had been taken down, and the only things left behind were some heavy lumps of lead, iron and iron ore. Carved onto one of the timbers of the palisade was the legend 'CROATOAN'.

In fact the apparently cryptic code reassured White greatly. As he explains in his own account, he had agreed with the settlers that the most sensible plan was not to stay on the island but to move, preferably '50 miles into the maine' (ie 80 kilometres/50 miles inland on the mainland). They had prearranged that if they were to move they would let White know where they had gone by making just such a carving as 'a secret token'. If they were in distress, they were to carve over the letters a Maltese (eight-pointed) cross – there was no such cross, so White assumed that the settlers were safe and had simply followed his instructions. Exploring further, White and his companions found that several chests buried on his departure were still there, although they had apparently been opened and many of the contents thrown around. This he interpreted as evidence that the colonists had taken whatever they needed and that the Native Americans had come along later and discarded items they did not understand. The boats that had been left with the colony were also absent.

White was confident that the inscriptions on the tree and timber indicated that the colonists had taken refuge with the friendly Native American tribe, the Croatans, on Hatteras Island. This was not exactly what they had agreed to on his departure, but it made perfect sense. The next day he and Captain Cooke agreed that they would make the short voyage to Hatteras Island, but fate and the elements intervened. Two of their cables (the lines attaching the ship to the anchor) broke and they narrowly avoided running aground, only for a hurricane to blow up. The ships were forced to abandon their attempt to reach Hatteras and had to return to England.

Rumours and sightings

Raleigh's patent to exploit the territory of Virginia lapsed in 1590, which may explain why he temporarily lost interest in organising further trips to America. White eventually had to reconcile himself to the fact that he would never see his family again. He retired to his estate at Killmore in Ireland. But it was generally assumed that the Roanoke colony, aka White's company, had survived and was still out there. Raleigh himself sponsored expeditions that were partly intended to look for them in 1602 and 1603, but both were sidetracked. Subsequent visitors and settlers in North America made repeated efforts to link up with them, in particular the settlers of the next, and more successful, attempt at a permanent colony, at Jamestown in Virginia. Indeed Lee Miller, author of *Roanoke: Solving the Mystery of the Lost Colony*, points out that many of the Jamestown colonists shared surnames with the 'Lost Colonists', and argues that they were probably relatives who were partly motivated by a desire to find their kin.

John Smith, leader of the new colony, heard stories from the Native Americans around Jamestown of other Europeans to the south, but neither he nor Christopher Newport, who was sent out from England in 1607 to help the Jamestowners and also specifically to look for White's company, were able to successfully investigate these tales. A 1609 expedition from Jamestown was similarly unlucky. Over the next few hundred years several visitors reported encountering or seeing people who looked or spoke English, or at least Native Americans who seemed to have Caucasian characteristics and a familiarity with English and Christianity, but no one was ever able to definitively claim that they had located the Lost Colonists. It seemed that 117 people had vanished, leaving a persistent mystery.

Theories about the Lost Colony

The most obvious explanation is that the Lost Colonists were never found because they were dead. They could have been killed by hostile Native Americans or starved to death. Both are plausible. The first attempt at colonising Roanoke Island failed to feed itself adequately, while the Jamestown colony 20 years later came perilously close to starvation. Perhaps the Lost Colonists simply ran out of food and were not familiar enough with local agricultural or foraging to cope. This explanation seems much more probable since the publication of a 1998 study on tree rings from old growth trees in the area. Conducted by the Tree-Ring Laboratory of the University of Arkansas' Department of Geography, the study showed that 1587–1590 saw the region's worst period of drought in the 800 years from 1185–1984.

If starvation had killed the colonists in Roanoke, however, White would probably have found the remains of the colonists on the site, and the colony itself would not have been carefully dismantled and stripped of most of its portable equipment. If the settlers did starve, they evidently didn't do it on Roanoke Island.

Hard times

The drought finding also increases the probability that the colonists came into conflict with their neighbours. At a time of extreme scarcity the indigenous peoples would have been less generous and more jealous of their scanty resources, and much more likely to take issue with newcomers attempting to take, steal or extort food, as the previous Roanoke colonists had tried to do. Although the Croatan Indians were friendly (when White left, at any rate), the other local tribes were not. This period also saw migrations and wars between Native American nations in the area, perhaps triggered or exacerbated by the drought.

The fact that the colonists had built a palisade in White's absence could be interpreted to mean that they felt threatened –

in fact we know they did, because this is one of the reasons White was sent back to England to drum up support. But such construction was probably routine for settlers, and again there was no evidence on site of battle or slaughter. It is conceivable that there was a siege scenario and the menfolk were picked off one by one as they ventured out of the palisade in an increasingly desperate search for food, eventually leaving only the women and children. They could have then been captured by the Native Americans and assimilated into the tribe, as was the custom, but there is no evidence to support this.

Going native

The most widely accepted explanation for the fate of the colonists is that they *were* killed by Native Americans, but only after leaving Roanoke Island. The primary source to back this up is Captain John Smith of the Jamestown colony. He had dealings with the hostile Native American King Powhatan (father of Pocahontas) and was specifically told by him that a group of white men had settled amongst friendly Chesapeake Indians on the south side of Chesapeake Bay – where they had originally intended to found the 'Cittie of Raleigh' before being dumped on Roanoke. Feeling increasingly threatened by the incursions of white men into his territories, and also hostile to the Chesapeake Indians who were not part of his confederacy, Powhatan had launched an attack and claimed to have killed most or all of the white men. He backed up his claim by producing for Smith's inspection 'a musket barrell and a brass mortar, and certain pieces of iron that had been theirs'.

This may not be the end of the story, however, as there is a lot of evidence that some colonists were assimilated into a Native American tribe in the Roanoke area, possibly because they did not join the group who went to Chesapeake Bay. The most probable candidates are the Croatan Indians. The colonists had good relations with them, and in particular with their chief, Manteo, who had previously travelled to England and become a firm ally of the English. Plus, of course, this location is suggested by the colonists' final message, 'CROATOAN'. It is now thought likely that some of the colonists stayed behind on Roanoke and later joined up with the Croatans on Hatteras Island, leaving the message for White to find, but that the collective was then forced to move to the mainland by the drought. The settlers and the Croatans then intermarried and eventually became known by a different name.

Some of the strongest evidence for this scenario is the tale of the Lumbee Indians of North Carolina. In the 19th century it was widely put about that the Lumbee were indeed descendants of the Lost Colony, and it was argued that their accents, appearance and many of their names clearly indicated this. Since then, this idea has gone in and out of fashion. Some anthropologists have argued that the 19th-century attribution was based on confused interpretation of the actual Lumbee ethnogenesis, which saw them migrate from the Roanoke area in the 18th century, and that Lumbee names do not resemble those of the Lost Colonists. More recently a DNA testing project has been launched to compare the Y chromosomes of Lumbee who share surnames with English people who might be descendants of the families who sent colonists to Roanoke. The whole issue is complicated by questions of race and segregation, for in the Lumbee area of North Carolina there was strict segregation until the Civil Rights era, and claiming mixed or white descent had important implications for personal and political treatment.

Other theories

This by no means exhausts the theories about the fate of the Lost Colony. The *Mary Celeste*-style disappearance of the colonists has lent itself to some whacky theories involving alien abduction. More plausible theories centre on the role the Spanish might have played. There was an established Spanish colony at

San Augustin (now St Augustine) in Florida, and they were keen to stamp out English presence in the New World. In fact they did just this to other attempted colonies.

It is now known that the Augustin colonists did hear about the Roanoke colony and that the Spanish did send out an expedition to reconnoitre and possibly destroy, but that when they arrived at Roanoke in June 1588, the colony was already gone. In other words it had survived *in situ* for less than a year.

In her book *Roanoke: Solving the Mystery of the Lost Colony*, Lee Miller argues that there is more behind the disappearance of the colonists than bad luck and poor planning. She asserts that the colony was deliberately sabotaged by Sir Francis Walsingham, chief of Elizabeth's intelligence network and Raleigh's enemy at court, who coveted the patent to exploit Virginia himself.

Miller claims that the account of a seaman who sailed with Fernandez's fleet carrying the White colonists, but was put ashore in the Caribbean before they reached North America, clearly shows that it was always Fernandez's intention to leave them on Roanoke and not transport them further to more promising regions. Supposedly he did this because he was in the pay of Walsingham, who had saved him from the gallows some years earlier. Miller further suggests that Walsingham also connived to block White and Raleigh's attempts to launch resupply/search expeditions.

The Dare Stones

In 1937 the story of the Lost Colony took an intriguing twist when a stone was found in a swamp, 100 kilometres (60 miles) west of Roanoke Island. The Eleanor Dare Stone, as it was soon dubbed, bore carvings which, when deciphered, seemed to indicate that it was a message from Eleanor Dare (daughter of John White and mother of Virginia Dare), explaining to her father that the colonists had fled from Roanoke Island under attack from Native Americans. Over the next three years 40 more stones were discovered, apparently tracing the colonists' epic journey from Carolina to Georgia. The stones created a media sensation but were revealed in 1940 to be an elaborate hoax.

Finding the relocated colonists

If the theory that at least some of the Lost Colonists joined up with the Croatan Indians and then moved to the mainland is correct, is it possible to discover the location of this new settlement and thus to finally say for sure what happened to the Lost Colonists? A team of researchers called the Lost Colony Center for Science and Research (LCCSR) think that it is. They have used a mixture of old and new techniques to attempt to locate and excavate the sites that the colonists might have occupied or passed through.

Their first major coup was identifying the site of the original Croatan settlement on what was then Hatteras Island. Excavations revealed a late-16th-century signet ring that probably, to judge from the design of the crest on the seal, belonged to one of the original Roanoke colonists (ie the Lane party). This proved that the Croatan Indians of this site had had contact with the Roanoke settlers at some point.

The researchers then turned to the hypothesis that the Lost Colonists and the Croatans joined up and moved inland, with a particular focus on John White's comment that the agreed plan had been to move '50 miles into the maine'. By looking at old land deeds they uncovered evidence that seemed to show that a group of descendants of Croatan Indians had owned land at a site called Gum Neck – precisely 80 kilometres (50 miles) inland from Roanoke Island, and one of the few sites suitable for settlement in an area that was previously swampy. The LCCSR now hopes to use aerial imaging and satellite photography to precisely locate the remains of a colonial-era settlement of some sort in or around Gum Neck.

Lost and found

For the moment the theories regarding the relocation of the Lost Colonists to Chesapeake Bay and mainland North Carolina are unproven. But they fit with the available evidence, and in particular with the suggestive tales of encounters with apparent European descendants in the area. Archaeological research, guided by remote-sensing technology such as airborne radar and magnetometer scanning, may eventually pinpoint the exact location, but not everyone is so keen to solve the mystery. Phil Evans – who helped to found the First Colony Foundation, a group of historians and archaeologists who are looking on Roanoke itself for the precise site of the Lost Colony, which has been lost through neglect and the shifting sands of the area – comments, 'As long as the Lost Colony is unexplained, it stays fascinating for a lot of people … I don't want to take away the mystery. That's what makes it different and exciting.'

On a less jolly note, however, there are suspicions about the motivations behind the effort to prove that the Lost Colonists intermarried with Native Americans and left descendants. In a racially fraught region it raises disturbing issues of ethnicity, and for some reflects a distasteful urge to create an artificial colonial–native legacy that might somehow undermine native claims. The Lost Colony is not simply a historical mystery; it is also the first act in the long and often tragic drama of colonial America.

Amelia Earhart's last flight

Her daring exploits made her a household name and a legend in her own lifetime, and subsequent generations have revered her as a feminist icon, but Amelia Earhart's fame was sealed not by success but by failure. On 2 July 1937, Earhart and her navigator

Fred Noonan went missing over the Pacific as they began the last leg of an attempted aerial circumnavigation of the world, engendering one of the 20th century's most enduring mysteries.

Electra down

Having already completed nearly three-quarters of their epic journey in a Lockheed L-10E Electra twin-engine plane, Earhart and Noonan set out from Lae, New Guinea, on 2 July at 0.00 AM to fly 4,113 kilometres (2,556 miles) to Howland Island, a tiny coral island in the Pacific that had been converted into a landing strip. They never arrived. American Coast Guard cutter *Itasca*, stationed at Howland to refuel the plane and also to act as a radio beacon to help guide her in, was able to pick up garbled transmissions from Earhart, but it was frustratingly obvious that she could neither hear them, nor find the island. The last known transmission came at 8.43 AM local time. It is now thought that conditions and a faulty chart conspired against Earhart and Noonan – the island was actually 10 kilometres (6 miles) further east than the position marked on their chart, while the rising sun and broken cloud cover casting island-like shadows on the water must have hindered their search.

Search at sea

Commander Thomson of the *Itasca* assumed the most obvious scenario – Earhart had run out of fuel and ditched somewhere around the location of her last transmission, to the north-west of Howland Island. He searched the area but found nothing. American naval officers reached a different conclusion after studying Earhart's last transmission. It read: 'We are on a line of position 157/337, will repeat this message, we will repeat this message on 6210 kcs [a different frequency]. Wait.' The 'line of position' is a line between two bearings (157° and 337°), which Earhart was following in a standard search tactic, and which Noonan had probably chosen because it gave them a chance of either finding Howland or, failing that, reaching islands to the south-east.

As Navy ships carrying planes steamed to the area to launch an air–sea search, garbled radio transmissions were picked up – they appeared to be from the lost aircraft. Encouraged by this evidence that Earhart had managed to land somewhere, the Navy focused its search on the area where some of the signals appeared to originate: the uninhabited Phoenix Islands to the south-east of Howland.

Over the next two weeks Navy planes criss-crossed the area but saw no evidence of life. One pilot reported what appeared to be 'signs of recent habitation' on Gardner Island, one of the Phoenix Islands, but although he buzzed the island several times no one made themselves known and there was no trace of air-craft or wreckage. The search widened to include the Gilbert Islands, a populated group that Earhart had flown over on her way to Howland, on the assumption that she might have tried to reverse her course. But there was no sign of the missing plane or aviators, and on 18 July the search was called off. The official verdict: Earhart had ditched at sea and the Electra had sunk without a trace, carrying pilot and navigator to a watery grave.

Conspiracy corner

Earhart's loss was a national tragedy and an international news phenomenon. Foreshadowing the suspicions that later sur-rounded the death of Princess Diana, it also quickly gave rise to a clutch of conspiracy theories. An Australian tabloid newspaper alleged that the American Navy had used the search for Earhart as a pretext to overfly the Marshall Islands, a Japanese mandate zone where it was suspected they were illegally building military bases. Later this theory inspired a successful 1943 movie, *Flight For Freedom*, starring Rosalind Russell and Fred MacMurray, in which the Earhart character was in on the plot, with her trans-Pacific flight merely a cover for her secret espionage work.

Flight For Freedom helped to fix in the popular imagination the suggestion that Earhart's disappearance was more than a simple accident. As soon as it was released, rumours began to surface that Earhart genuinely had been co-opted by the American government to alter her flight plans. The rumours and allegations culminated in a bestselling 1966 book, *The Search For Amelia Earhart* by Fred Goerner, in which it was sensationally alleged that she had crash-landed in the Marshalls and fallen into Japanese custody, meeting her death as a prisoner. It was further claimed that the incident had been covered up by America to prevent public outrage at the government's role in putting America's sweetheart in harm's way. Subsequent books and theories went even further, claiming that Earhart had been smuggled back to America to live out her days in anonymity, and that she was alive and well and living as one Irene Bolam in New Jersey, where she died in 1982.

Debunking the conspiracy

Evidence for these extraordinary theories included the apparent post-crash radio transmissions from various parts of the Pacific, photos alleged to be of Earhart and Noonan in captivity, reports from people who claimed to have seen the pair in custody, and the 'fact' that the American government still has classified documents relating to Earhart, which it refuses to release. Little of this evidence holds water. Analysis of the transmissions suggests that most of them were hoaxes or never happened (with one important possible exception – see page 195), that the photos were either taken before Earhart and Noonan set off from New Guinea, or were actually from *Flight For Freedom*, and that the reports of sightings could not be substantiated. The classified records are a myth, and never existed. It is now thought likely that the 1943 movie itself is the likely source for most of the rumours. Nonetheless, the theory has been taken seriously enough for two claims to be extensively investigated by archaeologists.

Digging on Tinian and Saipan

World War II soldier Saint John Naftel was in charge of a group of formerly captive workers on the Pacific island of Tinian, shortly after its liberation from Japanese occupation in 1944. He says that one of the workers showed him two graves, which he claimed were the last resting place of Amelia Earhart and her navigator Noonan. In 2004 Naftel attempted to point out the spot to a team of archaeologists and historians, but extensive excavations failed to reveal any bones or other evidence.

Another claim was that Earhart had been held captive on the island of Saipan. According to a BBC News report of March 2005, a French consul had wired the US Department of State in 1937 to inform them that she was on Saipan. Supposedly local rumour says that Earhart had been held captive in a Japanese jail, and that later she had died and been cremated behind the jail. In 2005 a permit was granted to excavate the site of the jail, but nothing was found.

Looking for Amelia

For serious Earhart researchers the conspiracy theories are simply a diversion from the two most likely scenarios: that Earhart ditched in the open ocean, in which case the wreck of the Electra may still be resting on the seabed, or that she made it to one of the Phoenix Islands but was never rescued and died there. Both theories have been the subject of recent expeditions.

The Nauticos hunt

The most straightforward explanation for Earhart's disappearance is the original one formulated by the captain of the Coast Guard cutter. Howland Island was at the limit of the Electra's range, and after circling for hours in a fruitless search for the island Earhart and Noonan must have run out of fuel and ditched the plane, hoping to make it out in one piece in their life raft and get rescued. Either they didn't survive the open water landing, or they perished in their life raft – either way, the wreck of the plane might still be intact on the sea bottom, 5 kilometres (3 miles) down.

This is the theory of the Nauticos Corporation, experienced deep-sea search and recovery experts, who believe that conditions on the floor of the Pacific could have preserved any remains remarkably well. According to Nauticos President, David Jourdan, 'The deep ocean is a very preserving environment. There are no currents or tides at that depth, and no human interactions that could have degraded what's there. Biological remains would have disintegrated quickly, but metals survive. We expect the plane to look pretty much like it did when it went down.'

In 2002 a Nauticos exploration vessel equipped with sophisticated seabed imaging equipment scanned 2,160 square kilometres (834 square miles) of an area near Howland Island pinpointed as the most promising spot by detailed study of Earhart's final radio transmissions. Unfortunately a blown hydraulic hose meant that they almost lost several millions worth of scanning equipment and the expedition was aborted two-thirds of the way through, having failed to find any sign of the downed aircraft. Although Nauticos claims to remain optimistic about its prospects, it is noteworthy that a planned 2004 follow-up expedition never took place.

Castaways

Perhaps the most convincing explanation of Earhart and Noonan's fate is the one advanced by The International Group for Historical Aircraft Recovery (TIGHAR). Their detailed research and analysis have led them to conduct extensive exploration and excavation on the tiny Pacific island of Nikumaroro, formerly known as Gardner Island. Previously it was thought that the Electra did not have enough fuel to make it this far, but TIGHAR have discovered that the plane was fitted with extra fuel tanks that would have allowed Earhart and Noonan several more hours in the air than formerly believed. Assuming that they were proceeding south-east on the 337° bearing Earhart reported in her last transmission, they could easily have reached Nikumaroro, which was within visual range of this course.

The TIGHAR hypothesis is that Earhart would have been able to put the plane down on a flat stretch of coral visible at low tide, where a ship, the SS *Norwich*, had run aground in 1929. Once landed, the aviators could have run the engines long enough to charge their batteries and send a last transmission, before the tide and high seas swamped the plane. This would account for the anomalous transmission, described as unintelligible but sounding like Earhart's voice, picked up by operators on the island of Nauru on the evening of 2 July 1937, on the same frequency that Earhart had previously said she would switch to.

With the plane swamped or swept away entirely, Earhart and Noonan would now have been castaways on a desert island. While a cursory search would have revealed a stash of supplies left there by the team that came to salvage the *Norwich* eight years earlier, lack of water and the manifold other perils of being marooned on a desert island – from disease and injury to storms and exposure – must eventually have done for the stranded aviators, especially once the overflying naval search planes had failed to spot the wreckage of the Electra (possibly because at high tide it was not visible/distinguishable from the wreck of the *Norwich*). What is not clear is why they did not make themselves known to the search flights, but there are many possible explanations (perhaps they were too weak or simply couldn't be seen through the thick island vegetation).

TIGHAR have accumulated an impressive array of circumstantial and suggestive evidence to back up their theory. In 1938 there was an attempt to colonise the island and the colonists reported finding evidence that someone had previously camped out on the island, and even claimed to have found a set of human bones, a sextant case and the sole of a woman's shoe. Excavation on the island itself has revealed evidence of aeroplane parts that had been scavenged and recycled as tools. Many of these undoubtedly came from other aircraft and were the work of the colonists or later visitors, but some may well be from Earhart's plane. In particular, TIGHAR have recovered fragments of dados – metal panels that were used in the cabin to conceal and protect wiring. These were not used in military craft, but *do* match ones believed to have been fitted in the Electra.

So far the definitive evidence that would finally confirm the TIGHAR theory has been elusive. Divers have searched the reef and the shoreline for wreckage that can be matched to the Electra but have yet to find it, while the dados and other artefacts cannot be linked to Earhart for certain. A search of colonial records appears to confirm the tale about finding the human bones, and the description of the remains recorded at the time matches what would be expected of a Caucasian female of Earhart's size, but so far efforts to find the bones themselves have not been successful. TIGHAR hope that if they do uncover them, DNA could be extracted for comparison with Earhart's living relatives.

Into the wide blue yonder

Lonely starvation on a desert island seems like a sad end for a figure as celebrated and admired as Amelia Earhart. Many people will not want to believe the TIGHAR theory even if they manage to prove it, and romantic notions of espionage and conspiracy will probably cling to Earhart's name for as long as she is remembered. Perhaps the most fitting outcome would be if the Nauticos theory proved to be correct, for it is probable that only the shell of the aeroplane would remain, with no corporeal remnants to bring Earhart's memory down to earth.

5

❧
Lost Wrecks
❧

Travelling the high seas has always been a risky business, and the sea floor is littered with wrecks to prove it. Very few of them have been located and identified, meaning that the vast majority remain 'lost' – undiscovered and unexplored. In fact United Nations Educational, Scientific and Cultural Organization (UNESCO) estimates that there are more than 3 million undiscovered wrecks on the world's ocean floors. Many of these ships carried cargo of importance and/or value. Many of them are themselves of historical or archaeological significance. This makes lost wrecks the most numerous category of lost things, and their pursuit can be the most lucrative of pastimes. Recovered cargo can be worth tens or even hundreds of millions. Perhaps the most famous example is the salvage of the *Nuestra Señora de Atocha*, a wrecked Spanish treasure galleon discovered by Mel Fisher in 1985, which eventually netted him around $400 million in recovered gold, silver, gems and jewellery.

Tracking down a lost wreck can be extremely difficult. Only relatively recently have ships been equipped to pinpoint and relay their exact position as they are going down, and they are often wrecked because of bad weather, which means they may not be where they are supposed to be. Once beneath the waves a ship can become as untraceable as if it were on the moon, particularly if sunk in deep water where only the most advanced technology can venture.

But this picture is changing with the increasing availability of underwater technology, especially new imaging techniques such as side-scan sonar, which can present a detailed three-dimensional picture of swathes of the sea bottom, or magnetometers, which can scan large areas for magnetic anomalies that may represent metal from wrecks. Advances in remotely operated vehicle (ROV) technology, which have made remote control mini-submarines cheaper and better, also mean that it is now much easier to explore potential sites, even in deep water. These technologies are becoming widespread enough to worry UNESCO, which in 2001 launched a new convention aimed at protecting wrecks from looters. It seems that lost wrecks are in increasing danger of being found.

However, all the technology in the world cannot overcome the greatest obstacle to the discovery of lost wrecks. The undersea environment can be extremely destructive, and for many wrecks there is only a slim chance that anything of note will survive. Metal rusts and is corroded, and wood is quickly consumed by a plethora of organisms, from corals and boring worms to bacteria. On the other hand, the undersea environment can also be uniquely preservative; if a ship is covered in silt it shuts out oxygen and thus reduces corrosion and consumption to a minimum, or if it sinks in particularly cold waters the biological breakdown processes are slowed or absent.

This chapter looks at four lost wrecks or groups of wrecks that span a vast range of history and geography, and which have so far defied the efforts of both looters and scholars. Whether they have survived the attentions of chemical and biological agents is another matter, but in each case marine archaeologists desperately hope so, as each is of massive historical significance.

The Persian invasion fleets

The ancient world was characterised by a number of epic struggles between mighty civilisations; Egypt vs Nubia, Rome vs Carthage, Greece vs Persia. The last of these had a major impact on the subsequent course of Western history, as the eventual victory of the Greeks allowed them to maintain their independence for another 300 years, during which time Greek culture and science flowered into the period now known as the Golden Age, helping to determine the shape of subsequent Western culture and thought.

Among the key incidents in the history of the conflict between the Persian Empire and the Greek city-states it sought to subdue were the disastrous fates that befell enormous Persian fleets no less than three times. According to ancient sources literally hundreds of ships and thousands of men sank to the bottom of the Aegean, where high rates of deposition of protective silt may well have preserved them for two-and-half millennia, offering a treasure trove of unparalleled archaeological significance to anyone who can locate them.

Darius and Xerxes

In the 5th century BCE the Persian Empire had conquered most of the known world and incorporated lands from the Himalayas to the Balkans, from the Upper Nile to the shores of the Caspian. Under the Persian aegis fell several of the Greek city-states of Asia Minor (modern-day Turkey), while the actions and attitude of the independent states of the Greek mainland irked the Persian emperors. Greek states such as Athens and Eretria had meddled in the affairs of Asia Minor, fomenting rebellions against the Persian overlords, and Darius the Great, emperor of Persia, determined to punish them. In 492 BCE he dispatched an army under his general and son-in-law Mardonius.

The sea monsters of Athos

Mardonius crossed the Hellespont that separated Asia Minor from Europe and marched down the Aegean coast of Greece, accompanied by a mighty fleet to offer naval and logistical support. The fleet sailed across the Aegean to the mainland and followed the coast down to Acanthus. To progress further it needed to detour around the peninsula of Mount Athos, which jutted out into the sea. According to Herodotus, whose *Histories* are the primary source for the Greco–Persian war, as the fleet 'made to double Mount Athos':

> A violent North wind sprang up, against which nothing could contend, and handled a large number of the ships with much rudeness, shattering them and driving them aground upon Athos. It is said that the number of the ships destroyed was little short of 300; and the men who perished were more than 20,000. For the sea about Athos abounds in monsters beyond all others; and so a portion were seized and devoured by these animals, while others were dashed violently against the rocks; some, who did not know how to swim, were engulfed; and some died of the cold.

Without naval support Mardonius was forced to turn back and the invasion was postponed for two years. The Persian's second invasion, in 490 BCE, was no more successful, and before he could plan a third attempt Darius died. It was left to his successor Xerxes to punish the upstart Greek states.

The greatest force the world had ever seen

By 480 BCE Xerxes had gathered what was probably the largest army in human history up to that point. It was said that he wept upon witnessing the serried ranks, overcome by the thought that within a few decades so many men would no longer be alive. The ancient estimates are probably wildly exaggerated – one speaks of the total land and sea forces numbering 2,641,610 men, accompanied by the same number of camp followers and hangers-on, giving more than 5 million people. Modern scholars scoff at these estimates, and it is widely assumed that they are out by a factor of ten. Nonetheless, Xerxes' army was unprecedented in scale and diversity, comprising warriors from 46 different nations, including many Greek states and colonies that were inimical to the mainland alliance of Athens and Sparta, which led the Greek resistance.

Accompanying the army was a vast fleet, said to number 1,207 triremes (battle galleys propelled by three rows of oars) and countless smaller support, troop transport and cargo vessels. The ships were drawn from Phoenicia, Egypt, Cyprus and Asia Minor, including many of the Greek states under Persian control, and therefore represented a unique cross-section of naval technology and design of the period.

The Magnesian disaster and the Hollows of Euboea

Determined to take no chances with the treacherous waters off Mount Athos, Xerxes had had a canal dug across the isthmus that separated the mountain from the mainland. He had decreed that it should be wide enough to admit two galleys abreast, and the work took two years. Ultimately this extravagant gesture was to little avail – although the fleet successfully negotiated the Athos peninsula, large numbers of ships were lost in two massive storms.

One struck the fleet as it was anchored off the coast of Magnesia in an unfavourable location where there was room for only a few ships in the relative safety of the bay, forcing the others to moor in rows eight deep, which left the outermost ships stuck far out to sea. When a fierce east wind blew up in the morning, only a few of the ships could be dragged up to safety on the beach. According to Herodotus, the ships caught in the open sea were exposed to the gale and dashed against the rocks and coast at Pelion, Cape Sepias, Meliboea and Casthanaea.

The Greeks put this stroke of good fortune (from their point of view) down to the intercession of Boreas, god of the north wind. Divine providence or not, the disaster cost the Persians both ships and loot. Herodotus tells us:

> The most conservative estimate of how many ships were lost in this disaster is 400, along with innumerable personnel, and so much valuable property that a Magnesian called Ameinocles the son of Cretines, who owned land near Sepias, profited immensely from this naval catastrophe. In the following days and months gold and silver cups were washed ashore in large numbers for him to pick up; he also found Persian treasure-chests, and in general became immensely wealthy.

While the main body of the fleet was suffering off the Magnesian coast, a detached squadron of 200 ships was attempting to round Euboea to outflank the Greek fleet. They too suffered from the storm. According to Herodotus the high winds smashed the ships against the shoreline known as the 'Hollows of Euboea', and all 200 of the galleys were lost.

In practice neither of these disasters made too much of a dent in the Persian fleet, vast as it was, but they helped to prevent it from gaining a tactical advantage over the outnumbered Greek navy, which got the better of subsequent naval engagements, including a battle in the Artemision Channel in which many Persian galleys were destroyed. These naval victories halted the Persian advance and effectively ended Xerxes' hopes of a swift and crushing victory in the war as a whole. Without naval support, Xerxes felt compelled to pull the bulk of his forces out of the Balkans, leaving Mardonius to pursue the war, which proved beyond him. Eventually the Persians were forced out of Greece forever.

Aegean treasure

Even if Herodotus was exaggerating the numbers of galleys and men involved and the numbers lost during the Persian invasions, the potential value of the wrecked fleets could be huge. There could be the remains of hundreds of ships, thousands of men and huge quantities of weapons, armour, stores and supplies and loot of all types resting at the bottom of the Aegean. All of it dates back 2,500 years to a period about which there is scant archaeological evidence, at least for ships and naval technology. The size and diversity of the Persian invasion forces mean that the remains would offer a unique picture of peoples and military and naval technology, not just from Persia and Greece but from across the ancient world. For the acquisitive there is also the promise of large quantities of precious objects and precious metals, like the 'gold and silver cups ... and Persian treasure chests' mentioned by Herodotus.

The ultimate prize for archaeologists, however, would be the discovery of the wreck of a trireme, the large galleys that constituted ships of the line for ancient navies. No trireme has ever been found, and historians are still in the dark about many aspects of this potent ancient naval technology. When a replica trireme was constructed, for instance, it was found that it could not match the performance capabilities ascribed to ancient galleys, which were much faster than modern experts are able to explain. Finding one of 1,000+ plus sunken galleys of the Persian invasion fleets could help to resolve decades of academic disputes. According to Dr Robert Hohlfelder, a maritime archaeologist at the University of Colorado, Boulder: 'Underwater archaeologists have wish lists. A trireme is certainly one of the top ones on most people's lists. And I think this [the waters off Mount Athos] is one of the best places to look for them.'

However, there are reasons why trireme remains have proved so elusive. Since ancient galleys did not use ballast, they did not sink when wrecked but floated on the surface. Ancient sources record how they were salvaged simply by being towed back to land, where they were either repaired or recycled for other purposes. Cargo would sometimes act as ballast, dragging a ship to the bottom, which is why ancient cargo ships have been recovered, but triremes were war galleys and hence did not carry heavy cargoes in their hold. The heaviest part of the trireme was probably the bronze ram on the prow that was used to smash enemy ships, and these may be lying on the bottom of the Aegean awaiting recovery, along with metal arms and armour carried by those on board.

Preserved in the deep

The Mediterranean is one of the most intensively exploited seas in the world, and has been so for millennia. This applies to treasure hunting and looting of wrecks, and there is considerable concern that many of the best/most accessible ancient wrecks have already been stripped of anything valuable, damaging and rendering them useless for archaeology in the process. Similarly, the prevalence of dragnet trawling, where fishermen drag heavily weighted booms with attached nets along the bottom of the sea, destroying everything in their path, has probably damaged or obliterated many ancient wrecks.

But the experts hope that the context of the Persian fleet wrecks may have preserved them from the looters. The fleets came to grief in deep water, especially the biggest potential wreck focus, off Mount Athos, where the sea bottom drops sharply to depths of 600 metres (2,000 feet) or more. This area is also quite remote, which should have helped to protect it from looters. An additional benefit is that silt is deposited quite fast in the Aegean, so that any remains may have been rapidly covered in a layer of preserving and protective silt.

Looking for the Persian fleets

In recent years the story of the Persian fleets has gained a new profile thanks to a concerted international effort to locate and study the wrecks, an effort made possible by new technology. The Persian Wars Shipwreck Survey (PWSS) – a joint programme by the Greek Ephorate of Underwater Antiquities, the Hellenic Centre for Marine Research and the Canadian Archaeological Institute at Athens, together with various other academics and institutions – uses side-scan sonar, mini-submarines and sub-marine remote-operated vehicles (ROVs) to map and explore the locations described by Herodotus.

In its three seasons of exploration so far the PWSS has explored the waters off the Mount Athos peninsula, the Hollows of Euboea (off the coast of southern Euboea) and the Artemision Channel, site of a major naval battle. The results have not been breathtaking. So far one of the main discoveries has been the location of the wreck of a cargo ship off Mount Athos, which was carrying amphorae identified as being from Mende, a Greek city to the west of Mount Athos. This could mean that the ship had nothing to do with Darius' fleet (it could date from up to a century earlier), or it could have been a supply ship carrying material requisitioned by the Persian invaders.

The headline discovery, however, has been attributed to the help of an octopus, likened to one of Herodotus' 'monsters beyond all others'. Alerted to the fact that local fishermen hauling in their catch had chanced upon two bronze helmets from the classical period (500–323 BCE), the PWSS crew searched in the same area and spotted a large jar on the seabed. The jar was home to an octopus, a creature renowned for occasionally retrieving sunken objects and squirreling them away in its lair. Sure enough, the octopoid loot proved to include a bronze *sauroter* – a pointed spear butt or butt-spike that fitted onto the end of a Greek hoplite's (infantryman) spear, allowing it to be stuck into the ground and also making it a double-ended weapon. Finding the weapon accessory where two pieces of armour have also been recovered has strengthened belief that the wrecks of the Persian fleet (which included many Greek soldiers from the vassal states in Asia Minor, as well as from Greek states inimical to Athens and Sparta) *do* lie in the area.

The PWSS team has had less luck in the waters around Euboea, but it plans to return in 2006 to continue mapping the sea floor and looking for promising targets to investigate using its submersibles. It also warns, however, that academics are not the only ones equipped with such technology. Katerina Dellaporta, director of underwater antiquities for Greece and one of the survey's leaders, has warned, 'Before, looters would only do scuba diving. But now, the technology [such as ROVs] allows everybody to have access to deeper waters.' While the assertion that 'everybody' might get access to deep water is perhaps an overstatement (buying and operating an ROV costs tens–hundreds of thousands), it is to be hoped that archaeologists and not looters are the first to locate the lost wrecks of the great fleets of Darius and Xerxes.

The *White Ship*

The year 1120 saw one of the most significant shipwrecks in English history; a tragedy that cost the lives of the flower of English nobility and would eventually plunge the nation into two decades of chaos and misrule – a period that has become known as The Anarchy. The heir to the throne of England and hundreds of scions of noble families perished when the *White Ship*, one of the most advanced vessels of the time, was lost with all hands. Its wreck and the potentially priceless cargo (in terms of historical and material value) it carried have never been located.

Between two kingdoms

Following the Norman Conquest of 1066, England was ruled by the dukes of Normandy. As overlords of two lands divided by the English Channel, it was routine for the Norman kings of England to shuttle back and forth between their dominions as they sought to preserve their territories on the Continent and in Britain. In 1120, Henry I, third of the Norman kings of England and youngest son of William the Conqueror, had been forced to travel to Normandy to confront the King of France, Louis VI. Accompanying him was his heir and only legitimate son, 17-year-old William Adelin. 'Adelin' is a latter-day rendering of 'Atheling' (the Saxon term for king) – he was named William the Atheling to show how the royal houses of the Saxons and Normans were unified in his person.

Henry had successfully resolved his dispute with Louis, gaining recognition for his son as the de facto Duke of Normandy, and was returning to England via the Norman port of Barfleur, from where his father had embarked for the invasion of England less than 60 years previously. The mood of the party was festive, especially since young William was habitually accompanied by a kind of 'youth court' – a youthful mirror version of his father's court, which included many of the most important heirs and offspring of the noble houses of England and Normandy. With the party were his own half-brother and sister – Henry I was the most prolific father of illegitimate children in the history of the English monarchy. Despite this, William was his only legitimate son (one of only two legitimate children), and was therefore absolutely central to Henry's dynastic ambitions.

Le *Blanche Nef*

On 25 November Henry was preparing to embark at Barfleur when he was approached by Thomas FitzStephen, master of the

Blanche Nef, or *White Ship*, a fine new vessel of the highest specifications. FitzStephen's father Airard had captained the *Mora*, the flagship of William the Conqueror's invasion fleet, and now he himself begged William's son for the honour of bearing him across the Channel in his splendid ship. Henry declined, as his own travel arrangements were already well in hand, but suggested that FitzStephen could carry his son, William Adelin, and his company. Henry boarded his own ship and departed not long afterwards, safely making the passage back to England.

Meanwhile William and his companions were feasting and drinking prodigiously, and their own departure was delayed while all the available casks of wine in port were loaded onto the *White Ship*. Once aboard, the partying continued, with the captain and crew apparently joining in. The company grew so inebriated that when a party of clerics led by the Bishop of Coutance arrived they were driven off with howls of derision. At least one of the passengers disembarked at this time: Stephen of Blois – possibly as a result of an attack of diarrhoea, or possibly because of an attack of common sense given the carryings on. It was a decision that would have fateful consequences.

Disaster strikes

By the time the *White Ship* was ready to depart everyone aboard was roaring drunk and night had fallen. On board were around 300 people, including 140 noblemen and at least 18 noblewomen. In relative terms, the Channel crossing was not especially dangerous – Henry had done it many times, while his father had made the crossing 17 times as king. But in the 12th century naval technology was still crude, and any sea journey was dangerous, particularly with a drunken crew, captain and pilot. To make matters worse, young William was keen to catch up with his father and get home first, and insisted that FitzStephen take the quickest route home.

This was to prove fatal. The correct route to take out of Barfleur harbour was to the south, avoiding dangerous shoals, after which the vessel would swing north towards England. The ship's drunken pilot tried to cut corners by heading directly north, but succeeded only in driving the ship onto a rock called the Quilleboeuf, about 2.4 kilometres (1.5 miles) out of the harbour.

The ship began to sink, but all was not lost for William. He was quickly hustled aboard the only 'lifeboat', but as he was rowed to safety he heard the piteous cries of his half-sister, Matilda, Countess of Peche, imploring him not to abandon her. William ordered the boat to turn back, but as it neared the sinking ship it was overwhelmed by the number of people who tried to climb aboard and it too was lost.

This at least was the tale told by a butcher of Rouen named Berthold, who had only gone aboard to chase up a debt. He clung to one of the masts that projected above the waves, and was rescued the next morning. He was the sole survivor: few people of that era could swim, and in the dark, amidst the waves and strong currents, a watery grave was inevitable. When the news reached England none of the barons or high officers of the court dared to tell the king; it was left to a child to tell him the terrible tidings. It is said that he fainted away, and that he never smiled again.

The lost generation

The impact on the world of power politics in north-western Europe must have been tremendous, not to mention the personal toll on bereaved parents. The feeling that might have been prevalent is well captured by Winston Churchill in his account of the disaster in *A History of the English Speaking People*:

> Two men remained afloat, the ship's butcher and a knight. 'Where is the Prince?' asked the knight above the waves. 'All

are drowned,' replied the butcher. 'Then,' said the knight, 'all is lost for England,' and threw up his hands [thereby casting himself into the waves].

The disaster has been likened to the sinking of the *Titanic*, which carried many rich and important people and had a colossal impact on Edwardian Britain. A more modern parallel might be the Thames' *Marchioness* disaster of 1989.

For 12th-century England the sinking of the *White Ship* was to have grim consequences. Despite his extra-marital fecundity, Henry was unable to produce another legitimate male heir. Although he forced his barons to swear allegiance to his legitimate daughter, also called Matilda, the idea of a female ruler simply would not wash with the medieval mindset. When Henry died in 1135 most of the English barons promptly ignored their oaths and acclaimed Stephen of Blois, Matilda's cousin and the same man who had so fortuitously stepped off the *White Ship* before it sailed to disaster, as king. Matilda was able to rally some support and attempted to reclaim the crown, plunging the country into nearly 20 years of civil war. It was a lawless and unstable time, when, in the memorable words of the contemporary *Peterborough Chronicle*, 'Crist and alle his sayntes slept.'

12th-century treasure trove

The wreck of the *White Ship* represents a potential gold mine of archaeological and material significance. William Adelin and his party would have been richly caparisoned and loaded with jewels. He would probably have been accompanied by a considerable treasury of plates, goblets and other loot. Discovering this today would amount to a unique record of courtly life in the early 12th century. The ship itself would also be of tremendous importance. As the cutting edge of naval technology it could reveal fascinating insights into the evolution of ship-building, from the longships used by William the Conqueror to the medieval galleons with their high fore and rear castles.

The real issue, however, is whether there might be anything of the wreck or its contents left. Some, if not most, of the treasure aboard was probably salvaged at the time. The strong currents and tides in the area may well have washed away much of the rest. It is known, for instance, that many of the bodies were swept away to be cast ashore along the coast of Normandy for weeks afterwards. Possibly the same forces may have done considerable damage to the wreck, while shipworms and other aquatic organisms would have reduced the wooden parts of the ship unless it was quickly covered in preserving silt.

In other words, the prospects for significant salvage are not great, but the potential archaeological interest makes even a slim chance worth pursuing. Despite this, and despite the apparent agreement of all sources that it is known where the ship was wrecked, there is no record of anyone having mounted a search or exploratory dive. The local conditions would make such an undertaking difficult and perhaps dangerous, but with modern technology such as side-scan sonar and ROVs it is worth at least a preliminary investigation. Perhaps, lying in a sandy hollow beneath a sheltering rock, the bejewelled bones of William Adelin himself await discovery.

Treasure galleons of the 1715 plate fleet

On 7 June 1494 Pope Alexander VI divided the New World between the Portuguese and the Spanish, setting under Spanish control all of the Americas west of Brazil and all of the East Indies to boot. This huge territory soon began to yield incalculable wealth, as all the treasures of empire flowed towards Spain. From the East Indies came spices, silks, woods, ivory and Chinese porcelain, for which there was an insatiable demand in Europe, and from the Americas came gold, silver and precious stones. Transporting this loot back to Spain proved difficult, and Spanish ships had to contend with everything from scurvy, crude navigational technology, vast blank spaces on the map, pirates, the privateers and navies of enemy nations and, above all, the unpredictable weather. At the same time, the Spanish government was desperate to impose tight controls on the massive trade between Europe and the colonies – to ensure that Spain alone reaped the benefits, that the government could extract taxes, including the monarchy's 20 per cent tithe, aka the *quinto*, and to preserve the jealously guarded monopolies issued to trading ports such as Seville.

The treasure fleets

The system adopted to meet these ends was the *flota*, or fleet system. It was decreed by law that all trade between the Americas and Spain should be restricted to a bi-annual fleet, which would carry manufactured goods from Spain to the New World, and the plundered resources of the colonies back the other way. These transatlantic fleets became known as treasure fleets because of the vast quantities of precious metals and stones they carried, and later the plate fleets, because of the Chinese porcelain (including plates) they carried. The porcelain arrived in the New World via the complementary Manila galleons system, whereby one or two (massive) galleons from the East Indies would cross the northern Pacific carrying porcelain, spices, wood, silk and other goods, and deliver their cargoes to the west coast of Mexico, where they were carried by mule train to Veracruz on the east coast, for trans-shipment to Spain.

The quantities of treasure and valuable cargo carried on these Spanish galleons were astonishing. The main precious metal was silver from the South American silver mines, but there were also prodigious quantities of gold, gems and finely crafted jewellery made by artisans in both the Far East and the New World.

Thousands of kilograms of silver and hundreds of kilograms of gold might be carried, with cargoes worth several millions. Because the modern value of such items is magnified by their historical worth, the present-day value of a typical Spanish treasure ship cargo might be measured in hundreds of millions of pounds or dollars.

Sinking feeling

Despite the hazards of trans-oceanic travel the treasure fleets had a pretty good record. The Manila galleons had the most perilous crossing, with about 40 going down over the 250 years that this system ran. The transatlantic plate fleet had a better record, despite being the prime target for greedy pirates, privateers and navies for two-and-a-half centuries. Because the fleets banded together and were protected by heavily armed galleons they were generally too much for their enemies to tackle. The weather was a much more serious threat, and it was particularly imperative for the fleet to make its return trip from the Caribbean to Spain before the onset of the hurricane season. The three biggest disasters for the plate fleet were caused by hurricanes, which in 1622, 1715 and 1733 wiped out entire fleets.

The 1715 fleet

The plate fleet of 1715 was one of the richest ever, owing to a unique set of circumstances. From 1701 until 1714 the War of the Spanish Succession had pitted Spain against other European powers – a state of war that extended to the high seas and made it dangerous for the fleet to attempt the crossing for fear of interception by an entire enemy fleet. For the previous two years the plate fleets had been kept in port, so that vast quantities of treasure had 'backed up' in the New World.

The usual practice was for two treasure fleets to be sent to different parts of the Caribbean. The *Nueva España flota* would sail to Veracruz in Mexico (aka Nueva España), while the *Tierra*

Firme flota would visit South American ports, of which Cartagena was the main stop. The two would load up and then rendezvous at Havana to sail back across the Atlantic in one armada, in good time to miss the hurricanes.

Held up in Havana

1715 was supposed to be no different. Captain General Don Antonio de Echeverz y Zubiza, in command of the Cartagena fleet, arrived in Havana on schedule, his ships groaning with an amazing fortune of Bolivian silver and gold coins, chests of Colombian emeralds and sacks of finely worked Peruvian jewellery. By mid-March he was ready to sail, but his superior, Captain General Don Juan Esteban de Ubilla, was late. The *Nueva España flota* was still moored at Veracruz, awaiting tardy mule-train shipments from the Pacific coast, bearing the booty delivered by two years of Manila galleon traffic. In the meantime Ubilla lined his holds with staggering quantities of gold bullion and silver ingots and coins. Finally the mule-train arrived and disgorged its bounty of silk, spices, ivory, hardwoods, indigo dye and precious porcelain. Ubilla finally arrived in Havana in mid-May.

To his dismay he was delayed still further. Every merchant in the New World had been waiting to ship cargo to Europe and the plate fleet represented their first chance for three years. All 11 ships in the combined fleet were stuffed to the gunwales with every bale and crate of merchandise possible. The Governor of Havana attempted to convince the two admirals to allow another ship – the *Grifon*, a French ship he had chartered himself – to join the convoy, a request that occasioned yet more wrangling before they assented.

The Queen of Spain's dowry

The real delay, however, was caused by the remarkable saga of the queen's dowry. King Philip V of Spain had recently lost his first wife, Marie Louise of Savoy, threatening to curtail the exercise of his wanton lust. A profoundly religious man, he would not countenance sex outside of marriage, yet was so unhinged by lust that he supposedly had to be dragged off his dead wife's corpse. His new bride, Isabella Farnese, Duchess of Parma, had reluctantly agreed to marry Philip before receiving a dowry, but refused to consummate the marriage until the full amount was delivered to her. Included in this enormous bride price was a host of the finest jewellery the Spanish dominions could deliver, and the king insisted that the plate fleet would not leave the Caribbean until the queen's dowry – all eight chests of it – was loaded aboard and stored in Ubilla's personal cabin.

Not until 24 July did the great fleet finally weigh anchors and leave Havana. It was carrying over 14 million pesos in declared treasure (plus a substantial quantity of undeclared, smuggled loot – perhaps even more than the declared amount), worth, according to one estimate, £220 million ($418 million) in today's money based on weight alone.

The gathering storm

The plan was to strike north and ride the Gulf Current along Florida's Atlantic coast until they reached the trade winds that would carry them across the Atlantic. At first they made good progress, but on 29 July they were becalmed and by the next morning the sea and sky took on an ominous cast. The sun struggled to break through a pervasive haze, while the sea rose in threatening swells despite the absence of any wind. The usual flocks of sea birds had vanished, and as the afternoon drew on the clouds gathered. Unbeknownst to the hapless sailors of the plate fleet, their northwards progress had shadowed the course of a huge cyclone brewing further out to sea. Now it changed course and swept westwards towards them – a full-blown hurricane, driving them towards the jagged reefs and shoals off the Florida coast.

In the early morning of 31 July all 11 of the Spanish ships met their end. Ubilla's flagship was the first to strike the reef. According to eyewitness accounts from survivors, it was picked up by a vast, 50-foot high wave and smashed onto the reef with such violence that the top half of the deck sheared off instantly. Soon the whole ship was smashed to splinters and the admiral and 223 of his crew were killed. The rest of the fleet soon followed, with the exception of the *Grifon*, whose captain had wisely sailed a more easterly course and left himself with enough weather room to ride out the storm. More than 700 men – possibly more than 1,000 – were drowned or smashed, and most of the precious cargo was scattered across the sea floor or plunged to the bottom amidst the wreckage. The only exception was the *Urca de Lima*, which was jammed fast against the bottom but survived relatively intact thanks to its sturdy hull. The survivors dragged themselves ashore and huddled together until the hurricane died down and the morning light revealed the full extent of the devastation. The wreckage and corpses littered 50 kilometres (30 miles) of Florida shoreline, between modern-day Fort Pierce and Sebastian Inlet.

Salvage

The ranking officer gathered the survivors into two camps and set them to salvage as much as possible as quickly as possible. Word was sent to nearby Spanish colonies and help soon arrived. The *Urca de Lima* was the first to be salvaged, because it had got off relatively lightly, but the other ships were either totally or partially broken up, making salvage extremely difficult. Native divers were worked relentlessly, despite poor visibility, variable weather and shoals of sharks.

A small fort was constructed to safeguard the recovered loot, but soon word got out and a plague of pirates, cut-throats and freebooters descended on the site to look for salvage of their own and poach other people's hard-won booty. The Spanish recovered an estimated 25–30 per cent of their treasure (including over 5 million pieces of eight), before finally giving up after three years. Before they left they burned to the waterline those parts of the wrecks that stood clear. Soon the freebooters left too, discouraged by the danger from others, from hostile natives and by the poor conditions. The locations of the wrecks remained evident for a few decades thanks to protruding spars, and it was common for passing ships to try their luck at fishing for treasure. Eventually however, their precise locations were forgotten and they were left undisturbed, the only sign of their existence being the harvest of coins, wood fragments and other debris that would wash up on the beach following a heavy storm.

Rediscovery of the 1715 fleet

The stretch of the Florida coastline where the 1715 fleet met its end is known as the Treasure Coast because of the number of wrecks offshore, and the tendency for some of the scattered cargo to periodically wash ashore. Many locals must have been dimly aware of the potential treasure trove just out to sea, but even after the *Urca de Lima* was rediscovered in less than 4.5 metres (15 feet) of water off Fort Pierce in 1928, and its cannons and anchors salvaged, there was no systematic search for the other wrecks.

Not until the 1960s did offshore treasure hunting begin in earnest. Kip Wagner was a local resident who had become interested in the tales of sunken treasure after finding coins on the beach near his home. He had first tried his hand at treasure hunting in 1949 but without success. In the late 1950s, however, Wagner struck up a friendship with a local history buff and they started to do some serious research on the possible source of the beach coins. From old maps and accounts of the region, together with a mass of documents from the Spanish Archives of the Indies, Wagner and his partner pieced together the story of the 1715 fleet and began to narrow down the location of the wrecks.

His real break came when he spotted a depression on the beach and noticed that his dog had unearthed a pool of fresh water. Wagner realised that he had stumbled upon the location of one of the original Spanish salvage camps (complete with the well they had dug), directly onshore from the wreck of the *Nuestra Señora de la Regla*. Recruiting a pilot and other helpers to his team, Wagner soon located first one wreck and later others, bringing in an increasing haul of treasure. Wagner and his partners found thousands of pieces of eight, gold coins, distinctive K'ang Hsi Chinese porcelain, rings, brooches, crosses, pendants, necklaces and eventually literal treasure chests stuffed full of coins and ingots.

Seven down

Since Wagner's pioneering work, many other salvors and treasure hunters have joined in the hunt for the 1715 fleet and its sunken riches. Six of the lost fleet have definitely been located, and possibly seven (it is not always possible to tell the date of a wreck, and there are many non-1715 fleet wrecks in the area). The original fleet was 12 strong, but the *Grifon* escaped the disaster, leaving 11 wrecks.

The identities of the lost 1715 fleet ships are: *Nuestra Señora de la Regla* (the flagship of the *Nueva España flota*, and hence also known as *La Capitana*), *Santo Cristo de San Roman, Urca De Lima* (aka *El Refuerzo*, or 'the resupply ship'), *Nuestra Señora de las Nieves, Nuestra Señora de Carmen y San Antonio, Nuestra Señora del Rosario, Nuestra Señora de la Concepcion, El Señor San Miguel*, another ship called *San Miguel* (aka *Señora de la Popa*), *El Ciervo*, and a Cuban *frigatilla* (a small transport ship, bought by Captain General Ubilla to add capacity to the fleet).

Of these, the ones that have been located are *Regla, San Roman, Urca de Lima, Las Nieves, Carmen* and *Rosario*. Reports indicate that *El Ciervo* and the Cuban *frigatilla* were lost in deep water; if this is true, it will require a serious, hi-tech salvage operation to locate them and recover any cargo. *La Concepcion* was reported to have broken up off Cape Canaveral. *San Miguel* was cast onto the beach nearly intact, possibly near Sandy Point south of Vero Beach. Officially it carried no treasure, but given the ubiquity of smuggling at the time it may be worth looking for remnants. An unidentified ship, possibly the *Señor San Miguel*, was reported as having wrecked on reefs near Nassau Sound, just south of Fernandina Beach. But to confuse the picture, news suggests that a 1715 wreck may have been discovered off Melbourne Beach. A silver-handed pistol discovered there in November 2005 has led salvors to what they believe could be one of the remaining undiscovered wrecks.

What's left?

It is believed that the wrecks that have been located and salvaged so far are those that were carrying the bulk of the fleet's treasure. With all the millions of pounds' worth of material recovered by salvors, both 290 years ago and more recently, it might be thought that there isn't much to dive for any more. It is certainly true that the undiscovered wrecks are increasingly likely to give up their secrets as modern technology – such as magnetometers and side-scan sonar – are brought to bear, but would-be treasure hunters should not despair for three reasons.

Firstly, there is the astonishing quantity of treasure that was carried by the fleet to begin with. One of the Wagner team's first prize recoveries was an actual 3-foot long treasure chest containing 85 kilograms (187 pounds) of silver coins. According to the manifest of the fleet's cargo, there were 1,300 such chests aboard, giving over 110,500 kilograms (111 tons) of silver in this form alone!

Secondly, it has become clear that official manifests were only half the story with the Spanish treasure fleets. In their desperation to avoid the heavy taxes levied on all goods brought back from the New World, merchants, noblemen and sailors alike went to extraordinary lengths to conceal and smuggle their loot. In one instance an enterprising captain actually had his anchor made out of gold and painted to look like iron. Recent investigations have concluded that some galleons actually carried more undeclared loot than they officially recorded. This state of affairs almost certainly applies to the 1715 fleet. One of the located and salvaged ships, *Las Nieves*, officially carried no treasure, yet its wreck has yielded millions of pounds of booty over the years.

Thirdly, the frequency with which coins and other treasures are still washed up on the beach proves that plenty of this treasure does still lie out to sea.

Perhaps the greatest prize that still lies beneath is Queen Isabella's dowry. It is not known exactly what it consisted of, but items that are known to have been part of the queen's prospective loot include a heart built up of 130 matched pearls, an emerald ring weighing 74 carats, a pair of earrings each of 14-carat pearls, and a rosary of pure coral pieces the size of small marbles. It is not clear how many recovered items belong to the queen's dowry, but it seems likely that much of it still awaits recovery.

How to look for sunken treasure

Having said which, treasure hunters should not get over-excited. Finding and recovering the remaining 1715 treasure will not be easy. A number of professional treasure-hunting/salvage operations have been working this area for decades now, including the company started by legendary sunken-treasure-hunter Mel Fisher – if anyone is likely to find the remaining lost ships it is they. Conditions in the area are also hard – as the Spanish salvors and their hapless Native American slaves discovered all those years ago. The weather only allows a short search season, and high winds and seas can frequently prevent access to the sites. Wreck diving and diving on reefs can be dangerous – combining them doubly so. The expertise and equipment needed for serious search and salvage are very expensive. There are also sharks to contend with, and variable visibility, as sediment from rivers to the north and kicked up by turbidity can make the water murky.

Bear in mind also that treasure hunting and salvage offshore are strictly controlled. Some of the wreck areas are off-limits to treasure hunters. For areas that aren't, it is necessary to apply and pay for a licence. Least popular of all is the law of the State's share, which means that the State of Florida is allowed to pick the first and best 25 per cent of any loot recovered at sea. This does not, however, apply to beachcombing finds, and simply walking along the beach with a metal detector is the easiest and most popular form of treasure hunting. Visit the beach after a storm and the chances are that you could find a piece of eight, a gold doubloon or even a priceless piece of antique jewellery, perhaps once destined to grace the hand of the Queen of Spain herself.

The Franklin expedition

In 1845 Sir John Franklin set off in charge of a British Navy expedition to chart the North American Arctic and the route of the fabled Northwest Passage. On 26 July of that year the two ships of the expedition – the *Erebus* and the *Terror* – were seen by whalers in Baffin Bay, at the gateway to the Northwest Passage. They were never seen by Europeans again. In the years that followed, the fate of Franklin's expedition became one of the great mass-media stories of its day, with a rapt public breathlessly following every new development and a stream of search expeditions flooding the Arctic in search of the missing men and ships. At least 40 expeditions have been launched over the 160 years since Franklin disappeared, and according to one estimate more men and ships have been lost in the hunt than perished on the original mission.

Today it is possible to piece together a fairly complete picture of the expedition's grim and drawn-out fate, but many mysteries remain. Indeed, the story of Franklin's lost expedition combines three of the topics of this book – lost ships, lost people and lost writings. Those hunting for them are convinced that, somewhere in the trackless Arctic wastes, they await discovery, ready to reveal their long-guarded secrets.

Eminent Victorian

Franklin's expedition was conceived as part of a programme of journeys of exploration undertaken by the Royal Navy, partly as a means of occupying their men and officers during peacetime and partly as a reflection of Victorian hubris, which saw the British Empire attempting to project the might of its technology, derring-do and pure British spunk to the farthest recesses of the globe. In particular, Franklin's expedition was part of an ongoing quest to open up the Northwest Passage, the fabled route between the Atlantic and Pacific oceans across the top of the North American continent, which, it was hoped, would dramatically reduce transit times between Europe and the Far East by obviating the need to navigate the Cape of Good Hope (at the southern tip of Africa) or Cape Horn (at the southern tip of South America). Even today, with the Suez and Panama canals, the Northwest Passage would be the preferred route for much of the world's maritime traffic.

Sir John Franklin had enjoyed a varied and not always illustrious career, seeing naval service in two of the major naval engagements of British history (Copenhagen and Trafalgar), narrowly surviving a land expedition to chart parts of the North American Arctic and being sent home early from a stint as governor of Tasmania. In 1845, despite poor health and relatively advanced years, he managed to get himself appointed commander of the latest British attempt to chart the Northwest Passage (although some historians claim that the real purpose of the expedition was the rather less glamorous work of taking magnetic measurements, and that Franklin was thus not quite the intrepid explorer of Victorian myth).

Bombs away

The Navy fitted out two bomb ships – sturdy vessels built to mount heavy mortars for ship–shore bombardment – with all the technology they thought appropriate for an Arctic expedition, which would have to contend with thick ice. The hulls of the ships were strengthened and armoured and they were fitted with central heating, screw propulsion and other cutting edge technology. In preparation for a long trip, the ships were supplied with everything from an extensive library and personalised tableware for the officers to three years of supplies, including quantities of tinned food (at this time still something of an untried novelty).

The two ships were named *Erebus* and *Terror*, and, with a combined crew of 129, they sailed on 19 May 1845. In July they encountered the two whalers in Baffin Bay, and then sailed into the channels and straits of the Canadian Arctic Archipelago. It was later discovered that they spent the winter of 1845–46 camped on Beechey Island, and were then able to make it as far as the north-western tip of King William Island, which is just off the Canadian mainland in what is now the Nunavut Territory. But the weather was against them and by September 1846 they were again trapped by sea ice in a gelid grip that would not relent for almost two years. What followed was only pieced together from the clues and rumours brought back by the search expeditions.

The hunt for Franklin

When two years had gone by without word from the Franklin expedition, the Navy and the government launched the first of a series of what were, initially, rescue missions, but later were sent simply to solve the mystery of the utter disappearance of the two ships and 129 men. Despite mapping much of the convoluted coastline of the region, the first 14 expeditions discovered only one trace of the Franklin party – their overwinter camp on Beechey Island, about a third of the way into the Northwest Passage, together with the graves of three crew members who had died of tuberculosis.

Not until 1854 did the first clues to the expedition's fate become clear. Dr John Rae, a surveyor for the Hudson's Bay Company, spoke to the Inuit, who reported encounters near King William Island four years previously, between Inuit and a party of 40 white men who were in a desperate state. There was no translator and the white men could only signal their intention to head south. Suffering a time of famine themselves, the Inuit were not able to offer any help and the two groups went their separate ways. Later the bodies of another group of white men were found by the Inuit near the mouth of a large river, with signs that they had been reduced to cannibalism. When Rae let it be known he was offering a reward for any material evidence to back up these tales he was able to obtain many artefacts that were obviously from the ships and crew, which the Inuit had salvaged.

Notes, boats and bodies

Franklin's wife, Lady Jane Franklin, raised enough money to finance a new expedition to follow up this new information, and by 1859 Leopold McClintock in command of the *Fox* had managed to reach King William Island. The McClintock expedition uncovered the evidence that, for the Victorian public, appeared to solve the mystery. On King William Island they found a cairn containing a brief note. Scribbled on a standard-issue Navy form, it had two parts. The first, dated 28 May 1847, recorded the ships' movements from 1845, including the winter camp at Beechey Island, their current location and some subsequent land explorations, and insisted, 'ALL WELL'.

The second part, dated 25 April 1848, was far grimmer. It recorded that the two ships had been abandoned after again 'having been beset' with ice, that nine officers and 15 other men had died, including Franklin himself, who had passed away on 11 June 1847, and that the surviving men were now striking out for Back's Fish River to the south (presumably with the intention of making their way up the river to outposts of the Hudson's Bay Company).

Investigating further, McClintock came across a trail of death – corpses, scattered equipment and one of the ship's boats, converted into a sled but then abandoned. It was laden with a bizarre range of equipment, including silver teaspoons, carpet slippers, a copy of the novel *The Vicar of Wakefield*, and unopened tins of meat.

Mystery solved?

To the Victorians the story now seemed relatively clear. Trapped by unrelenting ice and with provisions running low and men dying, the crew had bravely decided to try their chances on land. Overcome with cold, hunger and scurvy (from lack of vitamin C) they had perished along the way – 'the first and only martyrs to Arctic discovery in modern times,' in the words of Lady Jane Franklin (writing before Scott of the Antarctic). The ships themselves had sunk near King William Island, according to Inuit informants. The note and the relics were displayed for the public in a grim tableau and the incident was subsumed to the greater myth of exploration and empire-building.

Even with this version of events, however, many mysteries remained. Why had the men abandoned their ships to attempt the suicidal overland trip via Back's Fish River, which would have meant a 1,200-kilometre (746-mile) trek over falls and rapids? Why had they filled their makeshift sled with useless and heavy equipment? Why, if they were starving, were some of the tins of food unopened? Why, in addition, did the note in the cairn contain some simple errors (such as the date given for the winter spent on Beechey Island), but little information that would have been of any use to searchers?

Answers were suggested in the 1980s following the analysis of the bodies of the three men buried at Beechey Island. In addition to tuberculosis, they also exhibited low levels of lead poisoning. The finger of suspicion was pointed at the canned meat. The technology involved was still in its infancy and the company that had supplied the tins did not have a great safety record. The lead solder used to close the tins probably leached into the contents, resulting in progressive lead poisoning, which explained many things. Lead poisoning impairs memory, affects concentration and leads to poor judgement. This would explain the confused note, the suicidal overland plan, the bizarre contents of the sledge, and the uneaten tins of food (ie perhaps the men became aware that the tins were causing problems). Improper preparation of the tinned food may also have led to the build-up of botulinum toxin in the cans, adding to the party's woes by causing botulism. Perhaps this is what killed Franklin.

Where are the ships and their logs?

This apparently neat explanation of why and how the Franklin expedition turned into a disaster is not the whole story, however. There still remain several unanswered mysteries. Where is the body of Sir John Franklin himself – was it buried, and if so, where? Where, exactly, did the expedition's ships sink, and might they still be on the seabed? Where are the logs of the expedition, which would have been kept by the commanders and officers of both ships and could provide definitive answers to many of the questions surrounding the mission?

Some Franklin scholars, unconvinced by the 'official' line, have returned to the accounts of the Inuit to look for answers to these mysteries. In doing so they have uncovered evidence that the true fate of the expedition may have been much more drawn out than the established account allows.

Arctic gold

The missing people, ships and records of the Franklin expedition have enormous historical significance and interest. The expedition has become one of the most important episodes in Canadian and Arctic history, with the allure of a historical mystery and the drama of personal tragedy. The ships themselves would have genuine archaeological significance, as there are no extant bomb ships, let alone ones with special adaptations representing the height of mid-19th-century technology.

As for the missing records, they are the Holy Grail of Franklin enthusiasts. Indeed, according to Franklin-scholar Russell Potter, 'Of all the dreamed-for documents in all the unsolved mysteries of modern times, none matches the drawing power of these elusive Franklin papers.' It is hoped that they may be aboard the sunken ships, so that finding one will lead to the other.

Listening to the Inuit

McClintock was only able to find the remains, relics and clues that he did thanks to the information of Inuit informants – Rae's and his own. But not all the elements of the story related by these Inuit were accepted by the Victorians – partly because the accounts tended to sound vague, and partly because there were things people did not want to hear. For instance, the Inuit claim that the corpses they had seen proved the Franklin survivors had been driven to cannibalism caused outrage in Victorian Britain, and many, including novelist Charles Dickens, flatly declared it to be impossible.

More Inuit information was collated by journalist Charles Francis Hall, who made several trips to the Arctic in his own attempt to solve the Franklin mystery. Hall spoke to the Inuit who had seen the ships themselves, and they related how one of them had sunk close to where it was abandoned, smashed to pieces by the crushing ice, while the other had eventually made its way south where it sank in relatively intact condition. Strangely, the Inuit also told of seeing white men, first near the ships and then later attempting to make their way south – well after the date the entire party was supposed to have abandoned the ships and struck south, according to the note in the cairn. There were even tales that some white men had spent an entire winter with the Inuit. This did not gel with the popular account of the last days of the expedition.

The modern synthesis

Franklin expert David Woodman pieced together the Inuit testimony collected by Hall and others, together with his own researches, to arrive at a more complete picture of how the expedition really ended. It seems likely that after the initial abandonment of the ships, recorded in the note in the cairn, some of the men reoccupied the ships, but when one of the ships sank after being destroyed by the ice, many men and provisions were lost, possibly prompting abandonment of the other. Later, however, other Inuit came across the surviving ship some way to the south and there was clear evidence that it had only very recently been abandoned – in other words it had, again, been re-occupied, by at least a few of the surviving men. Perhaps they even piloted it to where the Inuit found it. Not long after this, the second ship was seen to have sunk, but its masts could still be seen above the water line, showing that it was relatively intact.

As for the survivors, some of the Franklin party may have lived with the Inuit for as long as a year, and some may even have made it to Back's Fish River and beyond, almost reaching the Hudson's Bay Company outposts. However, all of this took several more years than allowed for in the 'official' chronology. This explains how it was possible for Rae's Inuit informants to tell of the encounter with the desperate white men in 1850, two years after the date of the note in the cairn. All in all the picture is messy at best, with repeated abandonments and reoccupations of the ships and disparate groups of men struggling through the snowy wastes, but all meeting the same ultimate fate.

Searching for the *Erebus* or *Terror*

For those like Woodman, who seek Franklin's lost ships, the most interesting portion of the Inuit testimony was giving the location of the second ship. Several informants agreed that it had last been seen off the Utjulik Peninsula, known to the West as the Adelaide Peninsula, but they disagreed exactly where. Two possible locations are suggested – one to the north of O'Reilly Island, and one further south, just to the west of Grant Point, near Kirkwall Island, known to the Inuit as Umiartaliq, or 'ship island'.

Using this information, Woodman has led a series of expeditions to search for the wreck of the Franklin ship, to identify which of the two it is and set the scene for a detailed exploration/salvage. Initially the expeditions used a magnetometer to image the seabed in the two target areas, looking for anomalies that could reveal the presence of metal objects such as anchors, hull cladding, nuts and bolts, etc. Having identified a range of anomalies, subsequent expeditions used sonar units lowered through holes in the ice to look more closely at the seabed.

So far none of the many expeditions has found anything on the seabed, but they have gathered a lot of useful information. Profiling of the contours of the seabed has narrowed down possible search regions, because it is known that the ship must have sunk in water deep enough to conceal all but the tops of the masts, but shallow enough to leave them protruding. It has also shown that the seabed in this area is free from ice scouring, which means that anything that has sunk to the bottom should be intact and probably very well preserved. The cold water means that there are no corals or ship-borer worms – organisms that quickly destroy wooden wrecks in warmer waters. As

Woodman himself comments: 'I'm picturing this beautiful wooden wreck sitting upright with everything but the masts, pristine, probably one of the best-preserved wooden wrecks in the world.' Meanwhile discoveries on land – including artefacts and wood (probably derived from the Franklin ship), European campsites and even the skull of a Caucasian – have confirmed that this area was most likely the last resting place of the ship.

The community of Franklin scholars continues to hope that the wreck of the *Erebus* or *Terror* will be located and explored, perhaps to reveal one of the expedition logs that could finally explain the full story of the various abandonments, reoccupations, desperate land treks and tragic deaths. Perhaps it would even reveal where Franklin himself was buried. But finding it will not be easy. The last expedition to the Utjulik area, in 2004, concluded that only direct sonar scanning of the seabed could identify the possible wreck, and only a small percentage of the target areas identified from the Inuit accounts has yet been imaged in this time-consuming and labour-intensive fashion.

Ironically the changing climate, which could soon see a dramatic reduction in the ice that trapped and doomed the Franklin expedition, may make it much harder to search for its remains, as it is generally easier to work on a solid footing of thick ice. Global warming could also see the Northwest Passage, which Franklin and 128 other men lost their lives to explore, finally opened up to commercial shipping traffic. Franklin's dream could become a reality, even as the last clues to his fate slip further out of reach.

References

This is a selection of sources and reference materials used in the writing of this book, which may help to provide background material, subject overviews or specific information on points of interest or tangential aspects.

Some general sources that are highly recommended include the websites of *Wikipedia* (**www.wikipedia.org**), *The Catholic Encyclopedia* (**www.newadvent.org/cathen/index.htm**) and *Early British Kingdoms* (**www.earlybritishkingdoms.com**), *Fortean Times* magazine, and the book *Undiscovered*, by Ian Wilson (1987, Michael O'Mara Books Ltd, London), which is in many ways a precursor to this book, though the topics covered only overlap in a few instances.

Chapter 1

Atlantis

Christopher, Kevin (September 2001) 'Atlantis: No way, No how, No where', *Skeptical Briefs* newsletter, **www.csicop.org/sb/2001-09/atlantis.html**

Diamond, Jared (1998) *Guns, Germs and Steel*, Vintage, London

Gutscher, Marc-André (April 2005) 'Destruction of Atlantis by a great earthquake and tsunami? A geological analysis of the Spartel Bank hypothesis', *Geology*, 33 (8), pp 685–688

James, Peter (1996) *The Sunken Kingdom: The Atlantis Mystery Solved*, Pimlico, London

Plato (1997) *Complete Works*, ed D S Hutchinson, Hackett Publishing Co, Indianapolis

Rincon, Paul (6 June 2004) 'Satellite images "show Atlantis"', *BBC News Online*, http://news.bbc.co.uk/go/pr/fr//1/hi/sci/tech/3766863.stm

Rudgley, Richard (1998) *Lost Civilisations of the Stone Age*, Arrow, London

The Temple of Solomon

Dolphin, Lambert and Kollen, Michael (25 March 2002) 'On The Location of the First and Second Temples in Jerusalem', www.templemount.org/theories.html

Levy, Joel (2004) *Secret History*, Vision Paperbacks, London

Levy, Joel (2005) *The Doomsday Book*, Vision Paperbacks, London

Ritmeyer, Dr Leen (accessed October 2005)'The Temple and the Ark of the Covenant', *Ritmeyer Archaeological Design*, http://homepage.ntlworld.com/ritmeyer/temple.ark.html

Rowe, John (2005) 'The Temple at the End of Time', *Strange Attractor*, 2

Shragai, Nadav (27 November 2005) 'In the beginning was Al-Aqsa', *Haaretz*

The Library of Alexandria

Baldwin, Barry (July 2004) 'Classical Corner', *Fortean Times*, 187

Brundige, Ellen N (1995) 'The Library of Alexandria', *Perseus Digital Library*, www.perseus.tufts.edu/GreekScience/Students/Ellen/Museum.html

Canfora, Luciano (1989) *The Vanished Library*, tr Martin Ryle, University of California Press, Berkeley

Hannam, James (2003) 'The Foundation and Loss of the Royal and Serapeum Libraries of Alexandria', *Bede's Library*, www.bede.org.uk/Library2.htm

Jaegers, Beverley (27 September 2000) 'The Secrets of Alexandria', www.rense.com/general4/alex.htm

Whitehouse, Dr David (12 May 2004) 'Library of Alexandria discovered', *BBC News Online*, http://news.bbc.co.uk/go/pr/fr/-/1/hi/sci/tech/3707641.stm

Camelot

'Arthur at Viriconium' (20 October 2004), *Virtually Historical*, www.virtuallyhistorical.com/downloads/953_King%20Arthur%20at%20Viriconium.htm

Ashe, Geoffrey (1997) *The Traveller's Guide To Arthurian Britain*, Gothic Image, Glastonbury

Ford, David Nash (2001) 'Winchester: Malory's Camelot?', *Early British Kingdoms*, www.earlybritishkingdoms.com/archaeology/winchester.html

Veprauskas, Michael (2002) 'The Generations of Ambrosius part 3: Ambrosius Aurelianus', **www.vortigernstudies.org.uk/artgue/ mikeambr2.htm**

El Dorado

Daly, Vere T (accessed November 2005)'A Short History Of The Guyanese People', **www.geocities.com/TheTropics/Shores/9253/eldorado.html**

De Bry, Theodor (2005) *Grand Voyages,* 8, *Philadelphia Print Shop,* **www.philaprintshop.com/debrytxt.html#Dorado**

Pasteur, John (16 February 2004) 'The Persistent Legend of El Dorado', **www.btinternet.com/~j.pasteur/DoradoIndex.html**

Shuker, Dr Karl P N (1996) *The Unexplained,* Carlton Books, London

Trevelyan, Raleigh (2002) *Sir Walter Raleigh,* Penguin, London,

Chapter 2
The Ark of the Covenant

'Biblical Archaeology: Where is the Ark of the Covenant?' (13 November 2003) *Institute for Biblical & Scientific Studies,* **www.bibleandscience. com/archaeology/ark.htm**

Blackburn, Michael and Bennett, Mark (March 2006) 'Re-engineering the Ark', *Fortean Times,* 207

'Kabbalist Blesses Jones: Now's the Time to Find Holy Lost Ark', (20 May 2005), *Arutz Sheva,* **www.israelnationalnews.com/news.php3?id=82226**

Grierson, Roderick and Munro-Hay, Stuart (2000) *The Ark of the Covenant: The True Story of the Greatest Relic of Antiquity,* Phoenix

Grierson, Dr R and Munro-Hay, Dr Stuart (1999) *The Ark of the Covenant,* Weidenfeld and Nicolson, London

Hancock, Graham (1993) *The Sign and the Seal,* Doubleday, London

The lost *Dialogues* of Aristotle

Eco, Umberto (1992) *The Name of the Rose,* Vintage, London

Lukács, B (January 2006) 'A Note To The Lost Books Of Aristotle', **www.rmki.kfki.hu/~lukacs/ARISTO3.htm**

Owen, James (25 April 2005) 'Papyrus Reveals New Clues to Ancient World', *National Geographic News,* **http://news.nationalgeographic.com/news/ 2005/04/0425_050425_papyrus.html**

Oxyrhynchus Papyri Project, **www.papyrology.ox.ac.uk/POxy/**

Prince, C (July 2002) 'The Historical Context of Arabic Translation, Learning, and The Libraries of Medieval Andalusia', *Library History,* 18 (2), pp 73–87

Thom, Johan C (1995) 'Review of A. P. Bos, *Cosmic and Meta-Cosmic Theology in Aristotle's Lost Dialogues*', *Scholia Reviews*, 4 (11)

The Holy Grail

Anderson, Lady Flavia Joan Lucy (1953) *The Ancient Secret: In Search of the Holy Grail*, Gollancz, London

Ford, David Nash (2005) 'The Chalice Well', *Early British Kingdoms*, **www.earlybritishkingdoms.com**

Baigent, Michael, *et al* (1996) *The Holy Blood and the Holy Grail*, Arrow, London

'Spanish academic revives speculation about authenticity of the Holy Grail'(October 1999) *AD2000*, 12 (9)

Thornborrow, Chris (January 2006) 'An Introduction to Current Theories about The Holy Grail', **www.byu.edu/ipt/projects/middleages/ Arthur/grail.html**

Shakespeare's lost plays

Collins, Paul (2001) *Banvard's Folly*, Picador, New York

Delahoyde, Michael (2005) 'Cardenio', **www.wsu.edu/~delahoyd/ shakespeare/cardenio.html**

Kelly, Stuart (2006) *The Book of Lost Books*, Penguin, Harmondsworth

Gerald, Lawrence (February 2006) 'The Discovery of Eight Shakespeare Quartos in Bacon's Library', **www.sirbacon.org/eightquartos.htm**

Shaksper: The Global Electronic Shakespeare Conference, **www.shaksper.net**

Chapter 3

The treasure of the Dead Sea scrolls

Feather, Robert (2000) *The Copper Scroll Decoded*, HarperCollins, London

Feather, Robert (September/October 2003) 'Unfolding the secrets of the Copper Scroll of Qumran', *New Dawn*, 80

Fillon, Mike (1 May 1999) 'Searching for the treasures of the Bible', *Popular Mechanics*, **www.popularmechanics.com/science/research/ 1281756.html**

Gwynn-Seary, Richard (December 1996) 'Scroll with it', *Fortean Times*, 93

Hochman, Gary and Collins, Matthew (November 2004) 'Ancient Refuge in the Holy Land', *PBS Nova*, **www.pbs.org/wgbh/nova/transcripts/ 3118_scrolls.html**

Krystek, Lee (1999) 'The Mysterious Treasure of the Copper Scroll', *The Museum of Unnatural History*, **www.unmuseum.org/copper.htm**

Moss, Gloria (February 2000) 'Sects, drugs and rotten scrolls', *Fortean Times*, 131

King John's jewels

Burgess, Mike (2005)'Hidden East Anglia: Landscape Legends of Norfolk & Suffolk', www.hiddenea.com/norfolkw.htm

'Colourful characters associated with The Wash' (November 2005) *The Wash Project*, www.washestuary.org.uk/details.cfm?id=10

Dickens, Charles (1969) *A Child's History of England*, Everyman's Library, Dent, London

Ibeji, Dr Mike (1 July 2001) 'King John and Richard I: Brothers and Rivals', *BBC History*, www.bbc.co.uk/history/state/monarchs_leaders/john_01.shtml

Waters, Richard (2003) *The Lost Treasure of King John*, Barny Books, Grantham

Wilson, Ian (1987) *Undiscovered*, Michael O'Mara Books Ltd, London

The treasure of the Knights Templar

Demurger, Alain (2004) *The Last Templar: The tragedy of Jacques de Molay, Last Grand Master of the Temple*, tr Antonio Nevill, Profile Books, London

McClure, Kevin (October 2004) 'The Templar Deception', *Fortean Times*, 188

'Notes on the Knights Templar'(January 2006) *Grand Lodge of British Columbia and Yukon*, http://freemasonry.bcy.ca/anti-masonry/templars.html

Robertson, Ian (June 2003) 'Templar treasure', *Fortean Times*, 171

Rutter, Gordon (2003) 'Fortean Traveller: Templar treasures', *Fortean Times*, 167

Smith, Paul (March 2004) 'Priory of Sion', http://priory-of-sion.com

'The Temple Mount in Jerusalem' (March 2004) www.templemount.org

Montezuma's hoard

Bertola, Max (1996) 'Montezuma's Treasure', *Max Bertola's Southern Utah*, www.so-utah.com/feature/montzuma/homepage.html

Prescott, William Hickling (February 2006) 'Book VII: Conclusion – Subsequent Career of Cortes', *Acoyauh's Aztec Lore*, www.geocities.com/Athens/Academy/3088/hist-book7.html

Möller, Harry (July 1982) 'Has Moctezuma's treasure been lost again?', *México desconocido*, 68, www.mexicodesconocido.com.mx/english/historia/prehispanica/detalle.cfm?idsec=1&idsub=3&idpag=1915#,%20%2068%20/

Wood, Michael (2000) *Conquistadors*, BBC Books, London

Captain Kidd's buried treasure

'Captain Kidd on Raritan Bay' *Weird NJ*, 14

'Captain Kidd: Pirate's Treasure Buried in the Connecticut River'(accessed February 2006) *The Connecticut River Homepage*, **www.bio.umass.edu/ biology/conn.river/kidd.html**

Hawkins, Paul (2000) *The Ultimate Captain William Kidd Website*, **www.captainkidd.pwp.blueyonder.co.uk/index.htm**

Paine, Lincoln P. (1997) *Ships of the world: an historical encyclopedia*, Houghton Mifflin Company, Boston

Wick, Steve (2006) 'Legend of Capt. Kidd', *Newsday*, **www.newsday.com/ community/guide/lihistory/ny-history-hs324,0,984646.story**

The Oak Island Money Pit

Atherton, Joanna (2005) 'Sir Francis Bacon', *Oak Island Treasure*, **www.oakislandtreasure.co.uk/theory_bacon.htm**

Joltes, Dick (19 April 1996) 'A Critical Analysis of the Oak Island Legend', *Critical Enquiry*, **www.criticalenquiry.org**

Joltes, Richard (November 2003) 'Oak Island Mystery', *Fortean Times*, 176

'Money pit for sale' (July 2003) *Fortean Times*, 172

Nickell, Joe (March/April 2000) 'Investigative Files: The Secrets of Oak Island', *Skeptical Inquirer*, 24 (2)

Chapter 4

The lost army of Cambyses

'Cambyses Lost Army and *The English Patient*'(28 September 2003) Aurelian's Archives on the Ancient Worlds.net site, **www.ancientworlds.net/aw/Journals/Journal/172631**

Chen, Jiquan (2005) 'Searching for the Lost Army of Cambyses and …', *Newsletter of Sino-Ecologist Association Overseas*, 18 (1)

Dunn, Jimmy (December 2005) 'Cambyses II, the Persian Ruler of Egypt (27th Dynasty) And His Lost Army', **http://touregypt.net/ featurestories/cambyses2.htm**

Hawley, Caroline (16 April 2000) 'Looking for a lost army', *BBC News Online* 2000, **http://news.bbc.co.uk/1/hi/world/middle_east/ 715461.stm**

Ikram, Salima (September/October 2000) 'Cambyses' Lost Army', *The Archaeological Institute of America*, 53 (5), **www.archaeology.org/ 0009/newsbriefs/cambyses.html**

Kelly, Saul (2003) *The Lost Oasis: The Desert War and the Hunt for Zerzura*, John Murray, London

Shaltout, Prof Dr Mosalam (September 1998) 'The Egyptianism of the ancient Egyptian civilization: Between lies and reality', *El Allem* ('Science'), **www.m-shaltout.com/arch.htm**

Boudicca's grave

'Hampstead Heath: The Barrow' (December 2005), **www.cix.co.uk/ ~archaeology/hampstead-heath/barrow/barrow.htm**

Tacitus (December 2005) *The Annals, Perseus Project*, **www.perseus.tufts. edu/cgi-bin/ptext?lookup=Tac.+Ann.+14.33**

Trubshaw, Bob *et al* (November 1995) 'Did Boudicca die in Flintshire?', *Mercia Mysteries*, 25

The tomb of Genghis Khan

'The Chinggis Khan Expedition', (March 2006) **www.khanexpedition.com**

Cody, Edward (5 March 2006) 'Unearthing secret of Genghis Khan's tomb', *Washington Post*

McElroy, Damien (17 August 2002) 'Genghis Khan's curse strikes dig in Mongolia', *The Scotsman*

McRae, Michael (July 1996) 'Genghis On My Mind', *Outside*

Schonwald, Josh (11 April 2002) 'Research team to resume its search for burial site of Mongol ruler Genghis Khan', *The University of Chicago Chronicle*, 21 (13)

The Lost Colony of Roanoke

'Droughts Affected Both Roanoke and Jamestown' (May 1998) *Roanoke Colonies Research Newsletter*, 5.2, **www.ecu.edu/rcro/Newsletter/ 5-2/Droughts.htm**

Keech, Lawrence (26 May 2002) 'Artifacts detail Roanoke Voyages', *Washington Daily News*

Lost Colony Center for Science and Research (January 2006) **www.lost-colony.com**

Lucas, Ronesha *et al* (January 2006) 'Exploring the Migration of the Roanoke Colonists', **http://nia.ecsu.edu/ureoms2005/tms/ lost_colony/lcreport071405.pdf**

Miller, Lee (2002) *Roanoke: Solving the Mystery of the Lost Colony*, Penguin, Harmandsworth

Neville, John D (October 2005) 'Search for the Lost Colony', *National Park Service*, **www.nps.gov/fora/search.htm**

Payne, Patrick (2002) *The Roanoke Lost Colony DNA Project*, **http://papayne.rootsweb.com/Lost-Colony/index.html**

'The Roanoke Colonies' (October 2005) *The Lost Colony*,
   www.thelostcolony.org/voyages_3.html

Amelia Earhart's last flight

'The Earhart Project' (accessed 16 May 2006) *The International Group for
   Historical Aircraft Recovery*, http://www.tighar.org/Projects/
   Earhart/AEdescr.html
Gillespie, Ric (2005) *Finding Amelia*, Naval Institute Press, Annapolis
'Island prison hunt for Earhart' (29 March 2005) *BBC News Online*,
   http://news.bbc.co.uk/go/pr/fr/-/1/hi/world/asia-pacific/
   4390107.stm
Hile, Jennifer (15 December 2003) 'Expedition Scours Pacific for
   Amelia Earhart Wreck', *National Geographic News*, http://news.
   nationalgeographic.com/news/2003/12/1212_031215_tvearhart_2.html

Chapter 5

The Persian invasion fleets

Herodotus (October 2005) *The Histories*, Book 6, http://nautarch.tamu.
   edu/pwss/Ancient%20Sources/Ancient%20Sources.htm
'Persian War Shipwreck Survey 2003–2005' (2006) http://nautarch.tamu.
   edu/pwss/homepage/
Rincon, Paul (19 January 2004) 'Bid to find lost Persian armada', *BBC News
   Online*, http://news.bbc.co.uk/go/pr/fr/-/2/hi/science/nature/
   3401449.stm
'Scientists racing time, pirates for secrets of Persian Wars ships' (3 May
   2004) *Milwaukee Journal Sentinel*
Smith, Helena (20 June 2005) 'Search on for secret of Greek sea battle', *Guardian*

The *White Ship*

Adams, George Burton (1905) *The Political History of England*, Vol II,
   Longmans, Green and Co, London
Sayers, William (June 2005) 'Twelfth-Century Norman and Irish Literary
   Evidence for Ship-Building and Sea-Faring Techniques of Norse Origin',
   The Heroic Age: A Journal of Early Medieval Northwestern Europe, 8,
   www.mun.ca/mst/heroicage/issues/8/sayers.html
'The Tragedy of the White Ship'(21 December 2002), *Everything*,
   www.everything2.org/index.pl?node_id=1404899
Wilson, Ian (1987) *Undiscovered*, Michael O'Mara Books Ltd, London

Treasure galleons of the 1715 plate fleet

'1715 Fleet History' (April 2006) *Mel Fisher's Treasures*, **www.melfisher. com/SalvageOperations/1715Ops/1715history.asp**

Gaither, Catherine M (1996) 'The 1715 Spanish Plate Fleet', **www.tuspain. com/heritage/gold.htm**

Henley, Jon (3 November 2001) 'UN Shuts Lid on Sunken Treasure Chests', *Guardian*

The History of the Spanish Treasure Fleet System'(March 2006) *Academic diving programme of the Florida State University*, **www.adp.fsu.edu/ fleet.html**

'Taxation and Smuggling' (March 2006) *RS Operations LLC*, **www.rsoperations.com/History/Taxation/Taxation_Smuggling.htm**

Weller, Robert (1993) *Sunken Treasure on Florida Reefs*, Crossed Anchors Salvage, Lake Worth, Florida

The Franklin Expedition

'Arctic Passage', *PBS Nova*, **www.pbs.org/wgbh/nova/arctic/expe-nf.html**

'Long Forgotten Arctic Grave of Franklin Expedition Search Ship Revealed' (5 October 2004) **www.shipwreckcentral.com/livedive/archives/2004/10/**

Moore, Charles (2004) 'Irish-Canadian Franklin Search Expedition, 2004', *Maritime Heritage Consulting*, **www.ric.edu/rpotter/woodman/ 2004_Field_Report_short.htm**

Potter, Russell A (1996) 'Sir John Franklin: His life and afterlife', **www.ric.edu/rpotter/franklife.html**

Woodman, David C (1991) *Unravelling The Franklin Mystery: Inuit Testimony*, McGill-Queen's University Press, Canada

Index

About the Author

Joel Levy is a writer on science, psychology, history and the paranormal and author of several books, including: Secret History – hidden forces that shaped the past; The Doomsday Book – scenarios for the end of the world; Really Useful – the history and science of everyday things; Boost Your Brain Power – a guide to testing and improving your mental abilities; Scam: Secrets of the Con Artist – an inside look at the world and history of the con artist and his scams; KISS Guide to the Unexplained – a beginner's guide to historical secrets and mysteries , the paranormal and supernatural; and Fabulous Creatures – on creatures of myth and folklore.